PENGUIN BOOKS

THE BURGER YEARS

Herman Schwartz is a professor of law at the American University in Washington, D.C., and a consultant to People for the American Way. He was Chief Counsel to the Senate Anti-trust and Monopoly Subcommittee and Chief Counsel for Revenue Sharing, Department of the Treasury. The first person called in to mediate the Attica prison uprising in 1971, he founded the American Civil Liberties Union Prisoners' Rights Project in 1969 and has served as Chairman of the New York State Commission of Corrections (1975–1976). He is also an authority on the law and practice of electronic surveillance.

THE
BURGER
YEARS

RIGHTS AND WRONGS
IN THE SUPREME COURT

1969–1986

Essays edited and with an Introduction by

HERMAN SCHWARTZ

PENGUIN BOOKS

PENGUIN BOOKS
Published by the Penguin Group
Viking Penguin Inc., 40 West 23rd Street,
New York, New York 10010, U.S.A.
Penguin Books Ltd, 27 Wrights Lane,
London W8 5TZ, England
Penguin Books Australia Ltd, Ringwood,
Victoria, Australia
Penguin Books Canada Ltd, 2801 John Street,
Markham, Ontario, Canada L3R 1B4
Penguin Books (N.Z.) Ltd, 182–190 Wairau Road,
Auckland 10, New Zealand

Penguin Books Ltd, Registered Offices:
Harmondsworth, Middlesex, England

First published in the United States of America by
Viking Penguin Inc. 1987
Published in Penguin Books 1988

3 5 7 9 10 8 6 4 2

This work is an expanded and updated version of a symposium originally
published in the September 29, 1984, issue of *The Nation*. Two new
contributions have been added to this collection.

"Separation of Church and State: The Burger Court's Tortuous Journey" by
Norman Redlich from *Notre Dame Law Review* (1985), Volume 60, Issue 5. © 1985
by the Notre Dame Law Review, University of Notre Dame. Reprinted with
permission.

LIBRARY OF CONGRESS CATALOGING IN PUBLICATION DATA
The Burger years.
Bibliography: p.
Includes index.
1. United States. Supreme Court. 2. United
States—Constitutional law. 3. Burger, Warren E.,
1907–   . I. Schwartz, Herman, 1931–   .
[KF8742.B78 1988]   347.73'26   87-7270
ISBN 0 14 01.0818 1   347.30735

Printed in the United States of America by
R. R. Donnelley & Sons Company, Harrisonburg, Virginia
Set in Trump Mediaeval
Designed by Victoria Hartman

FOR MARY

"Somebody splendid
Someone affectionate and dear"

PREFACE

This book analyzes the record of the Supreme Court from 1969 to 1986, the period of Warren E. Burger's tenure as Chief Justice and one of the most turbulent and unpredictable periods in the Court's history. We consider not only the legal soundness of the Court's decisions, but also the real-world impact on those directly affected by them, such as blacks, women, the press, criminal defendants, labor unions, and others.

The contributors to this collection have a corresponding duality. Most have been actively involved as lawyers in the cases and social conflicts about which they write. All are also recognized scholars and experts as either teachers or writers. They accordingly analyze the Court's rulings from both practical and theoretical perspectives.

The book had its genesis in an issue of *The Nation* that was devoted to the work of the Burger Court on its fifteenth anniversary. The issue was well received, winning the American Bar Association Silver Gavel Public Service award for 1985, and it was decided that the essays should be given the more permanent book form. This also provided an opportunity to broaden and deepen the discussions, so that the book covers areas not treated in the *Nation* symposium and treats the subjects originally discussed much more intensively. Although size considerations have prevented analysis of the Court's decisions in some areas, we hope we have covered enough of the Court's work to give the reader a sense of what the Burger Court did during this period and what it meant to the American people.

This is the place to acknowledge how much this book owes to Victor Navasky, editor of *The Nation*. His support and encouragement while we gathered and edited the many contributions that make up the volume were indispensable. His wise suggestions at crucial points resolved delicate problems that often seemed intractable.

I also want to thank our wonderful editor Elisabeth Sifton, who guided us through the shoals of book publishing and often seemed to understand what we wanted to say better than we did ourselves. She has this rather astonishing notion that lawyers should write in English, and disconcerting as it was to many of us, insisted—with wit and good humor—that we at least try.

Most of all, thanks are due to the contributors who complied patiently with my nagging about deadlines, graciously responded to impertinent suggestions, and were willing to write and rewrite to accommodate new developments. They made putting the book together not just an exciting intellectual experience but also an occasion for enjoyable friendship.

Finally, my appreciation to my secretary, Yvonne Montanye O'Neill, who patiently typed and retyped much of the manuscript, often deciphering handwriting of near-hieroglyphic obscurity.

The essay by Dean Norman Redlich is adapted from an article originally appearing in Volume 60, No. 5, of the *Notre Dame Law Review* and is published with the permission of the *Notre Dame Law Review*, University of Notre Dame. The essay by Professor Yale Kamisar draws on a talk delivered at the Hofstra University Law School Supreme Court Conference on November 8, 1985, and on the Edward Douglass White lectures delivered by him at the Louisiana State University on March 27 and 28, 1985.

CONTENTS

Introduction

HERMAN SCHWARTZ

On June 16, 1986, Chief Justice Warren E. Burger announced his retirement from the Supreme Court after seventeen years. President Reagan promptly nominated the most conservative member of the Court, Justice William H. Rehnquist, as the sixteenth chief justice, and elevated Court of Appeals Judge Antonin Scalia, also a very conservative jurist, to be associate justice. The Burger Court became history.

This marks the beginning of a reshaping of the Supreme Court, the contours of which are still unknown. It coincides with the two hundredth anniversary of the Constitution. These concurrent events serve as a reminder that, with rare exceptions, major changes in the Court are never made on a clean slate, but almost invariably against a background of precedent, tradition, and institutional constraints that limit or channel the changes.

The record of the Burger Court is one of the best illustrations of that. Despite the many decisions criticized by the contributors to this volume, many basic principles and doctrines developed by the Court under Chief Justice Earl Warren to protect individual liberty and promote social justice have survived the Burger era intact, and some were strengthened. For example, the high points of the Warren Court's revolution in criminal procedure, *Mapp v. Ohio* (1961) and *Miranda v. Arizona* (1966), though battered and diminished, nevertheless survive; as Yale Kamisar notes, a 1986 opinion by the prosecution-oriented Justice Sandra Day O'Connor viewed *Miranda* as a serious effort to strike a proper balance between competing interests.[1] The basic church-state separation principles worked out over the last forty years were refined and firmly reasserted, and, with some important exceptions and backslidings, the Warren Court rulings on the rights of blacks and women, including the right to an abortion, also still stand.[2]

One would never have expected this in 1969, when Richard M. Nixon nominated Warren Burger to be the Chief Justice. During his 1968 campaign, Nixon had devoted a good deal of heated rhetoric to assailing Earl Warren and his colleagues for being soft on crime and too activist, and chose Burger because he had written some articles to the same effect. Radical change seemed even more likely when, just a few years later, three other Warren Court justices (Abe Fortas, John M. Harlan, and Hugo L. Black) were succeeded by Nixon appointees Harry Blackmun, Lewis F. Powell, and William H. Rehnquist. Later, Presidents Gerald R. Ford and Ronald Reagan replaced Justices William O. Douglas and Potter Stewart with John Paul Stevens and Sandra Day O'Connor, who were both more conservative than their predecessors. The Burger court thus had a solid six-member majority of appointees made by three presidents who had harshly criticized liberal judicial activism and vowed to change the Court's direction.

Part of the reason for this unexpected degree of continuity is that the problems confronting the Court changed. Abortion and other women's rights and gender issues, prisoners' rights, capital punishment, interdistrict busing, affirmative action, rights of the handicapped, of aliens, and of illegitimate children are all areas that the Warren Court barely touched.

Still, the Burger Court was discernibly more conservative than the Warren Court, even though by 1968 the latter was moving to the right along with the nation, in reaction to riots, assassinations, and the Vietnam War. The Burger Court's rightward shift was most explicit in two areas where its predecessor seemed to be making especially significant changes: access to the federal courts and national security. Just two years after his appointment, Chief Justice Burger cautioned young people against becoming lawyers in order to effect social or legal progress in the courts, because "that is not the route by which basic changes in a country like ours should be made." Evidently he had forgotten that for two hundred years the courts have indeed made "basic changes." He promised lawyers "some disappointments" if they tried.[3]

In chapter 1, Burt Neuborne documents the persistence with which Chief Justice Burger and Justices Rehnquist, Powell, and O'Connor worked to ensure such "disappointments" by shutting the courthouse doors. This shutdown was selective, however, limited largely to those seeking to enforce constitutional rights. When those same justices wanted to promote nuclear power, for example, "standing" and other courthouse-closing concepts became flexible indeed. And one might add to Neuborne's discussion of the standing, class-action, and immunity cases the Court's ruling requiring prior recourse to state courts in the name of "our federalism," and the very high barriers that the Burger Court erected against federal habeas corpus review of constitutional issues that might arise in state criminal trials.[4]

There were rulings going the other way, as Neuborne notes in his discussion of some Civil Rights Act cases. And where the regulatory agencies are concerned, Alan Morrison shows that the Court actually expanded judicial review of administrative rulings. Almost invariably, however, it supported governmental and other efforts to withhold information from the public by narrowly construing the Freedom of Information Act, at times so restrictively that several of its decisions were overturned by Congress.

Matters were almost totally one-sided, however, where national security was concerned. Here the Burger Court adopted what the late Edmond Cahn felicitously called "the imperial perspective"—what the government wants, the government gets because it is the government. In *Snepp v. United States* (1980),[5] as Morton Halperin points out, the Court did not even bother hearing arguments or reading briefs before giving the government broad authority to control disclosures by former Central Intelligence Agency employees. In *Regan v. Wald* (1984), the Court allowed the President to bar travel to Cuba, despite a 1977 law clearly intended to deny him that power.[6] And in the 1986 yarmulke case, *Goldman v. Weinberger*, the Court, in an opinion by now–Chief Justice Rehnquist, brushed aside a major claim of religious freedom—the right of an army psychologist who is an Orthodox Jew to wear a small skullcap—with a one-liner: "The desirability of dress regulations . . . is decided by the appropriate military officials, and they are under no constitutional mandate to abandon their considered professional judgment."[7] So much for the First Amendment.

Earlier precedents in the area of criminal procedure also suffered some heavy blows, as Yale Kamisar points out. However, there was some expansion of individual rights, such as the revival of a Sixth Amendment right to counsel for suspects during the interrogation process once adversary proceedings have begun.

In other fields there was more of a steady drift to the right than an explicit turnaround. This was particularly true in the business area. Jerry Cohen and Herbert Milstein show that in the antitrust and securities cases decided under Warren Burger, the Court became more and more a defendants' court, after issuing some antitrust decisions extending antitrust principles to professions and municipalities. David Silberman documents a similar tilt toward management in labor-management relations. But as Arthur Fox shows, where union members tried to enforce some union democracy, the unions generally came out ahead.

This rightward drift favoring business is part of a more general movement to protect property rights, which a number of observers of the Court have noted. Some conservatives have gone so far on behalf of those with money as to urge the Court to scrap almost the entire structure of modern social legislation.[8] They have proposed that the Court use the Fifth Amendment requirement that property not be taken for public use without just compensation, and the ban in Article 1, section 10, on state impairment of contractual obligations, to strike down rent control, zoning, the National Labor Relations Act, land-reform, minimum-wage, and maximum-hours laws, and other social legislation. The *Wall Street Journal* has editorially embraced this cause, urging judicial activism to protect what it calls "economic civil rights."

Even under Chief Justice Rehnquist, the Court is unlikely to accept these invitations to resuscitate such decisions as *Lochner v. New York* (1905),[9] which nullified a state's effort to limit working hours for bakers, drawing from Justice Oliver Wendell Holmes an angry complaint that the Court was writing Herbert Spencer's *Social Statics* into the Constitution.

Nevertheless, the labor and business cases discussed in this book support the view of those who believe that the Burger Court reemphasized protection for traditional property rights by, for example, banning the distribution of leaflets and labor organizing in shopping centers.[10] In a 1983 essay, Norman Dorsen and Joel Gora suggested that "with few exceptions, the key to whether free speech will receive protection depends on an underlying property interest, either private or governmental. . . . [F]ree speech has received diminished protection when [it] appeared to clash with property interests."[11] Recent decisions support this, like the one allowing Harper & Row to use copyright law to prevent *The Nation* from printing three hundred words from Gerald Ford's memoirs.[12] Laurence Tribe has also found in the Burger Court a "substantive tilt" against a redistribution of wealth and in favor of "those with sufficient economic clout to win bilateral contract protection vis-à-vis the government while providing virtually no protection for those whose only power lies in concerted political action."[13]

My own feeling is that these observers somewhat overstate the situation. Along with these decisions favoring vested and traditional property rights were others, either curtailing property rights[14] or favoring less conventional property interests. For example, the Burger Court refused to grant significant judicial protection for claims to welfare, shelter, or other "basic necessities," or to insist on equalization of school financing, housing, or welfare benefits.[15] Yet when Texas tried to deny all schooling to children of illegal aliens, when Pennsylvania tried to cut off all welfare benefits to a fifteen-year-old, when Maricopa County, Arizona, refused hospital care to recent arrivals, and when the federal government denied food stamps to households in which not all the members were related, the Court, often by top-heavy majorities, insisted that the benefits be provided. Equality of benefits—no; but a total denial of basic necessities to some when they are made available to others is beyond the pale.[16]

In other contexts, the Burger Court's performance was more mixed, and many decisions in its last years began to go against the claims of constitutional right. *New York Times v. Sullivan* (1964),[17] which imposed First Amendment limitations on the libel laws, was originally hailed as a great victory for the press. Lyle Denniston contends that it was flawed from the outset, however, and he analyzes just how those original faults resulted in sharply curtailing press freedoms during the Burger era. Sidney Zion supplements this with a report on how the Burger Court discriminated among different kinds of defamatory speech.

A more sharply demarcated reversal of form appears in two criminal contexts. As Michael Meltsner writes, in the mid-1970s, the Court was making capital punishment so difficult to administer within constitutional standards that it seemed doomed. By 1983, however, the Court had lost patience with lawyers trying to save their clients by insisting on fair procedures, and began to abandon its concern for fairness. In my essay on prisoners' rights, I chronicle a somewhat similar rise and fall in the Court's prisoners-rights cases. Between 1969 and June 1974, prisoners rarely lost a case in the Supreme Court. From June 1974 on, however, it became almost impossible for a prisoner to win one, as the Court, led by Justice Rehnquist, insisted on judicial deference to prison administrators, a throwback to the old "hands off" doctrine that many of us thought long since discredited.

Where the handicapped are concerned, the picture is more confusing. The Court did recognize some constitutional and statutory rights, but, as Norman Rosenberg explains, it often took away in practical application what it seemed to be giving in principle.

There remain, however, some very important continuities. Decisions from 1981 to 1984 seemed to signal a significant erosion of the wall of separation between church and state. Norman Redlich's comprehensive analysis of the decisions on the First Amendment's prohibition against official establishments of religion shows, however, that as a result of the 1985 and 1986 cases, the basic doctrines establishing the separateness of church and state still survived when Warren Burger left, though the decisions were often very close. And with some important exceptions, highlighted by Haywood Burns and Wendy Williams, the rights of racial minorities and women—including the right to an abortion—were still receiving substantial protection.

In the very last days of the Burger era, however, the Court reasserted and underscored its conservatism. In a cruelly traditionalist opinion by Justice Byron White, *Bowers v. Hardwick* (1986), a 5–4 majority of the Court refused to extend to private homosexual conduct the right to privacy recognized in the abortion, contraception, and other cases. In a biting comment, Yale professor Paul Gewirtz assailed the Court's opinion for responding to the arguments favoring such a right with nothing but insults, and its "failure to acknowledge in any way the human dimension of this issue . . . that this case involves human beings who have need for intimacy, love and sexual expression like the rest of us." It is not surprising that the five-member majority was composed of the four critics of the abortion decision and Justice Powell, who is frequently uneasy about developing new protections for individual rights.[18]

The Burger Court remained consistent, however, with respect to a matter we do not deal with separately but is basic to American constitutionalism: the respective roles of the federal government and the states, and how to reconcile conflicts between them. The Court consistently struck down parochial state efforts to favor in-state businesses at the expense of out-of-staters,[19] with Justice Rehnquist in frequent and sometimes solitary dissent. And despite a sharply split 1976 decision, *National League of Cities v. Usery,* which nullified a federal statute applying the minimum-wage and maximum-hour requirements of the Fair Labor Standards Act to state and local employees, the Court imposed few limits on congressional power over state authorities. *National League of Cities* was subsequently interpreted as not preventing application of federal energy standards to state utility commissions or the Age Discrimination in Employment Act to state employees. In 1985 the Court finally overruled the decision as "unworkable" in *Garcia v. San Antonio Metro. Transit Authority,* though two of the four dissenters in *Garcia*—Justices Rehnquist and O'Connor—warned that they would reinstate *National League of Cities* as soon as the Court composition changed in their favor.[20]

What of the future? How will the changes on the Court affect the Reagan administration's campaign to turn the clock back a half century and more in such matters as abortion, church-state separation, civil rights, criminal law and capital punishment, free speech and press, environmental and safety regulation, and a competitive economy?

One thing is clear already. Given the opportunity, President Reagan will appoint justices who will be eager participants in this effort, for based on their records to date, Chief Justice Rehnquist and Justice Scalia share the administration's hostility to the rulings of the Warren and Burger Courts.

The administration's campaign purports to be based on two fundamental principles, both of which are often invoked by Chief Justice Rehnquist and Justice Scalia: courts should exercise "judicial restraint," and judges should construe constitutional provisions in accordance with the framers' original intent.

"Judicial restraint" sounds like the reasonable notion that judges should not intrude on legislative and executive prerogatives. But in practice, Attorney General Edwin Meese III, Chief Justice Rehnquist, and others who share their views have given it a variable content. They support judicial restraint when the judiciary is asked to *protect* civil rights and civil liberties; while they unabashedly favor an energetic activism when it comes to *curtailing* such rights and liberties, or to promoting business interests.

The controversy over tax exemptions for schools that discriminate against minorities is a good example of this ambivalence. In *Allen v. Wright* (1984), the Reagan administration persuaded the Court to reject a challenge by black parents to enforcement procedures the IRS itself had found inadequate, on the ground that the courts should not mix into such matters. But one year earlier, in the *Bob Jones University* case, the administration urged the Court to ignore what was found to be clear congressional intent and to set aside the IRS regulations entirely; Justice Rehnquist was the administration's only supporter.[21]

The administration has also urged the Court to ignore one of the cardinal principles of judicial restraint—that it should decide cases on the narrowest ground possible, especially if that avoids deciding a constitutional question. In *United States v. Leon* (1984), in which the Court created a good-faith exception to the rule excluding illegally obtained evidence from criminal trials, and in *Grove City College v. Bell* (1984), in which the Court narrowly construed the statute barring discrimination by recipients of federal funds, the administration urged far-reaching outcomes, even though the decisions could have been based on limited, fact-specific grounds. Here, the Burger Court was far more receptive, and accepted the administration's broad position, ignoring the available narrow base.[22]

Under the Reagan administration, the Attorney General's zeal for judicial restraint also seemed limited where presidential power is involved. In a little-noticed address in September 1985, Meese challenged the constitutionality of the long-established congressional practice of delegating enforcement power to regulatory agencies. Justice O'Connor saw a similar implication in the government's argument in the *Gramm-Rudman* case (1986), and the lower-court opinion striking down the act, which is generally attributed to then-Judge Scalia, showed great sympathy for this position; the Supreme Court's decision affirming the nullification of the Gramm-Rudman Act—itself a major bit of activism urged by the administration—pointedly omitted all reference to the issue. If this position were adopted—and it would involve overturning a fifty-year-old precedent—it would place the now-independent regulatory agencies under the President's control.[23]

Consider also the Attorney General's reaction to the Supreme Court's decision in the *Garcia* case mentioned earlier. *National League of Cities v. Usery,* which ruled that the federal Fair Labor Standards Act could not constitutionally be applied to state and local employees, was judicial activism at its most vigorous, for it involved congressional action in economic matters, and judges had not overruled such actions since 1937. In *Garcia,* the Court advised the states to look to Congress for protection against federal action, a principle more than 150 years old. Although one would have expected applause from Meese for this judicial deference to the representative organs of government, he and other devotees of his brand of judicial restraint assailed the decision for leaving the states to the tender mercies of "political officials," bereft of a judiciary to "protect . . . the States from federal overreacting."[24]

Mr. Meese claims that his concern for federalism is partly behind his criticism of *Garcia.* But here, too, the Attorney General has shown a remarkable inconsistency. In the "Baby Doe" case, *Bowen v. Am. Hosp. Ass'n.* (1986), the Solicitor General asked the Supreme Court to approve the use of section 504 of the Rehabilitation Act of 1973 to justify sweeping federal intervention in decisions concerning the treatment of seriously ill infants. Child protection and medical treatment are areas traditionally handled by the states, and in 1977 the Secretary of Health, Education and Welfare had concluded that the act provided no authority for federal intervention. That, however, didn't stop the Solicitor General from asking the Court to allow the federal government to ignore what the states had done in such matters. The Court again rebuffed him, noting that Congress had shown no interest in overriding state and local authority in such matters.[25]

Where the interests of business are concerned, the administration has also not been shy about seeking judicial activism. As Jerry Cohen and Herbert Milstein document, it has continually asked the Court to rewrite the antitrust laws to favor business, which has drawn angry responses from Congress including a prohibition against presenting to the Court certain arguments for relaxing the ban on price fixing between buyers and sellers.[26]

In March 1986, *Congressional Quarterly* concluded that "despite its stated opposition to judicial activism, the Reagan administration has engaged in an unprecedented degree of legal activism before the Supreme Court. Since President Reagan took office in 1981, the Solicitor General—who speaks for the government before the high court—

has volunteered that administration's views to the justices more often than any of his predecessors."[27] The cases involved not just abortion and other social issues, but sexual-harassment problems, unemployment compensation, civil rights damages and attorney's fees, land-use legislation, and more. In all of these, the government was not a party but a volunteer, and it asked the Court to exercise vigorous judicial activism in support of property and against poor people, workers, and those whose civil rights were violated. More often than not, the Court turned down the government, on the ground that Congress had decided otherwise.

The justices do not really believe in judicial restraint either, as the Burger Court graphically demonstrated in two of the most important opinions of its entire seventeen-year history, decided in its last days. On June 30, 1986, the Court decided *Bowers v. Hardwick*, the homosexuality case. Writing for the Court, Justice Byron White stressed the need for judicial self-restraint. The same day, however, he wrote the lead opinion in *Davis v. Bandemer*, creating a new right to challenge political gerrymandering, over angry complaints about improper judicial activism from the dissenters (who had voted for healthy activism in other cases); Justice Powell, who in the sodomy case had joined the White opinion urging restraint, also voted to create the right to challenge gerrymandering.[28] Regardless of whether it is sound, the gerrymandering decision has put the courts in the business of remaking the political face of the country and will force them to adjudicate bitter partisan disputes without the benefit of objective criteria, since the Court offered none.

Indeed, the entire record of the Burger Court, from its first days to its very last, when it struck down the Gramm-Rudman Act, is one of activism. And so it will always be. Since its earliest years, the Supreme Court has been actively and deliberately shaping the social and political structure of the nation, and that will never change. The pertinent question is, activist for what goal?

The administration's "original intent" argument is cut from the same motivational cloth, though its threadbare and patchy quality is more obvious. In various speeches, Mr. Meese has criticized judges who engage in "chameleon jurisprudence, changing color and form in each era" and who think

> that what matters most about the Constitution is not its words but its so-called "spirit." These individuals focus less

on the language of specific provisions than on what they describe as the "vision" or "concepts of human dignity" they find embodied in the Constitution. This approach to jurisprudence has led to some remarkable and tragic conclusions.

In the 1850s, the Supreme Court under Chief Justice Roger B. Taney read blacks out of the Constitution in order to invalidate Congress' attempt to limit the spread of slavery. The *Dred Scott v. Sandford* decision, famously described as a judicial "self-inflicted wound," helped bring on civil war.[29]

The ludicrousness of this will be obvious to anyone who reads *Dred Scott*. Apart from the inherent implausibility of the notion that a decision "read[ing] blacks out of the Constitution" could be based on "concepts of human dignity," the fact is that Taney did precisely what Meese wants judges to do: he engaged in an extensively researched, strict reading of the framers' original intent, explicitly rejecting any "more liberal" (Taney's phrase) current views.[30]

Meese's fidelity to the original-intent doctrine is itself somewhat dubious. *Brown v. Board of Education* (1954)[31] is now so well established that only an occasional disinterested scholar like Raoul Berger criticizes it, and certainly not a politician like Meese, who has praised it as an example of fidelity to the original intent of the framers of the Fourteenth Amendment in 1866. But if anything is clear from the less than pellucid history of that enactment, it is this: the amendment was not meant to outlaw segregated schools. Indeed, as Alexander Bickel concluded, the Fourteenth Amendment

> was meant to apply neither to jury service, nor suffrage, nor anti-miscegenation statutes, nor segregation. . . . The evidence of congressional purpose is as clear as such evidence is likely to be.[32]

On the other hand, the historical record makes it equally clear that the framers of the amendment had no objection to racial preferences and affirmative action—the Freedmen's Bureau Act, also adopted in 1866, was bitterly opposed because, as one senator complained, it "gives them [blacks] favors that the poor white boy in the North cannot get."[33]

Obviously, Meese would not try to justify school segregation or antimiscegenation statutes today, and he is certainly not impressed by the thirty-ninth Congress's approval of racial preferences. But if there is discretion to pick and choose which intentions to honor and which to reject, by what criteria are those choices to be made? Except by exercising a contemporary moral and practical judgment, how can one reject the framers' views on some things, but not on others?

Also, circumstances have changed so much since the late eighteenth and mid-nineteenth centuries, how can we know how the various framers of the Constitution and its amendments would respond to today's problems? As Justice O'Connor observed last year in a school-prayer case, responding to an "original intention" dissent by Rehnquist, "it is unlikely that the [Framers or ratifying legislators] anticipated the problems of interaction of church and state in the public schools."[34] This holds true for almost every major problem we face today, even though since 1787 we have been basically consistent in our way of doing things. This consistency is reflected in our long-standing traditions and customs, in our general adherence to *stare decisis*, and in our continuing fidelity to the core ideas and values expressed in the Constitution. Meese is correct in saying that "those who framed the Constitution chose their words carefully." But the words and ideas they chose are rarely precise or confining, and the constitutional text was intended to accommodate what Thaddeus Stevens in 1866 called the "advancing progress of a higher morality."[35]

In any case, the framers' intent is often hard to discern. It is seldom possible to understand what people in earlier centuries meant by certain words without knowing the contemporaneous social and legal context. To an eighteenth-century lawyer, for example, "intent" and "intention" meant something quite different from what they mean to a lawyer today: they referred not to the subjective opinion of the draftsmen, but to the *objective* intent, as reflected in judicial precedents and other public meanings.[36] Also, the historical records are often incomplete and confusing. We do not have a verbatim transcript of the debates of the Philadelphia Convention in 1787, only a compilation of notes taken by many different, often partisan, participants. The editor Max Farrand has characterized these records as "carelessly kept," sketchy, and incomplete.[37]

Moreover, our understanding of history, like our understanding of all social sciences, is constantly being revised. In 1960, the noted historian Leonard Levy argued that the framers did not intend the First Amendment to repudiate the repressive common law of seditious libel. His conclusions became the commonly held view. Recent research, however, has led Levy to conclude that there was a much greater acceptance of vigorous expression in the eighteenth century than he originally thought.[38]

But even if we could reliably discern the framers' intention, why should their views govern? They didn't adopt the Constitution; they only drafted it. The state conventions adopted the Constitution, and an even larger constituency (two-thirds of both houses of Congress and three-fourths of the state legislatures) adopted the Bill of Rights and the Fourteenth Amendment. Why aren't the constituents' views— in all their multiplicity—the decisive ones? Certainly James Madison thought they were.

How will these rationalizations for ultraconservative decision-making fare on the Rehnquist Court? How much of a repudiation of the Warren and Burger Court rulings promoting individual rights and liberties are we likely to get?

That Chief Justice Rehnquist and Justice Scalia are not sympathetic to these rulings is hardly in doubt. Justice Rehnquist, for example, had dissented from all eight of his colleagues more than seventy times, something of a record, and generally in cases involving social justice or individual rights. To note just a few examples, he was the lone dissenter from otherwise unanimous decisions allowing aliens the right to get civil service jobs, illegitimate children to inherit, and indigent new arrivals to get free medical care; he frequently dissents alone when the Court refuses to hear a lower-court ruling favoring a civil rights plaintiff. In many more Bill of Rights cases, he and Chief Justice Burger were the only dissenters; for example, they were the only justices to vote to continue allowing prosecutors to exclude blacks from a criminal jury.[39] During his fifteen years on the Court, Justice Rehnquist rarely voted to sustain a claim of individual rights, and then only when the violation was so flagrant that the vote for the claim was unanimous.

Judge Scalia appears to be equally conservative. He has consistently voted against the press in libel cases,[40] has called the Freedom of Information Act "a disaster," and has lambasted affirmative action. He, like the Chief Justice, has specialized in developing ways to keep litigants attempting to challenge governmental abuses out of court.

Nevertheless, the net change in actual case outcomes is hard to predict. Although the last year of the Burger era saw more 5–4 votes than in the five previous years, Chief Justice Rehnquist will just continue to vote as he always has, and Justice Scalia will simply be replacing the second most conservative member of the Court.

There are more subtle factors, however, and they may affect outcomes. There is, first of all, the matter of interpersonal relationships on the Court. Although outside scholarship, election returns, and other matters inevitably influence the justices, one of the most important factors is the relationships among them and the respect they hold for one another.

Chief Justice Burger was not effective in this sphere. Few of his fellow justices had much respect for his intellectual powers, and they tended to mistrust him, partly because of his often punitive manipulation of his authority to assign opinions. Chief Justice Rehnquist and Justice Scalia are very different. Even those colleagues most hostile to their views have expressed admiration for their intellectual powers and affection for them as associates. Although it is unlikely that this will have much of an impact as far as Chief Justice Rehnquist in concerned—his fellow justices have worked with him for a long time and are not likely to be affected by his new eminence—Justice Scalia may sometimes be able to swing the more centrist judges, while Chief Justice Burger could not.

Justice Scalia may also prove more conservative than Chief Justice Burger, who in such matters as federally mandated affirmative action in *Fullilove v. Klutznick* (1980), abortion, and in other settings may be more sensitive to both precedent and nonideological considerations than Justice Scalia.[41]

In other respects, the new Chief Justice can make a significant difference. Since he controls the opinion-writing assignment when he is in the majority, Chief Justice Rehnquist can assign himself the most important decisions. Although Burger used to assign Rehnquist many of the important decisions anyway, more will now go to him. This can have a very real long-term impact, because when Justice Rehnquist wrote for the majority during the Burger years, he invariably wrote in broad, sweeping terms verging on sloppiness, with the obvious purpose of laying down rules that would be hard to limit to the facts of the particular case before the Court.[42]

The Chief Justice, moreover, often has great influence with new justices, no matter who appoints them, if only because of his opinion-assigning power.

Finally, the Chief Justice has two vital nonadjudicative roles: he administers the federal judiciary, a large and powerful institution, and he is the spokesman for the entire federal judiciary—he is, as Chief Justice Burger liked to say, "the Chief Justice of the United States," not just of the Supreme Court. As Alan Morrison has documented elsewhere,[43] the Chief Justice, through his control of the membership and staffs of the Judicial Conference and some twenty judicial committees, exercises great influence over the administration of justice throughout the United States. These committees deal with such matters as class-action rules, discovery, probation, sentencing, and jury rules. The Chief Justice is also the federal court's spokesperson on legislative matters and he appoints the members of special courts.

In addition, the Chief Justice is the spokesman for the federal courts to the community at large. In this respect, the appointment of Chief Justice Rehnquist is especially disturbing. What does it say to the poor, the victims of discrimination, the unpopular, and those socially, politically, or otherwise handicapped, who have come to look to the federal judiciary as the last resort for some justice, that its leader has consistently tried to turn them away?

We will not know whether the Burger Court was only a transition from the liberal activism of the Warren Court to the reactionary activism of a Rehnquist Court, until one or two more appointments are made. That, in turn, depends on which president makes the nominations and how the Senate reacts. And even then, not all the great landmarks of the last thirty years are likely to fall. Although the notion that justices frequently disappoint the presidents who appoint them is largely a myth (few presidents are disappointed with respect to the specific reasons for which they made their choices, but only with respect to other or unanticipated issues)[44], the Court continually surprises its observers, and even extreme conservatives may want to avoid the instability that comes with radical change and indifference to precedent.

In 1979, ten years after Warren Burger became chief justice, I wrote that "this Court may indeed be like Churchill's much-scorned pudding, without a theme." I wondered, however, "is that so bad, at a time when the theme set by the other branches of Government and the not-so-silent majority often seems so hostile to human rights?"[45] More appointments like Chief Justice Rehnquist and Justice Scalia may make us very nostalgic indeed for those pudding years.

·I·

ACCESS TO
THE COURTS

· 1 ·

Justiciability, Remedies, and the Burger Court

BURT NEUBORNE

Discussion of the Burger Court's seventy-odd decisions on "justi-ciability" issues—such as who has enough of an interest in the out-come of a case ("standing") to invoke a federal court's power, and when the court should hear a case—has taken place at a very high level, if you measure it in decibels. Critics have characterized the decisions as cynical attempts to close the courthouse doors to those trying to enforce their constitutional rights. Defenders have hailed them as a welcome return to a principled vision of a restrained ju-diciary in a functioning democracy.

In fact, the Burger Court's decisions on who can get into federal court and when are neither blueprints for majoritarian oppression nor expressions of judicial principle. Rather, they reflect a fundamental void in American political theory concerning the legitimacy and func-tion of judicial review.

There is nothing in our Constitution that explicitly authorizes courts to overrule other branches of government—state or federal—in the name of enforcing fidelity to the Constitution. Despite the fact that judicial review is the most distinctive and widely admired aspect of our political structure, we are two hundred years into the American experiment and we still haven't evolved a convincing theoretical ex-planation of where the Supreme Court's power comes from and how it should be used. When judicial review is discussed, we've tended to heed Bismarck's warning that lovers of sausages and law alike should not look too closely at what goes into the product.

3

The orthodox apologia for judicial review flows from John Marshall's brilliant attempt to establish his power to torment President Jefferson in 1803. In *Marbury v. Madison*,[1] Marshall projected the image of a Supreme Court justice as reluctant arbiter, an innocent bystander charged by Congress with responsibility for resolving controversies, but confronted by disputatious litigants asserting conflicting rules of law. When, Marshall argued, one proposed governing rule of law is established by the Constitution, while its competition is merely the creature of Congress or the President, the Court's duty must be to apply the constitutional rule as a matter of hierarchy. Judicial review, according to Marshall, is simply the accidental by-product of a judge's duty to select the governing rule of law in order to resolve a dispute between litigants. Moreover, according to Marshall, a judge has no real choice in the matter, since, in resolving the dispute the judge merely plays out a hand dealt by someone else— Congress tells the judge to resolve the dispute and the Constitution supplies the governing rule of law.

Marshall's opinion in *Marbury* shrewdly stressed those relatively rare provisions of the Constitution that are self-defining, like the requirement of two witnesses for a treason conviction. He carefully skirted the troublesome problems of how to deal with ambiguous constitutional phrases like "due process of law" and "privileges and immunities of citizenship" and, even, "abridgement of the freedom of speech." Nothing in Marshall's opinion in *Marbury* explains why the Supreme Court's reading of the Constitution should take precedence over a contrary reading by Congress whenever a constitutional provision invites more than one plausible construction. Thus, while Marshall's elaborate apologia for judicial review in *Marbury* provides a formal justification for the phenomenon, it has never provided an intellectually satisfactory explanation of the reality inherent in virtually all constitutional adjudication, including *Marbury* itself, in which judges first breathe meaning into an open-textured provision of the Constitution and then enforce that meaning against the other branches of government. We have been willing to accept the *Marbury* explanation, even to lionize it, without looking too closely at its warts because judicial review has become so integral a part of our political structure and has worked so well as a check on majoritarian overreaching that any theory purporting to explain the process, even one as flawed as Marshall's, is preferable to no theory at all.

When, however, judicial review is analyzed functionally rather than formalistically, every element of the *Marbury* explanation, which treats judges as passive figures forced by circumstances beyond their control to overturn the decisions of Congress as a necessary and essentially mechanical incident of a duty to resolve a dispute, breaks down. Nothing in the last one hundred years justifies painting Supreme Court justices as passive figures engaged in the mechanical process of playing out someone else's hand. Rather, American judges have creatively helped to determine the relationship between the individual and the state in ways that simply cannot be explained by reference to John Marshall's defense of judicial review. Instead of being passive figures, they have repeatedly played active roles in setting the national agenda. Instead of behaving like mechanistic robots, they have made law by choosing among a number of plausible readings of ambiguous constitutional phrases. Instead of acting solely, or even principally, as dispute resolvers, American judges, especially at the appellate level, have acted primarily as generators of behavioral norms for society at large.

Unfortunately, given the virtual canonization of *Marbury* as the definitive apologia for judicial review, few alternative defenses of the process have been attempted. The celebrated footnote 4 in *U.S. v. Carolene Products* (1938)[2] suggests that judicial review is a form of "virtual representation" of discrete and insular minorities, with courts acting as insulated forums exercising special responsibility to protect the interests of persons or groups who are unlikely to get a fair shake in the political process. Individual-rights theorists like Ronald Dworkin have attempted a functional explanation of judicial review, arguing that judges are more capable than political actors of enunciating principled decisions in settings of extraordinary importance to the individual.[3] Process theoreticians like John Hart Ely have argued that judicial review is a necessary corrective to attempts by transient political majorities to prolong their power by impeding the free interplay of the democratic process.[4] None of the relatively recent attempts to forge a theoretical justification for the reality of twentieth-century judicial review has, however, threatened to displace—or even to compete with—the *Marbury* model. The net effect is formal judicial doctrine clinging to *Marbury* as the sole justification for judicial review uneasily coexisting with a judicial reality that has, for a long time, gone far beyond Marshall's somewhat disingenuous description of the process. The tension created by attempts to shoehorn the reality of twentieth-century judicial review into the confines of the nineteenth-century *Marbury* model is what has made the Burger Court's justiciability decisions so controversial.

During the Warren years, while formal adherence to the *Marbury* model was maintained, the Court perceived its power to enforce the Constitution as flowing not from the accidental consequences of resolving a random dispute, but from the Court's preeminent political role as expositor and guardian of the Constitution. At the risk of oversimplification, if the *Marbury* model characterized judicial review as the accidental by-product of the need to resolve a dispute, the Warren Court appeared to view enforcement of the Constitution as its principal responsibility, with dispute resolution serving as an almost incidental by-product of judicial review. Thus, while adherence to the formal aspects of the *Marbury* model was maintained, the constraints of the model were not permitted to interfere with the effective enforcement of constitutional rights. For example, in *Baker v. Carr* (1962),[5] when voters challenged the constitutionality of grossly malapportioned state legislatures, the Warren Court brushed aside objections that no *Marbury*-style dispute existed. The objections were far from frivolous. After all, in *Baker*, the plaintiffs were voters whose alleged injury—the relative devaluation of their votes—was very difficult to quantify and was widely shared by large numbers of similarly situated voters. It is thus inaccurate to characterize *Baker v. Carr* as nothing more than a dispute between discrete litigants that just happens to have raised a profound constitutional question of general significance. In fact, the *Baker* "dispute" was worth resolving only because it concerned a significant issue that affected the lives of large numbers of persons sharing a common constitutional grievance. Even more dramatically, in *Flast v. Cohen* (1968),[6] the Warren Court agreed to decide the constitutionality of federal aid to parochial schools despite the fact that the challengers' only stake in the case was a passionate belief that it was a violation of the establishment clause to funnel federal funds to religious schools. Unlike *Baker*, *Flast* could not be made to fit even the formal constraints of the *Marbury* model. The Warren Court's response was to fashion an exception to the *Marbury* model for establishment-clause challenges to federal spending programs. Thus, while it required adherence to the forms of the *Marbury* model whenever possible, it did not hesitate to stretch the model to its outermost limits (as in *Baker*) or to jettison it entirely (as in *Flast*) in order to make sure that the Supreme Court fulfilled its role as enforcer of the Constitution.

The emergence of the Burger Court in the early 1970s was marked by two dramatic shifts in perspective, with obvious consequences for justiciability doctrine: a wholesale acceptance of Marshall's opinion in *Marbury* as the sole justification for judicial review, and an acceptance of individualized dispute resolution as the dominant, if not the only, function of courts. Unless a disagreement over the meaning of a constitutional provision can be presented in the context of a classic *Marbury*-style dispute, the Burger Court confessed itself powerless to decide it.

In *Laird v. Tatum* (1972),[7] for example, individuals challenging the legality of military surveillance of lawful political protest were rebuffed because the Supreme Court ruled that the challengers had not shown a sufficiently serious "injury-in-fact" to elevate the case to the level of a *Marbury*-style dispute. The legal questions raised by military surveillance of lawful protest were clearly substantial, yet because the injury is both difficult to quantify and widely shared, the Burger Court's strict adherence to *Marbury* removed the judiciary as a restraining force on an arguably unlawful military activity.

In *Schlesinger v. Reservists Committee to Stop the War* (1974),[8] the Supreme Court declined to consider the constitutionality of members of Congress continuing to hold reserve military commissions because the challengers could not be characterized as *Marbury*-style plaintiffs with particularized grievances caused by the unlawful activity, and could not articulate an individualized injury-in-fact. The significant issue of whether members of Congress who are called upon to pass on the military budget may also hold reserve military commissions was rendered incapable of judicial resolution. And in *United States v. Richardson* (1974),[9] the Court refused to entertain a constitutional challenge to the refusal to make public the general contours of the CIA's budget because the challengers were unable to point to a specific injury they suffered that differed from the injury suffered by the general public.

The *Laird*, *Schlesinger*, and *Richardson* decisions announced a radically altered view of the Supreme Court's role in enforcing the Constitution. Unlike the Warren Court, no matter how important the issue, no matter how clearly illegal the activity, and no matter how significant its impact on our citizens, the Burger Court refused to enforce the Constitution unless and until the question was presented in the form of a *Marbury*-style dispute. If the nature of the controversy did not lend itself to the *Marbury* model—as in the reapportionment or church-state cases—the Burger Court simply declared the constitutional provision beyond the range of judicial enforcement.

These first three justiciability cases—*Laird, Schlesinger,* and *Richardson*—rebuffed the attempts made by political activists to raise arguably esoteric challenges to ostensibly legitimate governmental activity. The next case—*Warth v. Seldin* (1975)[10]—revealed the full reach of the new doctrine into more traditional areas of constitutional law. In *Warth,* inner-city residents of Rochester, New York, challenged the restrictive zoning devices maintained by suburban communities which made it impossible or prohibitively expensive to build multiple dwellings accessible to poor people. Once again, the Burger Court by a narrow majority dismissed the challenge, holding that the plaintiffs had failed to point to a specific project that had been frustrated and had therefore failed to demonstrate a concrete grievance. Accordingly, the Court ruled, the inner-city residents had only a generalized grievance that failed to rise to the level of a *Marbury* dispute. In *Warth,* given the realities of the housing market, no specific project was feasible in the face of restrictive zoning; but, in the absence of a specific project, no challenge to the zoning was possible. The result is a Catch-22 vision of *Marbury* that denies powerless plaintiffs access to a judicial forum to adjudicate a serious constitutional question solely because the issue cannot be dressed up to look like *Marbury v. Madison.*

In *Rizzo v. Goode* (1976),[11] the Court carried the *Marbury* analysis even further by reversing an injunction requiring a police chief to take action to control a pattern of police brutality because the police chief had not himself been involved in the illegal acts. Since the *Marbury* model presumes the existence of a dispute between identifiable litigants, the Court reasoned that the police chief fell outside the model because he himself had done nothing to the plaintiffs. The net effect of this slavish adherence to *Marbury* was to limit the Court's power to issue effective remedial orders designed to protect constitutional rights.

In *City of Los Angeles v. Lyons* (1983),[12] the Court took its *Marbury* fetish to almost absurd lengths, holding that the victim of an allegedly illegal police chokehold did not qualify as a *Marbury* plaintiff for the purposes of seeking an injunction against the future use of the chokehold because he could not show a likelihood that he would be choked a second time and, thus, had no individualized dispute with the defendants.

And in *Valley Forge Christian College v. Americans United for Separation of Church and State* (1982),[13] the Court declined to apply the relaxed rules of *Flast v. Cohen* to a challenge to a government gift of land to a religious school. Instead, the Court dismissed the case because the plaintiffs could show no particularized injury from the gift. Thus, if the government channels tax dollars to religious schools, individuals may challenge the expenditure under the Warren Court's relaxed *Flast* test; but if the government gives property away, the case would not be heard by the Burger Court because it does not conform to John Marshall's defense of judicial review.

Rigid adherence to the *Marbury* model as the sole justification for judicial review in the cases from *Laird* to *Valley Forge* connotes more than the requirement of a particularized injury-in-fact. It requires, as well, a showing that the defendants' challenged actions caused the injury-in-fact and that judicial intervention will alleviate the injury. If, after all, resolution of a dispute between the plaintiff and defendant is the sole justification for the Court's power, a plaintiff must show that the requested judicial decision will actually benefit the plaintiff in order to justify its issuance. Not surprisingly, therefore, the Burger Court declined to resolve serious disputes over the legality of governmental action because plaintiffs could not show with certainty that a legal victory would alleviate their practical plight. In *Linda R. S. v. Richard D.* (1973),[14] the Court rebuffed a challenge to the failure of local officials to enforce the law because it was impossible to predict whether increased levels of enforcement would actually benefit the named plaintiffs. In *Warth v. Seldin*, the Court sought to justify its refusal to pass on the constitutionality of restrictive zoning by observing that no basis existed to predict that low-income housing would, in fact, be constructed if the zoning rules were struck down. In *Simon v. Eastern Kentucky Welfare Rights Organization* (1976),[15] the Court refused to decide the legality of granting tax-deductible status to hospitals that refused to serve the poor because no showing could be made that the threat of a denial of this status would lead to increased health services for poor plaintiffs. And, in *Allen v. Wright* (1984),[16] the Court refused to decide the legality of the grant of tax-deductible status to allegedly segregated private schools because the plaintiffs could not prove that the removal of this status would actually cause white children to return to integrated public schools.

In each of the so-called causation-in-fact cases, the Burger Court turned away from serious allegations of unlawful activity not because the issues were incapable of judicial resolution—the issues of law raised by the cases were no more troublesome than the issues raised in most constitutional cases—but because the resolution of the legal issue might not provide the precise tangible benefit to the plaintiff that he hoped for. The linkage between a rigid causation-in-fact test and the *Marbury* model is obvious: if a court's action will not, in fact, cure the plaintiff's injury, the dispute is not judicially resolvable; if the dispute is not judicially resolvable, the Court has no power to announce the governing law. When one links the injury-in-fact cases like *Laird v. Tatum* with the causation-in-fact cases like *EKWRO v. Simon*, the ability of the judiciary to enforce the Constitution becomes an appendage of its ability to entertain and resolve *Marbury*-style disputes. If, according to the Burger Court, an issue—such as the constitutionality of exclusionary zoning or military spying on protest activity—doesn't fit neatly into the *Marbury* model, the Supreme Court lacks not only the duty to seek to resolve it but the power even to try. Under a rigid application of *Marbury*, the Supreme Court's judicial review power—a central attribute of our political structure—is a hostage to the random question of whether a given constitutional issue is describable in traditional dispute-resolution terms.

The practical consequences of this rigid reading of the *Marbury* model as the sole justification for judicial review should not be overstated. One reason why the model has endured so long is that most issues lend themselves to resolution in the form of a classic *Marbury*-style dispute, especially if the model is generously defined. In most settings, identifiable plaintiffs exist with particularized grievances linked causally to an allegedly unconstitutional act by a government defendant. Given the strength of our attachment to the model and its undeniable functional value in assuring a spirited presentation of the issues by adversaries with a stake in the outcome, it is appropriate to require adherence to *Marbury* in most settings. As the Burger Court's decisions demonstrate, however, constitutional questions of major significance exist which lie at or over the model's borders. The price of a rigid acceptance of John Marshall's opinion in *Marbury* as the sole justification for judicial review is the placing of those questions outside the judiciary's ability to resolve.

The Burger Court's justiciability decisions can be analyzed in two ways. First, assuming continued adherence to the *Marbury* model as the sole justification for judicial review, has the Court drawn defensible and principled lines defining the limits of the model? Second, if a principled application of *Marbury* precludes the judiciary from enforcing significant provisions of the Constitution, can the model be supplemented?

Even if one accepts *Marbury* as the sole justification for judicial activity, many of the Burger Court's decisions appear to be unnecessarily narrow readings of the *Marbury* model. In *Laird v. Tatum*, for example, the Court was able to assert that the targets of allegedly unlawful military surveillance had not suffered an injury-in-fact and thus presented no *Marbury*-style dispute, only by ignoring allegations that they—and people like them—would refrain from lawful protest activity if the armed forces continued to collect the names and addresses of the protestors. In *United States v. Richardson*, persons complaining about the secrecy of the CIA budget were denied information which they claimed was needed to cast an informed vote. Whether or not they were entitled to the information on the merits, a deprivation of information should be viewed as a sufficiently serious injury to trigger the *Marbury* model. Nothing in Marshall's opinion supports the Court's suggestion that since the information was denied equally to everyone, no one had a sufficiently particularized injury to support a judicial challenge; such a rule invites the absurd consequences that the more widespread the injury from a constitutional violation, the less chance there is of judicial protection. Thus, two of the three cases announcing the Burger Court's new justiciability rules appear to manipulate the *Marbury* model to block judicial consideration of cases that fell within a principled view of the process.

The later cases are even worse. *Warth v. Seldin*, in which the Court declined to pass on the constitutionality of exclusionary zoning, cannot be defended under any view of *Marbury*. The impact of suburban exclusionary zoning on the ability of inner-city residents to escape from the ghetto is obvious. The case was brought in order to remove exclusionary zoning as an obstacle to the building of low-cost housing in the suburbs. The Court's refusal to decide the case simply used *Marbury* as an excuse for avoiding the issue, and left the powerless with no forum in which to protect their rights.

In *Rizzo v. Goode*, all the attributes of the *Marbury* model were unquestionably assembled. Plaintiffs had proved a pattern of unconstitutional activity by named Philadelphia police officers. When the district judge sought to prevent future abuses by directing the police chief to take action to stop the abuses, the Supreme Court reversed him, holding that the police chief wasn't a party to the *Marbury*-style dispute between the plaintiffs and the guilty officers. Nothing in *Marbury*, however, even purports to limit the remedial power of a court confronted with a *Marbury*-style dispute from going beyond the original parties to assure the termination of a pattern of unconstitutional activity.

Similarly, in *City of Los Angeles v. Lyons*, it verged on the bizarre to argue that *Marbury* precluded the courts from enjoining the use of unconstitutional force that had already almost killed the plaintiff because he allegedly lacked a sufficient interest in the future use of the force. If *Marbury* was designed to assure that judicial decision-making take place in the context of a real dispute, the *Lyons* damage action clearly filled the bill. Indeed, the Court conceded that the legality of the Los Angeles chokehold would be decided by the damage verdict. Nevertheless, the Court refused to permit an injunction against continuation of the illegal activity, ostensibly because it would violate the *Marbury* model. However, once the existence of a *Marbury*-style dispute has been established, there is nothing in the rationale of *Marbury* to prevent a court from taking necessary steps to prevent a repetition of the illegal activity that gave rise to the original dispute.

Finally, the causation-in-fact cases that deny access to the courts because the relief may not alleviate the plaintiffs' practical problems cannot be justified under *Marbury*. In each of the cases, a plaintiff identified an arguably unlawful official policy that contributed to his injury. In each case, the purpose of the lawsuit was to remove the policy in the hope that, absent the policy, the plaintiff's plight would improve. A reasonable expectation that the plaintiff's position will improve in the absence of an unlawful policy is the most one can ask in order to satisfy the *Marbury* model. Unfortunately, the Burger Court required as a precondition of deciding the legality of the policy, not a showing of reasonable expectation of improvement, but proof that actual improvement would occur.

Any suggestion that the restrictive application of *Marbury* present in most Burger Court decisions is a principled view of judicial self-restraint is belied by the Court's willingness to abandon *Marbury* constraints when that suits its political agenda. For example, in *Duke Power Co. v. Carolina Environmental Study Group* (1978),[17] a respected federal district judge had invalidated a federally imposed ceiling on liability for damages caused by a nuclear accident at a nuclear power plant. The ceiling, imposed in order to permit the plants to obtain financing, was challenged by residents living in the vicinity of a plant under construction, who argued that it would be unconstitutional to limit the plant's liability to them in the event of a future nuclear accident. The Supreme Court quite properly held that the challengers did not qualify as *Marbury* disputants, since the twin contingencies of a future nuclear accident and damages in excess of the ceiling were too speculative to give rise to a current *Marbury* dispute. If, however, the Court had simply dismissed the case as nonjusticiable, a serious cloud would have been placed on the liability ceiling, since the only judge to have passed on it had declared it unconstitutional. Even if that lower-court decision were to be technically vacated on standing grounds, no bond lawyer could give an unqualified opinion that the ceiling was valid in the teeth of the lower court's contrary finding. Thus, the practical effect of a justiciability dismissal would have been to complicate future bond financings for nuclear power plants. Confronted with such a prospect, the Chief Justice decided that the validity of the ceiling was justiciable after all, since the challengers alleged that the plant would create thermal pollution and, in the absence of the ceiling, it might be impossible to obtain financing to complete the plant. The "dispute" over the possibility of a lack of financing and the prospect of possible thermal pollution was deemed enough of a particularized grievance to permit the Court to reach the lower-court decision on the merits and to reverse it, thus removing the obstacle to the construction of future plants. It is, of course, impossible to explain why the challengers in *Duke Power* qualified as *Marbury* disputants but the inner-city residents in *Warth* did not. So much for principle.

Similarly, in *Bender v. Williamsport* (1986),[18] the Court was asked to pass on the constitutionality of student-initiated prayer meetings prior to the beginning of the high school day. The trial court had upheld the legality of the prayer meetings and the school board had declined to appeal. A dissenting member of the board had, nevertheless, sought to appeal. The Court's majority, applying classic *Marbury* theory, ruled that no dispute existed because the "contending" parties (the school board and the students seeking to hold their prayer meeting) were on the same side. Despite their insistence in *Rizzo v. Goode* that the police chief could not be made a *Marbury* party, Justice Rehnquist and Chief Justice Burger vigorously protested, arguing that the dissenting school-board member could be made an adverse party. Of course, the principal—if not the principled—difference between the police chief in *Rizzo* and the school-board member in *Bender* was the fact that Burger and Rehnquist did not wish to reach the merits and deal with the substantive issues in *Rizzo* and were eager to uphold the prayer meetings in *Bender*.

I do not suggest that the Court was wrong to have reached the merits in *Duke Power* or that the majority in *Bender* was incorrect in declining to reach the merits. I do suggest, however, that the willingness of Burger and Rehnquist to reach the merits in *Duke Power* and *Bender* destroys any pretense that their attachment to *Marbury* is strictly principled. In fact, the contrast between the inner-city residents in *Warth* and the affluent suburbanites in *Duke Power* and between the police chief in *Rizzo* and the school-board member in *Bender* illustrates the degree to which the *Marbury* model is susceptible to unprincipled manipulation.

Anger at the manipulation of the justiciability doctrine by the Burger Court is, however, nothing new. The more significant issue raised by its justiciability decisions is whether we are using the correct model to test for justiciability in the first place. As I have suggested, a generous reading of the *Marbury* model will usually permit the Court to fulfill its role as enforcer of the Constitution. That hasn't changed. But when the model is compressed to the point where an unacceptably high number of disputes about the meaning of the Constitution are placed beyond the judiciary's sphere of enforcement, fundamental questions about the model's use are inevitably raised.

Does the Supreme Court's power to serve as final interpreter and enforcer of the Constitution really hang on the slender thread of John Marshall's sophistry? I think not. It's simply too late in the game to pretend that judicial review is an accidental and automatic by-product of individualized dispute resolution. Whether or not the framers intended it, the institution of judicial review has evolved to the point where it doesn't need Marshall's crutch to justify its existence. Judicial review continues to exist not because it is a by-product of the dispute-resolution function, but because it provides an effective institutional check against majoritarian tyranny.

The unhappy history of the twentieth century has taught us that power to the people, whether couched in the benign form of a western democracy or in the more sinister garb of a totalitarian dictatorship, has the capacity to trample the interests of the politically weak in ways that we deem unacceptable. Judicial review has provided western democracies with an institutional vehicle through which majority rule can be tempered in the name of just treatment of the weak and despised. While no single theory has yet emerged to guide us in deciding when and how judicial review should be invoked, whatever one's theory of constitutional adjudication, the institution stands on its own feet without the necessity of Marshall's attempt to characterize it as an inevitable and essentially mechanistic process. None of this is meant to suggest that judges should be free to decide cases without constraints or that they should reach out and decide any issue that has not been properly placed before them.

This is not the place to attempt a full examination of the constraints that can and should limit a judge's freedom of action in construing the Constitution. At a minimum, though, such constraints include the text of the Constitution, the discernible intention of the framers, the work of past judges codified as *stare decisis*, the principled use of analogy and other conventional forms of legal reasoning, the force of public scrutiny and professional criticism, and the pressure generated by the adversary process. Taken together, such constraints seriously limit a judge's freedom of action, although they rarely reduce the task of constitutional adjudication to a mechanical exercise in finding the "right" solution. Rather, they provide the basis for argumentation and criticism against which the creative act of judging may itself be evaluated and from which a conscientious judge may derive her or his conception of the "meaning" of the precise constitutional phrase at issue.

In most settings, moreover, the *Marbury* model is an excellent format for the exercise of judicial review, precisely because it maximizes the prospect that the judge will be vigorously confronted with all sides of the controversy. When, however, either because the *Marbury* model has been excessively limited, as in many Burger Court settings, or because the issue genuinely falls outside the model, as in *Flast v. Cohen*, we cannot afford to have courts ousted from their review functions because of a misplaced allegiance to John Marshall's apologia for judicial review, an apologia that was outdated on the day it was written.

The problem with the Burger Court's justiciability theory is not its preference for the classic *Marbury* model—whenever possible, disputes should be presented to courts in the context of real-world disputes—but its insistence that the Supreme Court's power to carry out the role of guardian of the Constitution is tied to the model. The

Burger Court confused the general *desirability* of deciding constitutional controversies in the context of live disputes between identifiable litigants with its *power* to construe the Constitution. When a genuine disagreement about the meaning of the Constitution erupts that affects the lives of a significant segment of the population, the Court's duty is to construe the Constitution, whether or not the disagreement can be choreographed as a classic *Marbury* dispute.

In fact, we have already recognized that legal disagreements affecting large numbers of people transcend the classic *Marbury* model. The widespread acceptance of the class action is little more than a realization that, often, a given disagreement is more accurately characterized as a dispute affecting a defined group as opposed to a single dispute between individuals. If the named plaintiff in constitutional cases were viewed not merely as the isolated bearer of an individualized grievance, but as the representative of a *de facto* class consisting of the group of persons likely to be affected by the disagreement, the unnecessary shackles imposed by the Burger Court on the judicial review process would disappear. Under such an approach, even if the individual plaintiff's grievance failed to meet the *Marbury* model, the case could go forward on behalf of the absent group members. That is precisely what happens now in a *de jure* class-action setting. In *Sosna v. Iowa* (1975),[19] for example, the Burger Court ruled that the named plaintiff in a challenge to the constitutionality of Iowa's one-year durational residence requirement in divorce cases no longer presented a live dispute since, by the time she reached the Supreme Court, her one-year residence requirement had been satisfied. Under classic *Marbury* analysis, once the *Sosna* plaintiff satisfied the residence requirement, she no longer presented the kind of live dispute that required resolution by the Court and, thus, could no longer serve as a *Marbury* disputant. But the Burger Court did reach the merits in *Sosna*, holding that the lower court's formal certification of a class of similarly situated persons created an *ad hoc* entity—the class— capable of continuing the suit even after the named plaintiff ceased being a *Marbury* disputant.[20]

In the absence of formal class certification, however, the Burger Court often dismissed appeals like *Sosna*. In *DeFunis v. Odegaard* (1974),[21] for example, the Court declined to pass on the legality of an affirmative-action admissions plan because the named plaintiff had graduated while the case was wending its way to the Supreme Court.

But in another case, the Court strained mightily to find a continuing impact on the named plaintiff in order to justify retention of the case. Thus, in *Super-Tire v. McCorkle* (1974),[22] the Court hypothesized that the continued existence of a law authorizing unemployment compensation for strikers might affect future collective bargaining between the parties, thus creating a *Marbury* dispute, even though the strike that had initially precipitated the lawsuit had been settled.

It seems unduly formalistic, though, to force the Supreme Court's judicial review power to turn on the accident of formal class certification in the lower court or the kind of Rube Goldberg gymnastics exemplified by *Super-Tire*. Constitutional cases like *Sosna, DeFunis,* and *Super-Tire* are significant precisely because they have an impact far beyond the resolution of the named plaintiff's dispute. Were cases like the Los Angeles chokehold case or the challenge to exclusionary zoning treated as *de facto* class actions for justiciability purposes, the apparent tension between *Marbury* and the Court's role as enforcer of the Constitution would radically diminish. As in *Sosna,* the Court would be free to recognize that even if the plaintiff fails to satisfy *Marbury,* he could continue on behalf of the absent *de facto* class whose lives would be affected by the case's outcome. Until the Court frees itself from its self-imposed thralldom to the *Marbury* model, though, it will be locked into its current approach, which subordinates the Court's principal role as guardian of the Constitution to the existence of a *Marbury*-style dispute between formalistically defined parties.

Justiciability decisions affect access to the courts. Getting into the federal courthouse isn't worth the effort, though, if the court's remedial powers are inadequate. Unlike the cases that have limited the capacity of courts to resolve constitutional issues, the Burger Court's remedial decisions did, on balance, improve the lot of plaintiffs seeking judicial redress for violations of constitutional rights, often over the Chief Justice's dissent.

Prior to the Burger Court, a plaintiff seeking damages in federal court from a state or local official for violating the plaintiff's federal constitutional rights faced a narrow range of options. Although the Warren Court had ruled in *Monroe v. Pape* (1961)[23] that plaintiffs could seek damages in federal court for the violation of federal constitutional rights at the hands of state or local officials, the Warren

Court refused to permit a civil rights damage action against a local government entity. A plaintiff in a constitutional-damage action was forced to name as the sole defendants the flesh-and-blood government officials who committed the challenged act. If, as was often the case, the official defendant lacked the financial resources to satisfy a money judgment, the plaintiff was out of luck. Moreover, in those cases where the official defendant was merely carrying out the seemingly lawful policies of his government employer, the official was entitled to a defense that he or she acted in a good-faith belief that the act was legal, which often blocked a damage recovery. The result was a system that was unfair, more often than not, either to the plaintiff, by denying any compensation, or to the defendant, by imposing damages personally on an official who was merely carrying out official policy. One of the unheralded achievements of the Burger Court was to restructure that system to provide a more rational mechanism for allocating loss in constitutional cases.

In *Monell v. New York City Dep't of Social Services* (1978),[24] the Burger Court, with Justice Rehnquist and the Chief Justice dissenting, reinterpreted the phrase "person" in the 1871 Civil Rights Act, holding that it authorized damage actions against local government entities as well as individual officials. After *Monell*, when a local government official causes an injury by enforcing an unconstitutional government policy or custom, the loss falls where it belongs, on the government, not on the official. On the other hand, when the government is not guilty of having an unconstitutional policy or custom, the official who on his own inflicts unconstitutional damages remains personally liable for the damages.

The Burger Court, again with Chief Justice Burger and Justice Rehnquist dissenting, reinforced its new system in *Owen v. City of Independence* (1980),[25] by holding that the good-faith defense available to an individual defendant was not available to a government entity. Under a combination of *Monell* and *Owen*, a plaintiff injured by a local government's unconstitutional policy or custom is now entitled to recover damages from the government itself, without regard to the government's good-faith belief in the lawfulness of its policy. On the other hand, a plaintiff injured by an official acting contrary to or in the absence of any government policy may sue the official personally unless the official can establish that he or she acted in good faith.

Since an official acting contrary to or in the absence of policy will, often, be unable to pose a plausible good-faith defense, the new system is likely to assure compensation to an injured plaintiff from either the government entity or the wrongdoing official—with two caveats. First, if a local official injures a plaintiff in the absence of a "custom or policy," the financial ability to recover damages continues to depend on the ability of the official to satisfy a damage judgment. Unless the defendant has insurance, it is often impossible to collect a judgment. Second, a category of cases exists that falls between the cracks of the *Monell-Owen* structure. If an official does not act pursuant to official policy but nevertheless has reasonable good-faith belief in the legality of his actions, both the government and individual defendants will escape damage liability, forcing the plaintiff to bear the loss caused by unconstitutional action.

It is, of course, possible to chart the respective contours of "policy or custom" and the good-faith defense to minimize the prospect of falling between the two. Unfortunately, the Burger Court expanded the good-faith defense by reducing it to an objective standard of reasonableness,[26] while applying a relatively restrictive definition of custom or policy. Thus, a potentially wide crack in the *Monell* system has appeared. Even with the crack, however, the Burger Court (*sans* Burger and Rehnquist) took very real strides toward rationalizing the allocation of loss in constitutional cases involving local government officials.

The 1871 Civil Rights Act, which was the vehicle for the Burger Court's welcome decisions in *Monell* and *Owen*, applies only to acts by state and local officials. Congress has never seen fit to authorize damages against federal officials who violate the Constitution. The Burger Court (over the objections of the Chief Justice) closed that serious gap in *Bivens v. Six Unknown Agents* (1971)[27] by recognizing a cause of action for damages against federal officials arising directly from the Constitution. Thus, after *Bivens* and it progeny, thanks to the Burger Court (*sans* Burger's vote), federal officials may now be sued for damages for violating federal constitutional rights.

What the Burger Court gave with *Monell, Owen,* and *Bivens,* however, it partially took back in a series of decisions expansively applying common-law immunity from suit and extending the good-faith defense. While it certainly did not invent the notion that certain high-ranking officials are immune from damage actions even for willful violations of constitutional rights, the Court applied an expansive conception of immunity that now shields the President, judges, administrative adjudicators, local legislators, district attorneys, police witnesses, and military superiors from damages for such violations. Apart from presidential immunity, however, it held the critical line on immunity for executive officials, refusing to immunize governors, National Guard officials, and school-board members from potential liability for unconstitutional actions, remitting them instead to the necessity of establishing a good-faith defense.

Finally, although *Monell* and *Owen* opened the way for suits in federal court against local-government entities like counties or municipalities, the Burger Court was generally sympathetic to claims of governmental immunity, expanding the reach of the Eleventh Amendment immunity of states so that it covers enforcement of state-law claims in federal court, and refusing to permit suits against the United States for unconstitutional policies unless sovereign immunity was waived by the Federal Tort Claims Act. In fairness, the Burger Court invented neither the Eleventh Amendment nor sovereign immunity, and, when prospective relief is at issue, it was prepared to endorse the fiction that unconstitutional government action is *ultra vires*, thus rendering injunctive relief possible against a government official who has exceeded constitutional limits. The Court was even prepared to permit Congress to override Eleventh Amendment immunity. Thus, while serious gaps continue to exist in our constitutional remedial structure, it would be unfair to blame them unduly on the Burger Court, which, by and large, improved the process.

The appointment of Justice Scalia and the elevation of Justice Rehnquist to chief justice to fill the vacancy caused by Warren Burger's resignation should have little, if any, impact on the area of justiciability and remedies. As an associate justice, Rehnquist joined Chief Justice Burger in championing a highly restrictive view of the *Marbury* model and in dissenting from decisions such as *Monell* and *Owen* that reformed the law of constitutional damages. Presumably, Justice Scalia will be skeptical of any attempt to broaden the theoretical underpinnings of judicial review beyond the mechanistic outlines of the *Marbury* model and will be reluctant to expand the judiciary's remedial armory. Thus, we can expect the continued dominance of a view linking judicial review to the existence of a dispute that fits within John Marshall's description of the process, and a cautious, pragmatic approach to damages in constitutional cases that seeks to apportion risk of loss on rational, functional terms.

· II ·

LIBERTY
OF CONSCIENCE:
THE FIRST
AMENDMENT

·2·

The Burger Court and the Press

LYLE DENNISTON

Five years before Warren Burger became chief justice, the nation's press was celebrating its constitutional liberation. Never before had the First Amendment held such promise for both print and broadcast media; the libel law, a legal bogeyman that had been shadowing the press since the first decade of the Constitution's existence, finally had been interred. Hard, aggressive reporting about the government—tough enough, perhaps, to cause the nation or a community to turn away from its governors in dismay or even disgust—had the Supreme Court's implicit blessing and the First Amendment's explicit protection. The idea of sedition was dead; more particularly, seditious libel, the obsolete doctrine by which the government kept the press from inciting the governed to disaffection, was no more. "Muckraking" was making a comeback in the modern form of "investigative journalism," aimed at political corruption and chicanery. The Watergate exposé in the years to come proved just how free the press had become.

The year the press celebration began was 1964, and the occasion was the Court's decision in the case of *New York Times v. Sullivan*.[1] In that decision, the first that the Court ever issued on the First Amendment as it applies to libel, the Court gave the press much greater protection against public officials who sued for defamation. The Court ruled that the press could not be sued successfully by a public official unless that official could prove that a story was false, that it defamed the official, and that it was published with "actual malice"—that is, those responsible for its publication either knew that it was false or did not care whether it was true or false. The ruling was later extended to such public figures as celebrities.

The celebration lasted well into the "Burger years." Ultimately, however, *Sullivan* was shown to be unequal to its grand promise. Seditious libel, or something very close to it, had a revival in lawsuits filed by two famous generals, heroes in battle who had kept one eye on the political implications back on the homefront: America's William C. Westmoreland and Israel's Ariel Sharon. In time, the Supreme Court itself exposed the basic doctrinal flaw of the *Sullivan* decision for all to see. The Burger Court not only brought the celebration to an end, but left the press wondering whether celebration had ever been the appropriate response to *Sullivan*.

The press's fate under the Burger Court was and remains closely tied to the *Sullivan* decision and to its underlying theoretical premises. Even though among journalists and their lawyers it remains something of a heresy to speak ill of *Sullivan*, that decision and its legacy must be accepted as the ultimate source of the press's current deep doubts about its constitutional future. The political theory upon which *Sullivan* was built has translated into something fundamentally different for a society that has prided itself upon its rigorous openness: the flow of information is now more and more regulated by governmental mechanisms to satisfy public ends, often supplanting private choices serving private ends.

The legacy of *Sullivan*, as interpreted and handed on by the Burger Court, has come to mean that the press's protection against damages for libel has been narrowed significantly. Moreover, access to governmental information, for the press and the public, is permitted when it will serve public ends but is held in check to make certain that it *does* serve those ends. In addition, governmental demands for disclosure of privately held information that is deemed to be of governmental importance have been increasingly honored.

What is emerging imperfectly but certainly in the courts is an "information policy" that converts much of private expression into communication for public utility. The press clause of the First Amendment is becoming largely a "structural" aspect of democratic government. In a very real and practical sense, the press is being conscripted into the role of a "fourth branch of government."

To go back to the beginning: *Sullivan* was a libel decision, but it was much more than a libel decision. The Supreme Court, then still in the liberating mode of the Warren Court, intended the decision to be a profound declaration about the role of the press in American society, and how that role was to be enhanced by the press clause of the First Amendment. The Court discovered what it took to be "the central meaning of the First Amendment" in the political necessities of a self-governing society. The First Amendment, it made clear, was the sovereign people's reservation of power to themselves, the power to keep a check upon the performance of their governors. The government created by the people was powerless to punish criticisms of it or of its officials. Hence, the apparent demise of seditious libel, which had traced its American ancestry to the Alien and Sedition Act of 1798. For the press, *Sullivan* confirmed its right to join with the public in the "uninhibited, robust and wide open . . . debate on public issues." Understood as broadly as it seemed to be intended, the decision was a charter of press liberty.

Two decades later, what has happened? The Burger Court did not transform the constitutional dogmas of *Sullivan;* its basic principles, its fundamental political theory, remain intact. Rather, the Court simply let what was always implicit in *Sullivan* come to fruition. The press, uncomfortable with what the decision has become, has been forced to abandon its naïveté about what a regime of law can do for press freedom; the decision certainly did not mean liberation.

Even in the early days, the *Sullivan* decision revealed troublesome implications. Within a year of the decision, its author, Justice William J. Brennan, Jr., disclosed some of what had been in the back of justices' minds. In the Alexander Meiklejohn lecture[2] at Brown University, April 14, 1965, he acknowledged his and the Court's debt to Professor Meiklejohn's theory of the First Amendment. That theory held that free expression, as a constitutional concept, was bound up with notions of "the governing power of the people." It was a part of a "governmental responsibility . . . a public power." Viewed from that perspective, free expression by the press as by others was protected so that the governmental order could be assisted to function through popular review and criticism.

This argument is troublesome for two reasons: it incorporates a variable concept of press freedom or free speech, and it introduces notions of public accountability or responsibility as regulatory mechanisms astride the process of communication. In the Meiklejohn-

Brennan view, primary "social value" attaches to expression that is governmentally related and is entitled to the highest level of constitutional protection. At that level, press freedom is socially useful because it fulfills a governmental responsibility. Moving down the hierarchy of social value, however, other kinds of expression are found to be entitled to less protection or none at all. Expression that cannot be said to be serving the needs of self-government comes to be understood as a departure from responsible behavior.[3]

This emerging interpretation of the First Amendment's free-expression clauses was, indeed, a matter of line drawing, of inclusion and exclusion. Although the dreaded notion of "content regulation" was still treated, at least rhetorically, as constitutionally suspect, something logically akin to that was developing. Expression as expression would not always fall on the protected side of the constitutional line. Instead, expression with a public purpose or serving a public need would be on that side of the line, and purely private expression would wander variously on both sides, depending upon whether it could redeem itself by demonstrating that it had "social value."

In 1964, however, the press could see only the positive side of this mode of interpretation. The soaring "public issues" rhetoric of *Sullivan* fit the press's traditional perception of itself as a servant of something that it long had chosen to call "the people's right to know." The rhetoric of the press's constitutional self-defense always has been heavy with such public-service (or, if you will, public-utility) concepts. Contrary to the view of many of its critics, the press has claimed First Amendment rights not merely for self-aggrandizement or self-satisfaction, but rather as the means by which it is enabled to do good—in the elementary "good citizen" sense. At public convocations as well as in private discourse, journalists have articulated enthusiastically their belief that the press has a social responsibility along with its rights; it expects to be judged, and judges itself, according to a standard of public accountability.[4]

In a wonderfully innocent way, the press believed that it would be left alone as it carried out that public-service approach to its work. From decades of routine reliance upon the notion that the Constitution forbade all forms of governmental "prior restraint"[5] upon expression and upon press freedom in particular, it came to assume that the process of commercial communication would remain one of private choice, reinforced by an internal, private system of ethical restraint. The courts continued to hear libel lawsuits, to be sure, but with very few exceptions they were mere nuisances and did not interfere seriously with everyday, privately managed journalism.

Without bothering to analyze critically what it believed, the press proceeded upon the assumption that it enjoyed its rights as a matter of institutional autonomy for its organizations, and personal autonomy for its individual practitioners. The internal inconsistency of a private industry serving a public right, yet doing so under an ill-defined and probably indefinable code of private ethics, apparently never troubled the press, which failed to appreciate that, in any ultimate constitutional reckoning over its performance, public law would prevail over industry self-restaint. The "public's right to know" would be too important to be left to journalists.

The reckoning, of course, did come. It began with *Sullivan*. By constitutionalizing libel, the Court obviously sought to add to press freedom. In the process, though, it saw to it that journalistic performance became a public—that is, a governmental—question. A regime of tort litigation transformed issues of journalistic malpractice into questions of public accountability. The idea of a journalist's personal autonomy or the institutional autonomy of a news organization became secondary, at best, in that jurisprudence; ultimately, it was all but ignored.

From its opening to its closing lines, the *Sullivan* decision was a constitutional homily on the virtue of open criticism of official conduct. The Court, of course, need not have gone beyond that, even in *dicta*, because it was confronted with a five-hundred-thousand-dollar libel verdict in favor of a police commissioner in Montgomery, Alabama, whose public conduct had been criticized in an advertisement in *The New York Times* in 1960. But in reversing that judgment, and articulating a rationale for doing so, the Court clearly was according a higher level of constitutional protection to "public debate." This was made abundantly clear in the concurring opinion of Justice Arthur Goldberg, who chastised the majority opinion, written by Justice Brennan, for failing to accord citizens and press an *unconditional* freedom to criticize official conduct, yet commented in passing that "purely private defamation has little to do with the political ends of a self-governing society. The imposition of liability for private defamation does not abridge the freedom of public speech."[6]

The Court obviously had little difficulty extending the constitutional protections of *Sullivan* to other libel cases that bore upon "public debate" or "public matters." From lawsuits brought by elected public officials, the Court broadened the *Sullivan* rule so that it applied to lawsuits involving persons who are not public officials but can influence public policy, plus subordinate government officials in significant positions, persons who are "public figures," public hearings of governmental agencies, candidates for public office, and the contents of official government documents.[7] Several of those extensions came after Burger became Chief Justice in 1969. But there were indications early on in the "Burger years" that the theoretical boundaries of free expression under *Sullivan* were about to be reached. The first came when Justice Brennan could not muster a majority to extend the *Sullivan* protections fully to the press when it had been sued for libel by *private* individuals. In fact, in the case of *Rosenbloom v. Metromedia* (1971), Brennan attracted only the support of Chief Justice Burger and Justice Harry A. Blackmun for an opinion that sought to extend "constitutional protection to all discussion and communication involving matters of public or general concern, without regard to whether the persons involved are famous or anonymous." In seeking to justify such an extension, Brennan actually hardened the theoretical foundation of *Sullivan*; that standard, he said, was applied to a public official or public figure "to give effect to the [First] Amendment's function to encourage ventilation of public issues, not because the public official has any less interest in protecting his reputation than an individual in private life."[8]

Throughout the opinion of the *Rosenbloom* plurality, therefore, the stress was on the value of expression regarding "an event of public or general concern." Justice Thurgood Marshall, joined by Justice Potter Stewart, complained in dissent that "courts will be required to somehow pass on the legitimacy of interest in a particular event or subject; what information is relevant to self-government. The danger such a doctrine portends for freedom of the press seems apparent."[9]

The Court majority, however, was unprepared to abandon the public figure/private individual dichotomy. The rationale of Justice Brennan's plurality opinion was explicitly repudiated within three years. In *Gertz v. Welch* (1974), Justice Lewis F. Powell, Jr., ridiculed the *Rosenbloom* focus on the nature of the story rather than the identity of the plaintiff. That, Powell said, "would occasion the difficulty of forcing state and federal judges to decide on an *ad hoc* basis which publications address issues of 'general or public interest' and which do not. . . . We doubt the wisdom of committing this task to the conscience of judges."[10] *Gertz* established clearly for the first time that private individuals—that is, those who neither held public positions nor sought public notoriety or influence—had a stronger right to sue to protect their private reputations than public officials or public figures did to protect their more visible personalities or reputations. In a very real sense, this approach was entirely faithful to the basic theory of *Sullivan*, because it accorded a higher level of First Amendment protection to press coverage of "public controversies," as Justice Powell phrased it.

The public figure/private figure distinction became the basis for decisions further exposing the press to defamation lawsuits when its coverage fell on the wrong side of that line. Thus, the Court refused to apply the *Sullivan* protections to cases involving private persons' civil-court proceedings, private persons who receive public funds, and private persons charged with or convicted of crime.[11]

One thing was becoming starkly clear: editorial choices, made according to journalistic concepts of "newsworthiness," would not control the legal fate of the press when it was sued for libel. The desire to have the reporting and editing process remain free of legal restraints was having to yield to other "social values," at least when the eye of the news might focus on private individuals. When harm was done to private reputations, and fault could be assigned to the press for that injury, public accountability for the wrong followed, in libel verdicts.

But if the press had any illusions that the legal risk it was facing was confined largely to wrongs done to *private* reputations, those notions disappeared when the "celebrity lawsuit" became the new object of fascination for libel lawyers. The *Sullivan* decision had only made it more difficult for public officials (and, later, public figures) to win libel verdicts; it did not forbid them to sue. As celebrity journalism expanded, especially in the broadcast media, it became inevitable that more public figures would deem themselves wronged and would sue for defamation.

Perhaps without explicitly intending to do so, the Court gave strong encouragement to such lawsuits in one of the first major libel cases spawned by the electronic "muckraking" of CBS-TV's enormously popular weekly program "60 Minutes." In a case growing out of a program about military atrocities in Vietnam,[12] the Court rejected the argument that the First Amendment protected internal editorial processes from pretrial examination in public-figure libel cases. Because what went on in each stage of the story's origination, pursuit, and preparation might reveal the "state of mind" of the journalists involved with the story, the Court said, lawyers for libel plaintiffs could probe those processes intensively.[13] Since *Sullivan* required a public figure to prove that a story not only was false and defamatory but also had been published with knowledge of its falsity or with indifference toward its falsity, "state of mind" evidence was directly relevant, the Court said. That decision ensured that public figures could get access to more of the evidence they would need to win libel damages; it also ensured that, with or without any final damage verdict, they could get some satisfaction by exposing to public view the "malpractice" supposedly occurring in the nation's newsrooms. Vindication could be had in more than one way.

Perhaps the ultimate in celebrity libel cases emerged in 1982 and 1983 when Generals Westmoreland and Sharon sued CBS-TV and *Time* magazine, respectively. The Westmoreland lawsuit was aimed at a documentary about politically inspired decisions of military leaders during the Vietnam War, and the Sharon case was leveled at a magazine article about the general's alleged encouragement of atrocities during the Israeli invasion of Lebanon. Although neither case reached the Supreme Court (Westmoreland's was settled in 1985 before verdict, and in the same year Sharon's resulted in a split verdict partly for Time, Inc., and partly for the general), it was plain that those cases were entirely predictable in the evolution of libel law under *Sullivan* and related Supreme Court cases. Moreover, they were vivid illustrations that the Court had not prohibited, once and for all, the opportunity of a government official to challenge press or public criticism of official conduct by filing a lawsuit. Each case, in other words, concerned a species of seditious libel—despite Brennan's proclamations in *Sullivan*. To suggest that either Westmoreland or Sharon had at stake a personal reputation separate from his public performance in high office would be nonsensical; although there were those in the press, and among the press's defense lawyers, who suggested that the two cases showed the continuing vitality of the *Sullivan* doctrine, the fact that the cases were brought at all and were pursued as vigorously as they were, was hardly cause for jubilation. Under the libel rationale that had prevailed for twenty years, those two lawsuits were in no sense extravagant attempts to exploit what *Sullivan* had begun.

The burgeoning of celebrity lawsuits clearly changed the nature of libel litigation. It no longer could be said that libel law existed primarily to restore sullied good names. Celebrities with ample opportunity to create positive images for themselves now had the libel lawsuit as a further tool. What they could win was not so much a personal victory as an enhancement of their public persona; the libel lawsuit became a new stage upon which to exhibit that persona. The Supreme Court gave them explicit encouragement when it suggested in *Keeton v. Hustler* (1984) that a state could use its libel laws not only to protect the public reputation of a celebrity but also "to discourage the deception of its citizens." If a story about a public figure is false, the Court said, it harms "both the subject of the falsehood *and* the readers of the statement."[14] It was obvious that the Court, in keeping with the basic theory of *Sullivan*, was seeking further to protect the recipients of information from journalism considered to be of lesser social value.

Steadily, case by case, the Burger Court made it obvious that the First Amendment could do only limited service in protecting expression that wandered afield from "public debate" or "expression upon public questions," in the phrasing of *Sullivan*.

A final kind of certainty emerged in 1985, in what was otherwise an obscure case provoked by an unimportant business credit report by Dun & Bradstreet.[15] In a perverse twist of the *Rosenbloom* "public issue" concept rejected in *Gertz* as a basis for protecting the press, the Court decided that the constitutional protections articulated in *Sullivan*, as modified by *Gertz*, were not available whenever the information challenged in a libel lawsuit involved "no issue of public concern." Justice Powell wrote: "We have long recognized that not all speech is of equal First Amendment importance. It is speech on 'matters of public concern' that is at the heart of the First Amendment's protection. . . . In contrast, speech on matters of purely private concern is of less First Amendment concern." When the information touches on "no public issue," he said, libel law may be applied fully because "there is no threat to the free and robust debate of public issues; there is no potential interference with a meaningful dialogue of ideas concerning self-government; and there is no threat of liability causing a reaction of self-censorship by the press."[16]

In *Dun & Bradstreet,* the Court solidified the concept of variable protection for expression depending upon its relevance to "self-government." The *Sullivan* decision had come full circle, proving that it had always constituted an invitation to public law to mark the limits of responsible journalism—even Justice Brennan's dissent in *Dun & Bradstreet* accepted the notion that "speech about commercial or economic matters [did] not directly implicat[e] . . . 'the central meaning of the First Amendment' [because] not at 'the essence of self-government.' " Although the Court had insisted, along the way, that it was repudiating the *Rosenbloom* notion that courts should have the task of defining the subject matter that would be entitled to full constitutional protection, it had returned to exactly that point. The decison in *Dun & Bradstreet* was the Burger Court's strongest illustration that *Sullivan* had been doctrinally flawed. If the First Amendment was a shield against libel only when a publication acted in the service of public or governmental ends, a vast array of editorial choices and private expression could be beyond the pale of constitutionality.

Once more seeking to refine First Amendment theory as it relates to libel, the Court found itself again—and necessarily—pursuing legal categories which by virtue of the very fact that they are legal may have little or nothing whatever to do with editorial choices. As journalists function day by day, even story by story, they make many choices, each of which is driven by some concept of newsworthiness—a process that is inherently haphazard and often irrational. If there are internal ethical limits to the process other than the difficulty of defining what may be of interest to the reading or listening audience, they are highly variable, individualistic, even idiosyncratic, and not subject to easy or reliable codification. Much less can that process easily accommodate legal precepts that are categorical or imperative in nature.

The press literally has no way of knowing how any story will be regarded when measured by legal norms: Is the individual involved a "public figure" (or only a "limited purpose public figure") or a "private figure"? Is the subject matter of public or of private "concern" or a mix of the two? Does it touch upon or relate in any way to "the essence of self-government"?[17] Lawyers and judges struggle with these questions within a slowly unfolding legal process. Questions of this kind are likely never to be resolved satisfactorily from the journalistic perspective, and are certainly not of a kind that can be resolved within the fleeting lifespan of so fragile a thing as a news story (or even within the somewhat longer lifespan of a feature story, which, however meticulously prepared, must compete with news for each editorial cycle's rapidly diminishing amount of space).

To journalists, it has become painfully clear that when law becomes a part of the editorial process, it has an inherently limiting effect. And, contrary to the assumptions of the Supreme Court and the illusions of libel plaintiffs' lawyers, the limitation that it creates is not necessarily in the direction of fair, balanced, or even responsible journalism (whatever any one of those may mean in relation to a given story). Law can at most assure *safe* journalism: in the felt need to inhibit recklessness, law penalizes energetic journalism; in the search for an enforceable duty of care, it stifles legitimate experimentation; in the pursuit of propriety, it frustrates creativity. The journalistic imagination is not merely chilled; it may well be frozen.

What *Dun & Bradstreet* demonstrates, perhaps better than any decision on libel in the years since *Sullivan*, is simply that the tort of libel exacts too high a price for free expression. It now seems evident that the protection of reputations from the assault of ideas is not a manageable endeavor—at least it cannot be managed with faithfulness to the concept of an open society, a society that cannot guarantee against the risks and hazards predictably and routinely attending free expression. One may well deplore journalistic excess (as many journalists themselves sincerely do) without conceding that the only remedy is a regime of rationally determined and externally imposed law and regulation. However heroic (or perhaps even antisocial) it may seem, the harm to reputation may well have to go unredressed by legal remedy. That is the ultimate conclusion toward which *Sullivan* inevitably pointed.

The problems the press had with the Burger Court did not end with the public-service rationale for free expression. There developed a corollary theory: if some preferred kinds of information were deemed important to "self-government," there probably would have to exist some public "right" to that information. The Burger Court, indeed, ultimately found such a right in the Constitution.[18] It came slowly, and with evident reluctance, to accept the notion that there was something like a "public right to know" or, as it was phrased alternatively, a public "right to receive" information. Most of this occurred outside the field of libel law, in areas of press law that had been previously little explored, or not at all.

Again, the press, as in its initial reaction to *Sullivan*, at first saw only the positive side of a developing constitutional right of access. It could expect to benefit by being given access to governmental information to which the public was thought to be entitled. The development of theories of access, in fact, could lead the way to some "right to gather news"—a right ancillary to the right of expression or publication. The press, with its loyalty to the rhetorical concept of the public's "right to know" and its devotion to its self-image as a constitutionally endowed public-service institution, was quite ready to believe that the Constitution formally confirmed its function as a conduit of governmentally generated information.

But such a confirmation created dangers. If that function existed as a *constitutional* matter, it would depend for its existence and its growth or contraction upon judicial—that is, governmental—creation and limitation. Access would exist where the Supreme Court thought access served a public end, and would be narrowed or denied where the Court thought only private ends would be served. As in the area of libel, the Court would be the arbiter, and it could be expected to filter a question of right of access through a First Amendment concept of expression as an aid to self-government.

An even more threatening implication lay behind a public right to information: the press could expect that when it was itself in possession of information thought to be needed by the public, or to which the public had some "right," the government might well demand forced disclosure. The conduit, in other words, might well have to flow both ways: not only would the press be entitled to what the government had, but the government might demand access to governmentally relevant information in the possession of the press.

The press, in a bold and perhaps even brash way, had introduced the Burger Court to the notion of a "public right to know" in 1971, in the "Pentagon Papers" case.[19] The government was seeking to enjoin further publication of a secret study on the background of the Vietnam War. The Court found that the government had not justified such an injunction, and treated the case as a fairly classical "prior restraint" case. In passing, however, six of the nine justices suggested that the government might well have the constitutional authority to prosecute publishers of classified information for a criminal violation *after* publication. Between the lines, it was plain that a clear majority of the justices would have found foolhardy the notion that the public had any "right to know" or to receive such secret information. Chief Justice Burger took the occasion explicitly to discuss the newspapers' claim, under the First Amendment, to such a right. He ridiculed the notion, which he attributed to the *New York Times,* that the press was the "trustee" of such a right on behalf of the public. He suggested that the *Times,* like every other citizen down to the level of "taxi drivers," had a duty to report to authorities "the discovery or possession of stolen property or secret government documents."[20]

That, as it turned out, was not an isolated comment. Just one day short of a year later, a Supreme Court majority made it the law that the press had an affirmative obligation to provide information about crime to the government, if that information was properly demanded. The Court refused, in *Branzburg v. Hayes* (1972),[21] to provide constitutional protection for the withholding of information by the press. It flatly rejected the claim that the First Amendment conferred upon the press a "privilege" to keep to itself information sought in a criminal grand jury investigation—including the identity of news sources. "The press," said Justice Byron R. White for the majority, "has the right to abide by its agreement not to publish all the information it has, but the right to withhold news is not equivalent to a First Amendment exemption from the ordinary duty of all other citizens to furnish relevant information to a grand jury performing an important public function." The Court was not "convinced that a virtually impenetrable constitutional shield . . . should be forged to protect a private system of informers operated by the press to report on criminal conduct."[22]

The *Branzburg* case was a curious amalgam of variations on the public's "right to know" and the right of the press to "gather news." The majority obviously was relying upon the right of the people's representatives, in government, to force the disclosure of privately held information in order to serve public ends. "The public has a right to every man's evidence," Justice White declared.[23] The dissenters, too, focused on the "public right to know." Wrote Justice Stewart: "A reporter's right to protect his source is bottomed on the constitutional guarantee of a full flow of information to the public. A newsman's personal First Amendment rights or the associational rights of the newsman and the source are subsumed under that broad societal interest protected by the First Amendment. Obviously, we are not here concerned with the parochial personal concerns of particular newsmen or informants."[24]

On the "right to gather news," it was evident that the dissenters had provoked the majority into a grudging acknowledgment that such a right might exist under the First Amendment. Justice Stewart called such a right "a corollary of the right to publish. . . . The full flow of information to the public protected by the free press guarantee would be severely curtailed if no protection whatever were afforded to the process by which news is assembled and disseminated."[25] Responding, Justice White remarked: "We do not question the significance of free speech, press or assembly to the country's welfare. Nor is it suggested that news gathering does not qualify for First Amendment protection; without some protection for seeking out the news, freedom of the press could be eviscerated."[26]

Again, however, it was clear that both sides were relating this news-gathering right to the press's public-service function. As Justice William O. Douglas wrote tellingly in dissent: "The press has a preferred position in our constitutional scheme not to enable it to make money, not to set newsmen apart as a favored class, but to bring fulfillment to the public's right to know. The right to know is crucial to the governing process of the people, to paraphrase Alexander Meiklejohn."[27]

At no time since *Branzburg* has the Supreme Court modified this view of the press's responsibility to share information with government, when a proper demand had been made, or its perception of a "right to gather news" as conferring a right of access only to activity and information bearing upon self-government.

For the press, *Branzburg* is a threatening decision, on both the pragmatic and theoretical levels. The ruling has been criticized properly on pragmatic grounds: first, that it interferes with the news-gathering process, because confidentiality is a price that often must be paid for obtaining newsworthy information, especially information that is in any way sensitive; second, that it costs the press credibility because news organizations will be perceived as an information-gathering instrument of the government, especially in the criminal-justice process.

On the first point: "Investigative" reporters—mainly, those who pursue public or private wrongdoing—have always insisted that they must trade assurances of secrecy (often to people who, arguably, might not deserve to be left totally unaccountable when other social values are considered) in order to obtain information vital to the exposure of corruption or misconduct among those who clearly ought to be accountable, by virtue of their position, power, or station. On the second point: Reporters in general tend to believe that they are effective only when they are visibly independent of government or, for that matter, any aggregation of power outside their own news organization. For many, too-close cooperation with such outside entities or power centers is taken as a forfeiture of independence. But perhaps because both of those are highly impressionistic assertions that may not be provable empirically, and thus seem to be essentially self-serving, the press was unable to convince the Court in *Branzburg* that proper functioning of the press would be impaired by a forfeiture of confidentiality or compelled cooperation with government.

Another threat, of equal seriousness, is posed by *Branzburg*, and that results from the decision's theoretical underpinnings. Once again, the press is understood to be worthy of its freedoms when it acts to fill governmental needs, whether by handing over information that the government wants or by communicating governmental news presumed to be of value to the people as political sovereign. The Court's view of the First Amendment remained consistent, and the free-press clause was still understood as importing a public-service rationale.

That rationale emerged with new strength as the Court worked its way toward a definite declaration of a right to gather information and, flowing from it, a right of access to government information—a right shared equally by the press and the public generally. The process continues today: the Court has yet to clarify in any final way the exact scope of either right. What has been obvious, however, from *Branzburg* on (and consistent with the rejection of special rights for the media in *Dun & Bradstreet*), is that press access would be derivative only of general public access. For eight years after that decision, press pleas for access were rejected on the theory that there was no right of "special access" for the press, only a right shared with the "public generally." That provided justification for the Court's rulings that denied press access to prisons and jails, that placed limits on broadcasters' opportunity to copy tape recordings used in open court as criminal evidence, and that refused the assurance of open pretrial hearings in criminal cases.[28]

Then, in 1980, the Supreme Court, speaking through a variety of justices' opinions, finally acknowledged a First Amendment right of access for the public and press to governmental information. In *Richmond Newspapers v. Virginia*, over the solitary dissent of Justice William H. Rehnquist, the Court declared criminal trials generally open, prompting Justice John Paul Stevens to remark in concurrence: "This is a watershed case. Until today the Court has accorded virtually absolute protection to the dissemination of information or ideas, but never before has it squarely held that the acquisition of newsworthy matter is entitled to any constitutional protection whatsoever." As the right developed in later cases, it was supported primarily by a public-utility rationale: access would exist where that would demonstrably serve the governmental, constitutional, or civic interest of the activity or function to which access was sought. In his concurring opinion in the *Richmond* case, Justice Brennan articulated an idea that has guided the Court on this issue continuously since then: "Analysis is not advanced by rhetorical statements that all information bears upon public issues; what is crucial in individual cases is whether access to a particular governmental process is important in terms of that very process."[29]

In subsequent cases, the Court has relied upon the public's interest in criminal trials to justify extensions of the *Richmond* ruling; it has barred judges from automatically excluding the press from a trial to protect teen-age victims of sex crimes, and from excluding the press from the process of selecting jurors in criminal cases (although it permitted potential jurors to insist on answering "personal" questions in private). The Court, after initially finding in the Sixth Amendment guarantee of a "public trial" a right of defendants to insist upon press access to pretrial hearings in criminal cases,[30] ultimately found that the press had a First Amendment right of access to those pretrial proceedings.[31] But the Court found insufficient public interest in pretrial proceedings in civil cases to justify press or public access to depositions and interrogatories taken in preparation for trial. It remarked: "Restraints placed on discovered, but not yet admitted, information are not a restriction on a traditionally public source of information."[32] Thus the Court once again stressed that openness of government depended on tradition or long-standing custom, where government did not affirmatively choose as an act of grace to provide access to information it held. The Court has yet to repudiate or even to alter meaningfully a comment by Chief Justice Burger in 1978: "There is no discernible basis for a constitutional duty to disclose."[33]

There has been, however, a more serious denial of access than that suffered by the print media or by the "public generally." News-gathering by videotape is still not constitutionally protected; there is no "right of access" for broadcast journalism to the sights and sounds of governmental proceedings where the government does not on its own choose to grant access.

Since 1965, when the Court made the rather anxious discovery that television had become a presence in the courthouse,[34] it has treated that medium as constitutionally second-class. Perhaps that treatment represents only the silent assumption that, since it is already a licensed medium functioning on a governmentally regulated, limited spectrum, television has a different legal status. The suspicion abides, however, that the justices are more troubled by its techniques of news-gathering, its pattern of editorial selectivity, its style, its very content.

The broadcast industry, of course, does not concede that, if the press has a "right of access," it is a right exclusive to print journalism or to the reportorial techniques of print reporters. The industry has shown itself to be quite interested in gathering news about the courts and other institutions to which the print media has been pursuing access, and television itself has not hesitated to litigate questions of access. Nevertheless, it is treated as a stranger to the courthouse, including the Supreme Court. That may be so, at least in considerable part, because of an unarticulated fear felt by some judges, including justices of the Court. As Justice Tom C. Clark remarked in 1965: "The television camera is a powerful weapon. . . . [O]ne cannot put his finger on its specific mischief."[35]

There are intimations from the Court that some of the anxiety over television access has to do with the "theater" and "entertainment" aspects of that medium. Television techniques themselves—in other words, program content—seem to be of acute concern to the Court. The Court has never wavered from its understanding, stated first in 1965, that any desire of broadcast reporters for access can be fully satisfied by allowing them into the courtroom, but bearing only the same working tools as print reporters. "It is true that the public has the right to be informed as to what occurs in its courts, but reporters of all media, including television, are always present if they wish to be, and are plainly free to report whatever occurs in open court through their respective media."[36] The Court in 1981, in the case of *Chandler v. Florida*, removed the remaining constitutional barrier to television cameras in the courtroom by permitting states to experiment with broadcast coverage of criminal trials. But Chief Justice Burger, writing for the Court, noted with a hint of satisfaction that the Florida Supreme Court in that case had "pointedly rejected any state or federal constitutional right of access" for the broadcast press. Justice White, concurring, remarked that the decision did not render any state less free to "forbid cameras in the court rooms in *any* criminal case"[37] (emphasis added).

The "public generally" (the citizen-sovereigns for whom the Court has discovered a "right to know" that may be implemented by a "right of access") does not have a right to receive information in the form of sight and sound when the government is not prepared to accord such a right. If access is genuinely a First Amendment issue, differential treatment of broadcasting media based on the different content of each medium would seem to be a considerable contradiction of conventional constitutional theory. Moreover, if access is a function of "self-government"—and the Court has treated it precisely as that— it is difficult (at best) to rationalize the exclusion of the most pervasive medium in modern American society. The Court, however, seems entirely comfortable with that exclusion, however aberrant that may be in terms of its own view of the First Amendment.

By contrast, it has not hesitated to allow *compelled* communication *by* the broadcast industry when it could be satisfied that the "public right to know" would thereby be served. In upholding the constitutionality of the "fairness doctrine" in 1969,[38] the Court made it clear that there is a public right to receive in the broadcast press all points of view on public controversies. Similarly, the Court in 1981 found an enforceable right to broadcast political advertising by presidential and congressional candidates.[39] While the Court has never been tolerant of an enforceable right of access to the print media,[40] it is not so troubled about something closely akin to that when the medium of communication is the broadcast press, so long as the licensed broadcaster is left with some discretion. The Court has made it clear that a constitutional price has been exacted for a broadcast license.

There remains one other area of the access issue, and an exploration of it provides a revealing insight into the Burger Court's philosophical ruminations over the First Amendment. That is the issue of press access to copyrighted material prepared by a public official and bearing upon that official's service. The Court has had only one opportunity to explore what might be seen as the underlying tension between copyright protection and free expression, and that opportunity came in a case involving distinctly governmental information: a former president's memoirs.

In the case of *Harper & Row v. Nation* (1985), the Court established the right of public officials to damages for infringement of a copyright on a manuscript bearing directly and solely upon information gathered in public office. *The Nation* magazine, the Court concluded, infringed upon former president Gerald Ford's copyright of his memoirs, entitled *A Time to Heal,* by printing excerpts of those portions of it dealing with Ford's pardon of President Richard Nixon for his Watergate crimes. "We see no warrant," Justice Sandra Day O'Connor wrote for the Court, "for expanding the doctrine of fair use to create what amounts to a public figure exception to copyright."[41]

In view of the Court's studied effort to assure the strongest First Amendment protection for information that is related to self-government, it is interesting to trace the First Amendment rationale in the Ford case. The Copyright Act's economic-incentive premises become controlling in this equation. "In our haste to disseminate news," the Court remarked, "it should not be forgotten that the Framers intended copyright itself to be the engine of free expression. By establishing a marketable right to the use of one's expression, copyright supplies the economic incentive to create and disseminate ideas. . . . It is fundamentally at odds with the scheme of copyright to accord lesser rights in those works that are of greatest importance to the public." But the Court also found in copyright the premise of a "countervailing First Amendment value": a right to refrain from expressing oneself. "Freedom of thought and expression includes both the right to speak freely and the right to refrain from speaking at all."[42] The economic right of first publication becomes, as fully for the public figure as for the exclusively private author, a right to choose when and where to communicate. For the public figure, however, such a right operates to control the dissemination of information of the utmost public concern. A "public right to know" becomes exclusively a matter for determination and definition by a government official, and the public end to be served would be only a hoped-for, perhaps even secondary, consequence of that official's personal appetite for private economic gain.

The Court in *Harper & Row* seemed to be engaging in a labored effort to invent constitutional consistency, to fit the controlled distribution of presidential memoirs into a regime that seeks to assure the free flow of information related to self-government. Once more, it convinced itself that it had acted to keep open the channels of expression upon "public issues" or "public questions"; it no doubt was content to believe that it had acted to maximize the potential for public debate upon the official matters explored in the Ford story. But there may well have been some self-delusion in that. The decision invites suspicion that the Court was subjectively determined to do what it had to do to protect the private publishing opportunities of governmental officials in general, judges and bureaucrats as well as presidents.

Implicit throughout the Court's decision is the acknowledgment of a highly debatable proposition: that people working in the government are acquiring by that service a property right in the manner of expression they choose for their current or subsequent discussions of the public business they managed or participated in. The right does not seem to spring forth upon a public official's retirement; rather, it would appear to exist from the moment that official's public service begins. The apparent existence of such a right alerts the press to a serious legal risk should it undertake to quote verbatim from an official's accounts of his or her service—even when verbatim quotation would be the most authentic rendition of what the official had in mind in telling his or her story. The words and phrases actually employed by the officials are animated by their own subjective perceptions of the way they functioned in office, and thus are as much a part of the substance of their memoirs as are the facts they choose to recite. When the press is put in legal peril for accurately passing on those perceptions, and is thus forced or at least encouraged to rely solely upon paraphrasing, much that is valuable (because newsworthy) in the officials' accounts may be lost in translation.

Moreover, the press cannot really know (because *Harper & Row* does not delineate it precisely) what part of an official's memoir may be quoted with impunity and what part may not. The parts given copyright protection tend, under the ruling, to envelop those parts that are not copyrightable because they convey mere information and are not parts of the form of expression; only expression may be protected by copyright, not the underlying facts. This, too, is an inducement to excessive caution by the press when dealing with information that is undoubtedly newsworthy.

The *Harper & Row* decision proved conclusively how flexible—manipulable, one might say—the constitutional doctrine flowing from *Sullivan* can be. It has required only a modest amount of rationalizing genius to fit all of what the Burger Court wrought on press law into a First Amendment the "central meaning" of which is the political necessities of self-governing America. In this perspective, the belief that the First Amendment exists to serve the autonomous individual seeking self-fulfillment seems disturbingly radical.

As the Burger years came to a close, any notion that the First Amendment might in time be viewed more expansively, focusing more on its implications outside the felt needs of self-government, seemed to represent a forlorn hope or a romantic illusion. Chief Justice Burger's retirement, with Justice William H. Rehnquist succeeding him, placed at the Court's head a determined foe even of the *Sullivan* principles—a jurist who had voted repeatedly to allow the states more, rather than less, authority to regulate libel, and who also had voted to permit states to deny the press access even to concededly open governmental proceedings.

Moreover, the selection of Circuit Judge Antonin Scalia to become an associate justice brought to the Court a jurist whose record on First Amendment issues during his service on the United States Court of Appeals for the District of Columbia Circuit seemed to parallel quite closely that of Justice Rehnquist.

In *Ollman v. Evans* (1984),[43] Judge Scalia argued strenuously, and with notable sarcasm, against a continuing evolution of doctrine in First Amendment cases in general, and in libel cases in particular, because of what he perceived to be the "general risk of judicial subjectivity." Regarding libel cases involving public figures, he wrote: "Defamation liability under existing standards not only does not impair but fosters the type of discussion the First Amendment is most concerned to protect." He added that "high libel judgments" might well be taken "as no more than an accurate reflection of the vastly expanded damage that can be caused by media that are capable of holding individuals up to public obloquy from coast to coast and that reap financial rewards commensurate with that power." In *Tavoulareas v. Washington Post* (1985),[44] he joined opinions declaring that juries would be permitted to take into account in determining "actual malice" any evidence offered by the suing party seeking to show that a news organization had an editorial policy favoring "sensational" or "muckraking" stories and evidence suggesting that a reporter had had "a preconceived plan to 'get' the subject of a defamatory story." In *Anderson v. Liberty Lobby* (1984), he wrote an opinion declaring that the standard of proof to be met by libel plaintiffs is lower at the summary judgment stage before trial than in deciding the case at trial, a decision reversed by the Supreme Court.[45]

Judge Scalia also made it clear that he would read narrowly any right of access to government documents, unless there had been the clearest demonstration that such documents traditionally had been open to public and press inspection.[46]

The beginning of the "Rehnquist Court," then, may well have marked the opening of an era in which the *Sullivan* decision and all that had flowed from its basic principles would be found to have been a constitutional aberration, a rash experiment in judicial activism seriously in need of revision if not eradication. The press, despite its earnest belief that *Sullivan* ultimately would redeem its grand promise, had not in fact prospered under that decision or from the principles upon which it was based. It was all the more appropriate, therefore, to anticipate the post-Burger era with the deepest foreboding.

·3·

Freedom of the Press: A Tale of Two Libel Theories

SIDNEY ZION

In law as in love, the surest way to know how far you've fallen is to see what picks you up. When the press won a victory in the Supreme Court in April 1984 in a case brought by a manufacturer of stereo systems against Consumers Union for criticizing the stereo system,[1] the rapturous treatment the press accorded the decision would lead one to think the ruling was a breakthrough victory for First Amendment rights. In fact, the decision was nothing of the sort. It merely reaffirmed a rule of twenty years' standing that in cases involving First Amendment rights, appellate courts will look closely to ensure that those rights are not trod on.

That the press crowed mightily about its success, however, was hardly surprising. It had been ten years since the press won a libel case in the Supreme Court. In fact, journalists' praise for the decision came less from joy than from relief. For a change, the Burger Court had not done them in.

The First Amendment has known plenty of troubled times, but what an awesome trashing it has suffered at the hands of the statists who controlled the Supreme Court during the Chief Justiceship of Warren E. Burger. Reporters jailed for refusing to disclose confidential sources. Newsrooms fair game for police ransacking. Telephone records secretly subpoenaed by law-enforcement officials on the hunt for reporters' sources. Journalists' inner thoughts and discussions with editors and colleagues opened for discovery by libel plaintiffs. Courtrooms closed by judicial fiat to press and public.[2] All that, and more, in a period of relative tranquility. No Alien and Sedition Acts here, no Joe McCarthy there. Is it coincidence that the Burger Court hit its stride after Watergate, just when journalism was getting its best press from the citizenry, in best-selling books and in movies?

None of this would have happened under Earl Warren. Indeed, had only Justices Hugo Black and William Douglas continued to serve through the Burger years, the press would have won every case it in fact lost before the Supreme Court. So much, too, for the impartial application of legal principles by a majority that promoted itself as "conservative" and "strict constructionist." What the Burger Court looked for is the identity of the defendant. Here is a trio of cases—selected from many—that tell the tale.

In 1976, Justice William Rehnquist, writing for a five-man majority in *Paul v. Davis*,[3] held that a person's good name and reputation are not protected by the Constitution. In that case, Edward Charles Davis III had been arrested for shoplifting by a private security guard in a store in Louisville, Kentucky. Davis, a photographer for *The Louisville Courier-Journal & Times*, had pleaded not guilty; the charge had been "filed away with leave to reinstate," meaning the police never intended to prosecute. Seventeen months later, the police chiefs of Louisville and Jefferson County, Kentucky, sent out a flier to area merchants containing mug shots and names of "active shoplifters." Davis's picture and name appeared on the flier, though he had not been tried on the charge and had never been convicted of a crime. Six days after the flier was distributed, the shoplifting charge against him was dismissed in court.

The next day, Davis filed suit in federal court against both police chiefs. He sought damages, an injunction against further dissemination of the flier, and an order that the chiefs retrieve all copies of the flier and instruct the merchants who had received them that Davis was not a shoplifter. He based his action on a federal statute providing redress to persons whose constitutional rights are violated by those acting under "color of law"—that is, acting under the authority of their office. The chiefs conceded that their conduct had been intentional and had been undertaken in their official capacity.

The Supreme Court had to decide whether Davis had been deprived of liberty or property without due process of law. "We hold," wrote Rehnquist, "that the interest in reputation asserted . . . is neither 'liberty' nor 'property' guaranteed against state deprivation." Therefore, "however seriously" the flier may have harmed Davis's reputation, he had no recourse under the statute because reputation itself was not a protected constitutional right.

It is interesting to compare that reasoning, which Justice William Brennan's dissent termed "frightening for a free people," with Rehnquist's opinion for the Court three years later in *Wolston v. Reader's Digest Association*.[4] In 1958, Ilya Wolston had pleaded guilty to criminal contempt for failing to respond to a subpoena directing him to appear before a federal grand jury in New York City. The grand jury was conducting a major investigation into the activities of Soviet intelligence agents in the United States. Wolston received a one-year suspended sentence and was placed on probation for three years; a condition of the probation was that he would cooperate with the grand jury in any further inquiries regarding Soviet espionage.

In 1974, the Reader's Digest company published a book entitled *KGB: The Secret Work of Soviet Secret Agents.* The book contained a passage that identified numerous alleged Soviet agents operating in the United States after World War II. Wolston's name appeared in that passage, in which it was explained that those listed had been "convicted of espionage or falsifying information or perjury and/or contempt charges following espionage indictments."

Wolston sued for libel. The federal district court in Washington, D.C., threw out his complaint on the grounds that Wolston was a "public figure" and so had to prove "actual malice" to recover. While agreeing that the book appeared to state falsely that Wolston had been indicted for espionage—his contempt conviction did not follow an indictment—the court held that the First Amendment precluded damages because it was clear that the falsehood was not made with "reckless disregard of whether it was false or not"—that is, with actual malice. The circuit court of appeals affirmed.

But the Supreme Court reversed, per Justice Rehnquist, in an opinion so concerned for the right of privacy you'd think it had been written by Justice Louis Brandeis. After allowing that Wolston's conduct was "newsworthy"—it had been the subject of fifteen stories in the New York and Washington press—and that Wolston had later been identified as a Soviet agent in two other publications, Rehnquist nevertheless held that Wolston had not become a "public figure." The reason: he had not "voluntarily thrust" himself into the investigation but was "dragged unwilling" into it by the government. Characterizing Wolston's conviction as a "mere citation of contempt" followed by passive acceptance of punishment, Rehnquist wrote, for a six-man majority:

> We find no basis whatsoever for concluding that Wolston relinquished, to any degree, his interest in the protection of his own name.
>
> This reasoning leads us to reject the further contention that any person who engages in criminal conduct automatically becomes a public figure for purposes of comment on a limited range of issues relating to his conviction.... To hold otherwise, would create an "open season" for all who sought to defame persons convicted of a crime.[5]

Whatever one may think of Rehnquist's sensitivity to the right of criminals, it takes some doing to think of Wolston without thinking of Edward Charles Davis III of Louisville.

Davis, an innocent man branded a criminal by police officers who admitted they knew better, could not collect damages for harm that, the Court majority conceded, was done to his good name. Wolston, who pleaded guilty, was entitled to collect from a publisher and an author who, at most, negligently overstated the grounds of his conviction.

Taken together, the two cases stand for the proposition that so far as the Constitution is concerned, the press may not, in good faith, defame convicts, while government officials may, in bad faith, defame the innocent. It is a hard combination to follow, but the Burger Court was equal to the challenge. On the day Wolston was decided, the Court, again per Rehnquist, ruled, in *Baker v. McCollan*, that a person who is falsely imprisoned is not deprived of a right that is "secured by the Constitution."[6]

Linnie Carl McCollan was stopped for running a red light in Dallas; he was then arrested and held in jail for eight days on a bail-jumping charge in a narcotics case. Despite his repeated protests that he was a victim of mistaken identity, the authorities did not bother to check the file. When they finally did, the prints and mug shots showed he was indeed the wrong man. The guy the cops wanted turned out to be his brother.

Linnie McCollan sued under the same statute that Davis had used against the Kentucky police chiefs—with the same result. The Burger Court ruled that McCollan had failed to satisfy the "threshold requirement" of the statute because he had not been deprived of liberty without due process of law, as the Court defined the constitutional meaning of that phrase.

In dissent, Justice John Paul Stevens—jointly with Justices Thurgood Marshall and William Brennan—noted that under the theory of the majority, McCollan would not have been entitled to release through a writ of habeas corpus, "since his detention is not a violation of his constitutional rights." Of course, a newspaper would have been subject to punitive damages in a libel suit if, under similar circumstances, it had accused the wrong man of a crime.

Likewise, had Davis been called an "active shoplifter" or even a "former shoplifter" by the press, or for that matter by an ordinary citizen, he would have had a right to money damages that could have reached astronomical figures if the defamation was intentional and therefore "malicious."

False imprisonment and official stigmatization are surely more harmful than defamation by the news media, and they are obviously far worse than slander by a private person. Yet the Court held that one's interest in freedom and reputation, while not protected by the Constitution, is, nonetheless, sufficient to overcome the First Amendment's prohibition against any abridgment of freedom of speech or of the press.

If that's not statism, what's statism?

·4·

The National Security State: Never Question the President

MORTON H. HALPERIN

Before the emergence of the Burger Court as a distinctive judicial voice, it was possible to argue that the Supreme Court had dealt in a responsible and relatively coherent way with the task of balancing the rights of individuals with the requirements of national security. It is no longer possible to do so. In a few broad and extraordinarily dangerous decisions, that Court swept away most of the limits established in earlier cases and laid down a standard of extreme deference to the executive branch when it asserted that certain limits on constitutional rights must be accepted to protect the national security.

In cases involving the exercise of the nation's powers in foreign affairs, the Supreme Court has historically deferred to the political branches of the government and to their findings as to what is necessary to protect the country. Until recently, however, the Court was not willing to defer when constitutional rights were at stake. It was especially vigilant when the President was acting without a clear delegation of authority from Congress. The record is not wholly commendable. The Court upheld the basic structure of the Japanese internment program during World War II,[1] and it was slow to rein in the excesses of McCarthyism. Nevertheless, it blocked President Truman's efforts to seize the steel mills during the Korean War, upheld the right of Americans to travel abroad, and limited the government's power to refuse to hire those it considered subversive or to strip draft dodgers of their citizenship.[2]

Indeed, as late as 1977 it was possible to write, as I did with Daniel Hoffman in our book *Freedom vs. National Security: Secrecy and Surveillance*,[3] that the overall record of the Court was surprisingly sensitive to claims of civil liberties when juxtaposed with claims of national security. There was not a single case in which the Court had permitted the President, acting without clear congressional authority, to override the fundamental rights of Americans. Even when the President was acting with congressional sanction, the Court was unwilling to defer to the judgments of the political branches; instead, it made a searching inquiry to determine for itself if sufficient harm would result. Nowhere was this clearer than in the "Pentagon Papers" case, *New York Times Co. v. United States* (1971),[4] in which the Court refused to accept at face value the government's claims that grave injury to the nation would result from release of the papers. Having listened to the arguments and read the secret briefs, a majority of the Court was not persuaded and would not order the newspapers that had copies of the Pentagon Papers to halt publication of them.

That decision, much praised by civil libertarians when it was handed down, was in fact the harbinger of a more deferential attitude toward national security claims. A majority of the justices were clearly willing to contemplate situations in which they would approve a prior restraint on publication of information. Justices Byron White and Potter Stewart, who cast the swing votes in the case, demanded that, at least in the absence of legislation, the government prove the publication would result in grave and irreparable harm to the national interest. However, as shown by the government's efforts to suppress Howard Morland's 1979 article about the making of the hydrogen bomb, written for *The Progressive* magazine, even that standard permits stopping publication for a significant time while trial and appellate courts decide whether the government has met its burden of proof.

Finally, the dissenting justices accepted the government's determination without any scrutiny whatsoever. In a little-noticed and now-forgotten indication of what was to come, Justice John Marshall Harlan, speaking also for Chief Justice Warren Burger and Justice Harry Blackmun, wrote:

> I agree that . . . the judiciary must . . . [satisfy] itself that the subject matter of the dispute does lie within the proper compass of the President's foreign relations power. . . . [It]

may properly insist that the determination that disclosure
of the subject matter would irreparably impair the national
security be made by the head of the Executive Department
concerned—here the Secretary of State or the Secretary of
Defense—after actual personal consideration by that officer. . . .

But in my judgment the judiciary may not properly go
beyond these two inquiries and redetermine for itself the
probable impact of disclosure on the national security.[5]

Today, that dissent clearly commands the support of the majority of
the Court. We are just beginning to experience the full weight of this
profound change. Four decisions reflect the Court's sharp break with
the past.

The manner in which the Court disposed of the first of these cases,
Snepp v. United States,[6] in 1980, showed its utter disdain for the basic
principle that had guided the Court in dealing with this issue in the
past: unless based on legislative authority, claims to limit constitutional rights on grounds of national security would be rejected.

Frank W. Snepp, a former Central Intelligence Agency operative,
published a book entitled *Decent Interval*, about the CIA's activities
in Vietnam. The Agency sought damages because he failed to clear
the manuscript, and it asked the Court to impose a requirement that
he submit all future writings for review before publication. The Court
was so little troubled by the absence of any statutory basis for the
CIA's action that it decided the case without benefit of briefs or oral
arguments. It did not deal in any serious way with the separation-of-
powers issue raised by the lack of congressional authorization. Even
the First Amendment prohibition against prior restraint was dismissed in a brief footnote:

When Snepp accepted employment with the CIA, he voluntarily signed the agreement that expressly obligated him
to submit any proposed publication for prior review. He does
not claim that he executed this agreement under duress.
Indeed, he voluntarily reaffirmed his obligation when he
left the Agency. We agree with the Court of Appeals that
Snepp's agreement is an "entirely appropriate" exercise of
the CIA Director's statutory mandate to "protec[t] intelligence sources and methods from unauthorized disclo-

sure." . . . Moreover, this Court's cases make clear that—
even in the absence of an express agreement—the CIA could
have acted to protect substantial government interests by
imposing reasonable restrictions on employee activities that
in other contexts might be protected by the First Amendment. . . . The Government has a compelling interest in protecting both the secrecy of information important to our
national security and the appearance of confidentiality so
essential to the effective operation of our foreign intelligence service. . . . The agreement that Snepp signed is a reasonable means for protecting this vital interest.[7]

The second opinion marking the Court's radical departure from
established law came a year later, in another case relating to a former
CIA official. In *Haig v. Agee* (1981)[8] the Court showed no interest in
finding a narrow way to uphold the government's contention that it
had the authority to remove Philip Agee's passport to keep him from
traveling to Iran. The executive branch claimed the right to limit an
American's foreign travel whenever the Secretary of State determines
such travel is "likely" to damage U.S. national security or foreign
policy.

Conceding that some delegation of power from Congress was necessary, the Court found it in Congress's failure to act following a few
scattered and ill-publicized cases in which passports were denied on
national security grounds. In so doing the Court ignored—as it was
to do again in the Cuban travel case, *Regan v. Wald* (1984)—a 1977
amendment to the Passport Act that severely limits the executive
branch's power to curtail travel.[9]

Once it had established congressional authorization, the Court was
unwilling to balance the proposed restriction on Agee's First Amendment rights against the possible harm of his trip. It simply declared,
contrary to the 1957 decision in *Kent v. Dulles*,[10] that there was no
such right. Thus the Secretary of State is free to deny passports for
any travel that he believes is likely to injure national security or
American foreign policy, as he defines it.

The full import of the *Agee* decision was made clear by Justice
William Rehnquist, writing for the majority in *Regan v. Wald*.[11] Taking some language from a 1965 decision out of context, he held that
free speech is involved only if restrictions are based on the beliefs of
the would-be traveler. If the government denies a passport to someone

who wants to go to a country to find out what is going on there, the First Amendment is not at issue. So much for the right to know.

Rehnquist then gave short shrift to the Fifth Amendment right to travel. It is "insufficient to overcome the foreign policy justifications supporting the restriction," he wrote. Neither the citizen nor the courts can challenge the government's evidence of the need or value of the restriction in support of foreign policy objectives—"given the traditional deference to executive judgment."[12] Rehnquist seemed not to know or care that there is no precedent for such deference in cases relating to constitutional rights.

The final case in this brief but devastating list also illustrates the Burger Court's unwillingness even to take into account legislation designed to limit the powers of the President in relation to national security. Just as Rehnquist did not think Congress's amendment to the Passport Act was relevant to a travel case, so he ignored the 1974 amendments to the Freedom of Information Act in his opinion for the Court in Weinberger v. Catholic Action of Hawaii/Peace Education Project,[13] which involved an effort to stop the navy from storing ammunition at a Hawaiian location. The Court merely accepted the government's assertion that it could not confirm or deny the presence of nuclear weapons at a particular location on the ground that the information was classified. In so doing, it ignored a provision of the FOIA that requires courts to determine on their own whether information is properly classified. It did not insist on the assurance of a senior official, as Justice Harlan would have required in the Pentagon Papers case, let alone the proof that a judge finds persuasive, as the FOIA clearly demands.

The decisions of the Burger Court in national security cases during its latter years add up to this: If the executive branch asserts that injury to the nation's foreign policy would result from the actions of its citizens, the Court will accept that judgment without any independent inquiry. Moreover, it will accept the President's definition of what needs to be done to avoid the injury without making its own determination of whether that is the least intrusive means. Finally, it will permit the President to act without congressional authorization, or it will, if necessary, stretch a point to find that authorization.

The trouble we face is underscored by Justice Lewis Powell's dissent in the Cuban travel case, in which he warned his colleagues that their job was to detemine what the law is and not what they think would be a good policy. Anyone who would defend these decisions as signaling an end to judicial activism needs to contend with Powell's clear and brief dissent:

> As the Solicitor General argues, the judgment of the Court may well be in the best interest of the United States. The regulations upheld today limit Cuba's ability to acquire hard currency, currency that the Executive has found might be used to support violence and terrorism. Our role is limited, however, to ascertaining and sustaining the intent of Congress. It is the responsibility of the President and Congress to determine the course of the Nation's foreign affairs. In this case, the legislative history canvassed by Justice Blackmun's dissenting opinion unmistakably demonstrates that Congress intended to bar the President from expanding the exercise of emergency authority under Sec. 5 (b) [claimed by the President].[14]

In 1967, in a case striking down a statute making it unlawful for a member of the Communist party to work in a defense plant, the Court pointed out that claims of national security cannot be invoked as a "talismanic incantation" to support any exercise of power that would violate constitutional rights.[15] Two decades later such claims, in the eyes of the Burger Court, sweep everything before them.[16]

·5·

The Separation of Church and State: The Burger Court's Tortuous Journey

NORMAN REDLICH

THE PRE-BURGER YEARS

The opening words of the Bill of Rights—"Congress shall make no law respecting an establishment of religion, or prohibiting the free exercise thereof"[1]—have provided a constitutional framework for this country's unique blending of religious freedom, diversity, and harmony. Although separation of church and state, embodied in this establishment clause, is deeply rooted in American history, Supreme Court involvement in this area is comparatively recent, dating from the *Everson v. Board of Education*[2] case in 1947.

Everson concerned a New Jersey statute that permitted a local board of education to reimburse parents for the costs of bus transportation to Catholic parochial schools. Both the majority and the dissent in *Everson* drew heavily on events in Virginia in 1784 that led to James Madison's famous Memorial and Remonstrance Against Religious Assessments, written in 1785 to protest a proposed bill that would have required each taxpayer to pay an amount to a church of the taxpayer's own choosing.[3] There were no public schools in Virginia at the time, and education was a principal function of the churches. Madison condemned the tax as an "establishment," and the bill's defeat in Virginia was followed by enactment of Jefferson's Bill for Religious Liberty.

In light of recent attacks on the historical underpinnings of the

Court's view of the establishment clause,[4] it is useful to review the *Everson* opinion. Both Justice Hugo Black's majority opinion and Justice Wiley Rutledge's dissent relied on the Virginia experience to argue that separation of church and state, and not merely the avoidance of a state religion or the favoring of one religion over another, was the guiding principle of interpretation of the establishment clause. In his now-famous *dicta*, Justice Black wrote:

> The "establishment of religion" of the First Amendment means at least this: Neither a state nor the Federal Government can set up a church. Neither can pass laws which aid one religion, aid all religions, or prefer one religion over another. Neither can force nor influence a person to go to or to remain away from church against his will or force him to profess a belief or disbelief in any religion. No person can be punished for entertaining or professing religious beliefs or disbeliefs, for church attendance or non-attendance. No tax in any amount, large or small, can be levied to support any religious activities or institutions, whatever they may be called, or whatever form they may adopt to teach or practice religion. Neither a state nor the Federal Government can, openly or secretly, participate in the affairs of any religious organization or groups and *vice versa*. In the words of Jefferson, the clause against establishment of religion by law was intended to erect "a wall of separation between Church and State."[5]

This theme was echoed in Justice Rutledge's dissent: "Not simply an established church, but any law respecting an establishment of religion is forbidden. . . . Madison could not have confused 'church' and 'religion,' or 'an established church' and 'an establishment of religion.' "[6]

Scholars and justices have disagreed over whether the First Amendment was intended to embody these principles developed in Virginia a few years earlier, or whether Madison's and Jefferson's views of separation were intended to be applicable to the states through the Fourteenth Amendment, or whether they are applicable to the different factual settings of public schools in the mid-twentieth century.[7] There is little doubt, however, that Madison and Jefferson emphasized the principles of separation of church and state at least prior to 1789, and that starting with *Everson* Supreme Court majorities have consistently adopted that interpretation of the establishment clause.

But agreement on general principles of interpretation did not lead to agreement on the constitutionality of the practices in *Everson* itself. Justice Black's majority opinion upheld the bus-reimbursement program on grounds that it was "public welfare legislation" designed not to benefit religion but to help children get to school safely.[8] To the four dissenting justices the expenditures constituted a tax to support religion.

In 1948 and 1952, the battlefield shifted to "released time," and it is not surprising that in the first of these cases, *McCollum v. Board of Education* (1948),[9] the Court's emphasis on the concept of separation of church and state led to an 8–1 decision invalidating the teaching of religion on school premises. But four years later, a bitterly divided Court in *Zorach v. Clauson* (1952)[10] held that releasing children for religious school instruction on non-public-school premises, while other students remained in school, was a permissible accommodation to religion. Justice William O. Douglas, who was with the majority in *Everson*, wrote his oft-criticized comment:

> We are a religious people whose institutions presuppose a Supreme Being. . . . When the state encourages religious instruction or cooperates with religious authorities by adjusting the schedule of public events to sectarian needs, it follows the best of our traditions. For it then respects the religious nature of our people and accommodates the public service to their spiritual needs. To hold that it may not would be to find in the Constitution a requirement that the government show a callous indifference to religious groups.[11]

In *McCollum* and *Zorach* a distinction emerged that was to find more detailed expression in the opinions of the Burger Court: teaching religion on public-school premises is an impermissible endorsement of religion, but a program of cooperation that enables the public and religious schools to perform their independent functions in their own ways might be permissible. Of course, the compulsory attendance requirement, which enforced a child's attendance at the religious school, could be viewed as something more than reasonable cooperation, and it was precisely on this point that the majority and the dissent in *Zorach* differed most sharply.

In light of the principles that evolved in *Everson, McCollum,* and *Zorach,* the 1962 decision in *Engel v. Vitale,*[12] invalidating the New York Regents' Prayer, should have come as no surprise, although the controversy it generated created the impression that new constitutional ground had been broken. Surely the *Everson dicta,* which barred a state from passing laws that "aid one religion or prefer one religion or another," precluded a state-prescribed prayer. With only Justice Potter Stewart dissenting, Justice Black's majority opinion concluded that neither the alleged neutrality of the "non-denominational" prayer nor the "voluntary" participation by students "can free it from the limitation of the Establishment Clause."[13]

One year later, in *Abington School District v. Schempp* (1963),[14] *Engel* was extended to a Pennsylvania law requiring Bible reading and the recitation of the Lord's Prayer at the beginning of the school day. Justice Tom Clark's majority (8–1) opinion emphasized the importance of neutrality in relations between government and religion, and set forth two parts of what was ultimately to become a three-part test in establishment-clause cases: "[T]o withstand the strictures of the Establishment Clause there must be a secular purpose and a primary effect that neither advances nor inhibits religion."[15]

Despite the near-unanimity, *Engel* and *Schempp* did not preclude subsequent litigation over whether the challenged practices were religious, as the Regents' Prayer and Bible reading clearly were, or whether they were educational, cultural, or otherwise secular, as might be the case with the teaching of religion, or possibly the singing of Christmas carols.[16] Indeed, one year before *Engel* the Court rejected an establishment-clause challenge to Sunday closing laws, concluding that whatever may have been the original religious motivation for such laws, the "present purpose and effect of most of them is to provide a uniform day of rest for all citizens."[17]

Toward the end of the Warren Court, disagreements within the Court related more to the application of its establishment-clause doctrine to particular cases than to the doctrine itself. Outside the Court, however, some believed that the Court's basic approach displayed a hostility toward religion. This sentiment was to grow more intense with the rise of the so-called Religious Right during the 1970s and 1980s. The focus of this criticism, as it had been since *Engel,* was on the school-prayer cases, which represented the core of the Warren Court's establishment-clause interpretation.

The final major decision in which the Warren Court interpreted the establishment clause[18] was a prelude to an issue that became very important to the Burger Court—financial aid to parochial schools. In *Board of Education v. Allen* (1968),[19] the child-benefit rationale stressed by Justice Black in *Everson* was extended to uphold a New York law requiring school officials to lend books without charge to students attending private as well as public schools. The Court accepted the argument that the financial benefit accrued to the children and their parents, rather than to the school; the books were selected by the public-school authorities, and ownership remained with the state. Justice Black, who wrote *Everson*, was one of the three dissenters.[20] The *Allen* case demonstrated that despite the near-unanimity that the Court had reached on such issues as school prayer, the secular educational purpose behind many financial-aid programs and the potential expansion of the child-benefit theory created the possibility of massive government support for religious schools. Whether the Burger Court could develop a constitutional approach to meet this challenge to the separation of church and state was the principal issue of establishment-clause law when Earl Warren left the Court in 1969.

FINANCIAL AID TO RELIGIOUS SCHOOLS: THE BURGER COURT SETS THE RULES

The "released-time" and school-prayer cases established that religious schools could not expect government money for the teaching of religion. But might they not expect government money to teach secular subjects? The purpose (education) would be arguably secular, and the effect would be to benefit the child, encourage parental choice, or relieve public-school overcrowding, rather than to promote religion. It would be a logical progression from the bus transportation in *Everson* and the lending of textbooks in *Allen*. And if government could "accommodate" religion by using the compulsory attendance laws to make sure that the children attend religious classes *(Zorach)*, why not "accommodate" by paying for the costs of purely secular subjects like history, mathematics, and science? Many religious schools were clamoring for public funds, and many parents, dissatisfied with the public-school system, were looking favorably on the alternative of religious schools. Those believing in church-state separation needed a constitutional doctrine to reinforce the principles that had evolved in the prayer cases.

The first case to articulate such a doctrine, *Walz v. Tax Commission* (1970),[21] involved the real-estate tax exemption uniformly provided by state and local governments. After concluding that the purpose of the exemption was not to establish religion but to spare "the exercise of religion from the burden of property taxation levied on private profit institutions," Chief Justice Warren Burger turned to the effect of the exemption:

> We must also be sure that the end result—the effect—is not an excessive government entanglement with religion. The test is inescapably one of degree. Either course, taxation of churches or exemption, occasions some degree of involvement with religion. Elimination of exemption would tend to expand the involvement of government by giving rise to tax valuation of church property, tax liens, tax foreclosures, and the direct confrontations and conflicts that follow in the train of those legal procedures.[22]

And the Court, with only Justice Douglas dissenting, upheld the exemption on grounds that its denial would have the effect of excessive government involvement with religious institutions.

One year later, the idea of "entanglement" emerged as the third part of a test that helped to close the door on most forms of significant financial assistance to church-related elementary and high schools. *Lemon v. Kurtzman* (1971) and its companion cases[23] were the first in a series in which the Burger Court grappled with state laws providing grants and support services to religious schools. In all of them the Court applied the test articulated in *Lemon* by Chief Justice Burger. "First, the statute must have a secular legislative purpose; second, its principal or primary effect must be one that neither advances nor inhibits religion [citing *Board of Education v. Allen*]; finally the statute must not foster 'an excessive government entanglement with religion' [citing *Walz*]."[24]

At issue in *Lemon* were Rhode Island and Pennsylvania statutes that provided for payments to supplement the salaries of teachers of secular subjects in private elementary schools (Rhode Island), and for the "purchase" of "secular educational services" from private schools

(Pennsylvania). Both statutes required private schools to use books used in public schools and precluded payment for subject matter that involved religious teaching.

The state's need to monitor the religious-school teachers to ensure their compliance with the statutory restrictions, wrote the Chief Justice, meant an excessive and continuing entanglement between government and religion. "Unlike a book," wrote the Chief Justice, "a teacher cannot be inspected once so as to determine the extent and intent of his or her personal beliefs and subjective acceptance of the limitations imposed by the First Amendment."[25]

The Rhode Island law also required surveillance of the religious school's records to determine the amount of the salary supplement spent on secular education. The Pennsylvania law had the "further defect of providing state financial aid directly to the church-related schools,"[26] which necessitated greater surveillance and control than payments to students and parents.

Direct aid to religious schools to teach basic secular subjects thus involved one of two unacceptable risks: either the government funds might be used to support the teaching of religion or the government would become entangled with the religious authorities in trying to make certain that this result did not occur. Neither alternative was compatible with the "dictates" of the religion clauses: "[G]overnment is to be entirely excluded from the area of religious instruction and churches excluded from the affairs of government."[27] The establishment clause protects all of the people from government endorsement of religion, and also protects religion from the control that inevitably accompanies extensive financial support.

A particularly interesting portion of the *Lemon* opinion struck a chord that had been sounded in Madison's Remonstrance in 1785: the danger of political divisiveness. Describing this phenomenon as a "broader base of entanglement," the Chief Justice wrote: "[M]any people confronted with issues of this kind [aid to parochial schools] will find their votes aligned with their faith. . . . [P]olitical division along religious lines was one of the principal evils against which the First Amendment was intended to protect. . . . The history of many countries attests to the hazards of religion's intruding into the legitimate and free exercise of religious belief."[28]

Finally, the Chief Justice seemed to be acutely aware of the need to create a constitutional standard that could counter the tendency of religious organizations to use prior decisions, such as *Everson* and *Allen*, to obtain more financial aid to religious schools. Perhaps in the hope that the "entanglement" test might brake the threatened flow of financial support for such schools, he wrote:

> We have already noted that modern governmental programs have self-perpetuating and self-expanding propensities. These internal pressures are only enhanced when the schemes involve institutions whose legitimate needs are growing and whose interests have substantial political support. Nor can we fail to see that in constitutional adjudication some steps, which when taken were thought to approach "the verge" [see Justice Black's opinion in *Everson*], have become the platform for yet further steps. . . . The dangers are increased by the difficulty of perceiving in advance exactly where the "verge" of the precipice lies. *As well as constituting an independent evil against which the Religion Clauses were intended to protect, involvement or entanglement between government and religion serves as a warning signal* [emphasis added].[29]

Lemon may have effectively blocked direct government support for elementary and secondary schools, but the Court has been far more lenient with regard to aid to church-related colleges. Decided with *Lemon* was *Tilton v. Richardson*,[30] which sustained federal construction grants to church-affiliated colleges for facilities devoted exclusively to secular educational purposes.[31] The majority noted that religious indoctrination was not a substantial purpose of the colleges and that college students were not so susceptible to religious teachings. Moreover, the very nature of a college curriculum tended to curb sectarian influence and reduce the risk that the primary effect would be to encourage or support religious activities. Entanglement was found not to be excessive because the inspection necessary to determine that the facilities were devoted to secular education would be "minimal."

These 1971 cases set the stage for a decade of intensive litigation, as state governments tried to channel money to religious schools while avoiding the interdictions of *Lemon*.

THE BURGER COURT APPLIES THE RULES: FINE LINES AND A DIVIDED COURT

Tax Benefits to Help Pay Tuition

State aid to reduce tuition costs was a natural fallback from the direct-assistance plan held invalid in *Lemon*. If parents could receive grants or tax breaks in the form of credits or deductions of tuition payments, then these benefits could be passed along to the religious schools through tuition increases that would be cost-free to the parents. This was behind the New York State plan held invalid in *Committee for Public Education and Religious Liberty v. Nyquist* (1973),[32] the first decision on financial assistance to religious schools to be decided by a Court with Nixon's four new appointees: Chief Justice Burger and Justices Harry Blackmun, Lewis Powell, and William Rehnquist.

The statute in *Nyquist* created three programs of financial assistance to religious schools, two of which involved tuition assistance. The first provided for grants of thirty to forty dollars per year per student (depending on the age of the facility) for "maintenance and repair of . . . school facilities and equipment to ensure the health, welfare and safety of enrolled pupils" in nonpublic schools serving a high concentration of low-income families. The maintenance and repair provisions were struck down in a unanimous opinion written by Justice Powell "because their effect, inevitably, is to subsidize and advance the religious mission of sectarian schools."[33]

A second program reimbursed parents with incomes below five thousand dollars for half of the tuition they paid to nonpublic schools up to an amount not exceeding fifty dollars for grade school and one hundred dollars for high school. (In New York State 85 percent of the children attending nonpublic schools were in religiously affiliated schools.) This tuition-reimbursement program similarly failed the "effect" prong of the *Lemon* test, for as Justice Powell emphasized, "By reimbursing parents for a portion of their tuition bill, the State seeks to relieve their financial burdens sufficiently to assure that they continue to have the option to send their children to religion-oriented schools. . . ."[34]

The third statute allowed families with incomes between five thousand and twenty-five thousand dollars whose children attended nonpublic schools to deduct a specified amount from their adjusted gross income. The deduction was based on a formula that was designed to make the tax benefit "comparable to, and compatible with, the tuition grant for lower-income families." The majority of the Court therefore concluded that "there would appear to be little difference for purposes of whether such aid has the effect of advancing religion, between the tax benefit allowed here and the tuition grant."[35]

In a separate portion of the opinion Justice Powell emphasized that while it was not necessary to consider the "entanglement" issue, "the importance of the competing societal interests implicated here prompts us to make the further observation that, apart from any specific entanglement of the State in particular religious programs, assistance of the sort here involved carries grave potential for entanglement in the broader sense of continuing political strife over aid to religion."[36]

If the establishment clause prevents direct government assistance to religious education,[37] the result in *Nyquist* was as necessary as that in *Lemon*. There could be no "neutrality" in such programs; both would have involved the government in massive funding of religious schools. Religions that support schools would benefit at the expense of those that did not. The programs posed threats to religious diversity, harmony, and, ultimately, religious freedom.

Nyquist helped to shut the door on direct aid to religious elementary and secondary schools, but the Burger Court continued to permit expanded aid to church-related colleges. In *Hunt v. McNair* (1973),[38] decided on the same day as *Nyquist*, the Court upheld a construction-aid program that permitted all colleges, regardless of religious affiliation, to borrow funds at low interest rates through the use of state-issued revenue bonds. And three years later, in *Roemer v. Maryland*[39] the Court upheld annual noncategorical grants to private colleges, regardless of church affiliation, as long as the money was not used for sectarian purposes.

Support Services

Having failed to obtain either direct or indirect grants, the proponents of financial aid to religious schools turned to a more selective approach—reimbursement for the cost of providing specific auxiliary secular services such as student testing and diagnostic, therapeutic, and remedial services. The Burger Court's decisions appeared to draw very fine, arguably arbitrary, distinctions. The evolution of the Court's thinking on these issues made it inevitable, however, that the results would turn on narrow issues of fact. In *Everson* and *Allen* the Court had ruled that some programs of state assistance to children attending religious schools (such as transportation and medical care), and even to the schools themselves, were permissible even though religious schools were the indirect financial beneficiaries. On the other hand, in *Lemon* and *Nyquist* the Court had rejected open-ended financial aid. By eschewing an all-or-nothing approach, the Court committed itself to a case-by-case evaluation in an effort to limit the quantity of government aid and the nature of its involvement, so that church and state would not become financial and administrative partners.

In the first of these cases, *Levitt v. Committee for Public Education and Religious Liberty* (1973),[40] decided the same day as *Nyquist,* the Court struck down a New York law that reimbursed private schools for the cost of administering state-mandated tests, both state-prepared and teacher-prepared. Because the latter involved the discretion of teachers supervised by religious institutions, Chief Justice Burger's 8–1 opinion concluded that there was a substantial risk that the tests could be used for religious indoctrination. Later cases permitted reimbursement for the cost of having private-school personnel administer and grade state-mandated and state-prepared tests.[41]

Meek v. Pittenger (1975),[42] dealt with Pennsylvania's efforts to overcome the "entanglement" hurdle by allowing public-school personnel to furnish a range of auxiliary support services in private schools— counseling, psychological services, speech and hearing therapy, testing and related services for exceptional or educationally disadvantaged students, and educational material and equipment such as maps, charts, films, records, periodicals, projectors, recorders, and laboratory paraphernalia. Of the nonpublic schools eligible for the assistance, 75 percent were church-affiliated.

The state sought to distinguish *Lemon* on the basis of the subject matter of the services and the fact that the public-school personnel would perform the services. Justice Stewart's plurality opinion[43] rejected both these distinctions. Relying both on "effect" and "entanglement," the Court concluded that the State must be certain that the subsidized teachers did not teach religion, whether the class be "remedial arithmetic" or "medieval history,"[44] and excessive entanglement would result if the State had to oversee its own personnel to ensure that they remained religiously neutral. The opinion also mentioned the danger of political divisiveness.[45] The loan of instructional material was found to be similarly invalid.[46]

Significantly, however, the near-unanimity of *Levitt* was absent in *Meek*, as the Chief Justice and Justice Rehnquist now joined Justice Byron White in bitter dissent.[47] *Meek* was the first indication that a growing minority was prepared to accept government aid to parochial schools in the form of secular support services furnished by public-school teachers.[48]

Ohio responded to the majority's objections in *Meek* with a scheme whereby diagnostic services (psychological, hearing, and speech) would be performed by public-school personnel *on* parochial-school premises; these were presumably analogous to health and welfare services provided by the state to all children. Therapeutic and remedial services, on the other hand, would be performed *off* the premises of the private school. In *Wollman v. Walter* (1977)[49] a divided Court upheld these provisions. To the majority, the limited contact between diagnostician and child in the parochial school did not pose the risk of the teaching of religion, and performance of the remedial tasks by public-school personnel on sites not identified with sectarian schools minimized the dangers of entanglement. The provision authorizing funds for textbooks was sustained, but the reimbursement for instructional materials, equipment, and field-trip services was struck down, consistent with the prior decisions.

Thus, the Court, by 1977, had distinguished between remedial services, permissible only if performed by public-school employees off the premises of the religious school, and diagnostic services, permissible if performed by public-school employees even on religious-school premises. Justices Powell, Blackmun, Stewart, and John Paul Stevens seemed to draw the line for remedial services at the parochial-schoolhouse door. The other five rejected the distinction but Justices William J. Brennan and Thurgood Marshall would find a constitutional violation no matter where the services were performed, while the Chief Justice[50] and Justices White and Rehnquist would reach the opposite conclusion. On diagnostic services, only Justice Brennan dissented from the Court's approval in *Wollman* of reimbursement for diagnostic services performed by public-school employees on religious-school premises.

These sharply disputed distinctions bore some relationship to establishment-clause concerns, even if one believed that they did not warrant the different conclusions as to constitutionality. Teaching religion is less likely to occur while diagnosing a learning problem or administering a state-prepared test; surveillance is less necessary and the consequent "entanglement" less likely. Remedial teaching, on the other hand, may be indistinguishable from "normal" teaching, especially in "enrichment" courses. To allow public-school teachers to do remedial teaching in religious schools would open the way for extensive financial support of religious schools and would require constant policing. Admittedly, remedial teaching outside religious schools could also trigger substantial government expenditures and some administrative entanglement, but religious schools are probably not inclined to rely on such programs, since that reliance tends to defeat the very purpose for which the schools are established—to have the children in a pervasively religious environment for most of their formative educational years. If the public-school teachers were permitted to do remedial work in the religious schools, however, they would be more likely to be drawn into the process of religious education. Thus, by insisting that only public-school employees may render educational support services (whether remedial or diagnostic) and that actual instruction of students (remedial or otherwise) be performed off the religious-school premises, the Court used the "entanglement" test to keep public- and religious-school systems separate.

THE REAGAN ELECTION: A NEW POLITICAL AGENDA

As the 1970s drew to a close, one might have concluded that a rather solid Court majority agreed on the broad principles of establishment-clause law: the government cannot support religious practices and institutions; government must be neutral in its dealing with religion; and secular programs must be conducted so as to avoid government support for, and excessive entanglement in, religious institutions and activities.

The first significant church-state case in the 1980s certainly gave no indication of any change in direction. In *Stone v. Graham* (1980),[51] the Court invalidated a Kentucky statute that required public-school officials to post a copy of the Ten Commandments, purchased with private contributions, in every public classroom, each plaque bearing a notation explaining that the display was a secular application of the Ten Commandments "in its adoption as the fundamental legal code of Western Civilization and the Common Law of the United States."

The Court concluded that the statute served no secular purpose. Since the Ten Commandments is "a sacred text in the Jewish and Christian faiths, no legislative recitation of secular purpose could blind us to that fact." Only Justice Rehnquist dissented.[52]

But political events were starting to run counter to the Court's constitutional doctrines. The election of President Reagan in November 1980 brought to the White House a president supported by a religious constituency that had long been critical of the Court's school-prayer decisions.[53] A constitutional amendment to overturn *Engel v. Vitale* was high on the "social issues" agenda of the Reagan presidency. As part of his "pro-religion" program, the President also promoted financial aid to religious schools, focusing primarily on a tuition tax-credit proposal similar to the New York program found unconstitutional in *Nyquist*.[54] As has happened so often, the Supreme Court's judicial agenda soon reflected the country's political agenda.

Widmar v. Vincent: *"Equal Access" for Religious Speech*

Although separation of church and state has been a principal theme in establishment-clause law, a countervailing theme has been "accommodation." In upholding the New York released-time program in *Zorach v. Clauson*, for example, Justice Douglas wrote that when the state encourages religious instruction it "respects the religious nature of our people and accommodates the public service to their spiritual needs."[55]

Of course, some "accommodation" with religion is necessary in order to recognize an individual's rights under the free-exercise clause. A 1963 case, *Sherbert v. Verner*,[56] held that a state could not deny unemployment benefits to a woman whose religious beliefs prevented her from working on Saturday. To regard this exception to an otherwise valid secular law as an "establishment" would place the two great religion clauses in irreconcilable conflict. The state may also alleviate burdens on free exercise, even if the burdens do not rise to the level of a constitutional violation. In one of the Sunday closing-law cases,[57] for example, while holding that a New York Sunday closing law did not violate the free-exercise rights of an Orthodox Jew, the Court suggested that the state could make an exception for those whose religious beliefs required that their businesses remain closed on Sundays.[58]

The aggressive posture of some evangelical religious groups has led them to claim that students in public schools should have a "right" to engage in group prayer at the start of the day, and that children at parochial schools are discriminated against if they are denied educational programs available to others. It was but a small step to argue that state support for public religious observances, or government financial support for religious schools, would be an "accommodation" to religious belief of the type the establishment clause permitted, even if it was not required by the free-exercise clause.

Widmar v. Vincent (1981),[59] lent some support to this argument. The University of Missouri at Kansas City prohibited the use of university buildings or grounds "for purposes of religious worship or religious teaching." The prohibition was challenged by an evangelical Christian students' organization on First Amendment and equal-protection-clause grounds. Justice Powell's majority (8–1) opinion concluded that once the university created a forum generally open to student groups, it could not exclude religious speech. As a free-speech case, *Widmar* was unexceptional: an urban public university, unlike a school, has many of the characteristics of a public forum, and the university's own regulations created a forum for student groups.

The case had establishment-clause ramifications, however, because the university contended that religious teaching and worship on the premises of a public university was an establishment of religion. Although Justice Powell's opinion emphasized that the case was decided on the "bases of speech and association rights,"[60] and that there was no conflict with the establishment clause, the Court appeared to be mandating a practice—religious activity (even prayer)—on the premises of a public educational institution. That result could threaten the establishment principle if it could be argued that student activity of the kind in *Widmar* should be allowed as an "accommodation" to free-speech rights even in those cases where, unlike *Widmar*, there was no free-speech violation. This was essentially the claim now raised by religious groups that wanted to use the decision to bring organized religious activity into public elementary and high schools, an argument generally rejected by the lower courts.[61]

Mueller v. Allen: *Tax Benefits Approved*

It will be recalled that in *Committee for Public Education v. Nyquist*, the Court concluded that the State could not use the tax system to reimburse a taxpaying parent for tuition paid to religious schools.

Nyquist involved benefits for parents of children in private schools in states where the programs effectively gave benefits only to those attending religious schools. Moreover, since they involved specified cash benefits to individual taxpayers, the easily calculated savings could be passed along to the private religious schools by allowing them to charge higher tuition. A benefit in the form of a deduction from taxable income, rather than a specified dollar amount, extended also to parents of children in public schools, might survive constitutional challenge.

Minnesota exploited this possibility with a law that provided for a deduction from taxable income of up to five hundred dollars in some grades and seven hundred dollars in others, not only for parents of children in private schools, but also for parents of public-school students. Deductible expenses included tuition to attend school outside the home district and summer school, tuition for physically handicapped children, and costs of transportation and textbooks.

On the basis of these differences, in 1983 a 5–4 majority in *Mueller v. Allen*[62] upheld the Minnesota statute. Justice Rehnquist, one of the *Nyquist* dissenters, wrote the majority opinion, joined by the two other *Nyquist* dissenters, the Chief Justice and Justice White, and by the newest member of the Court, Justice Sandra Day O'Connor. The decisive switch was that of Justice Powell, who had written the *Nyquist* opinion but who now joined the new majority. Justice Stevens, who had not been on the Court in 1973, seemed firmly aligned with Justices Brennan, Marshall, and Blackmun in opposing financial support for religious schools.

In deciding that the Minnesota law did not have the "effect" of advancing the sectarian aims of the nonpublic schools, Justice Rehnquist placed principal emphasis on the availability of the deduction to all parents. He also noted that this was one of many deductions permitted under the Minnesota tax system. And though *Widmar* had been explicitly based on the free-speech rights of the student religious groups, Justice Rehnquist cited it as authority for the proposition that when benefits are extended to a broad spectrum of groups, it is an "important index of secular effect."[63] The "effect" prong of *Lemon* was satisfied, even though, as Justice Marshall noted in a strong dissent, fewer than one hundred of the ninety thousand children in Minnesota public schools paid a "general tuition.... Parents who send their children to free public schools are simply ineligible to obtain the full benefit of the deduction."[64] Moreover, approximately 96 percent of the private-school children attended religious schools. Thus, the overwhelming portion of the tax benefits flowed to parents of religious-school children. Although the identity of the beneficiaries was clearly a factor in *Nyquist,* Justice Rehnquist concluded: "We would be loath to adopt a rule grounding the constitutionality of a facially neutral law on annual reports reciting the extent to which various classes of private citizens claimed benefits under the law."[65]

In his dissent, Justice Marshall also emphasized that the entire scheme was intended to enable the religious schools to charge higher tuition. While the amount of the benefit resulting from a deduction varied in accordance with each parent's taxable income, virtually all of them benefited to some extent, and private schools would have little difficulty in becoming the indirect beneficiaries of the state's generosity.[66]

The danger of political divisiveness in such programs—emphasized in *Lemon, Nyquist,* and *Meek*—was casually disposed of in a footnote by the *Mueller v. Allen* majority. Justice Rehnquist simply ignored *Nyquist* and concluded that the references in *Lemon* to this subject "must be regarded as confined to cases where direct financial subsidies are paid to parochial schools or to teachers in parochial schools."[67] This very limiting interpretation of an important component of the "entanglement" prong became significant in later cases.

Legislative Chaplains: Historical Exception or Still More Accommodation?

At the close of the 1982–83 term, the Court, in *Marsh v. Chambers* (1983), held that paid legislative chaplains and prayers at the start of each session of the Nebraska legislature were not establishment-clause violations. Chief Justice Burger's majority opinion (6–3) was based almost entirely on historical analysis, emphasizing that the practices challenged were identical to those adopted by the very Congress that approved the First Amendment in 1789. Moreover, the framers of the First Amendment had considered the issue of legislative chaplains and apparently had not viewed them as representing the evil that the establishment clause was designed to prevent. Chief Justice Burger also rejected the argument that the clause should be given a more expansive reading when applied to the states through the due process clause of the Fourteenth Amendment. Supporting this narrow view of the case was the reference to the fact that the complaining party was an adult, an obvious gesture of deference to the school-prayer cases.[68]

Justice Brennan's dissent, joined by Justice Marshall, may have been accurate in describing the majority opinion as "narrow and, on the whole, careful . . . [with a] limited rationale [that] should pose little threat to the overall fate of the Establishment Clause."[69] But the Chief Justice's opinion did more than characterize the Nebraska practice as an historical exception to the establishment clause. In words that might be applied to school prayer, or other manifestations of government-supported religious practices in public life, he compared the hiring of a legislative chaplain (in this case the same one for sixteen years) to the "conduct" approved in the Sunday closing-law cases, and described the practice as "simply a tolerable acknowledgement of beliefs widely held among people of this country."[70]

Justice Brennan's dissent questioned the emphasis on the intent of the members of the First Congress, arguing that the Constitution is not a "static document" and that "practices which may have been objectionable to no one in the time of Jefferson and Madison may today be highly offensive to many persons, the deeply devout and the nonbelievers alike." He concluded that the Nebraska practices were not *de minimis* or nonsectarian but "will inevitably and continuously involve the State in one or another religious debate."[71]

The differing emphasis given to history in the opinions of the Chief Justice and Justice Brennan shifted *Marsh v. Chambers* from the earlier pattern in establishment-clause cases. Starting with the *Everson* case, separationists had virtually monopolized the historical turf, relying on the Virginia experience in 1784 and 1785 to justify reading into the establishment clause the views of Madison and Jefferson that were articulated so forcefully at that time. The debates in the First Congress were far less clear, and one's conclusions about them depended in large part on how one viewed Madison's efforts to infuse his own views on limitations of state power into an amendment that limited the federal government. The Chief Justice had relied on history in order to justify the tax benefit in *Walz*, as did Justice Rehnquist in *Mueller v. Allen. Marsh v. Chambers* was further indication that history was rapidly becoming a weapon for all sides to use.

The Crèche Case: Accommodation Triumphant

Placing a Christmas nativity scene—a crèche—at public expense on a private park in front of city hall in Pawtucket, Rhode Island, would appear to be a classic example of conduct that undermines virtually all of the values that the Court had attached to the establishment clause since 1947. Justice Black's *Everson* dicta and Chief Justice Burger's three-part *Lemon* test were designed to guarantee neutrality and maximum noninvolvement by government in matters of religion. Here was the absence of neutrality and the essence of involvement—government financial support for the depiction of an event that was of profound religious significance to one religion and that was, as a matter of religious belief, rejected by most others.

Nor did the case raise significant countervailing establishment-clause themes. Since citizens did not have a First Amendment free-speech right to a government-funded crèche, the "accommodation" argument in *Widmar* did not exist. Nor could the state be viewed as burdening religion by refusing to pay for a crèche, as it might in imposing property taxes[72] or drafting conscientious objectors.[73] The crèche could not be equated with a textbook; it provided no secular benefit to individuals to warrant even an analogous argument to the child-benefit theory. And there was no long historical exemption that could be traced back to the First Congress. Indeed, there was persuasive evidence that the secular observance of Christmas was not a common practice at the end of the eighteenth century.[74]

Both the district and circuit courts had ruled that the Pawtucket crèche was unconstitutional. In furtherance of the political-religious agenda of the Reagan administration, the Justice Department, in an *amicus* brief, urged the reversal of these lower-court rulings. And it succeeded 5–4.

Chief Justice Burger's majority opinion in *Lynch v. Donnelly* (1984) was based on an expanded notion of "accommodation" to religion and on what the Court perceived to be the essentially secular nature of the Christmas display and celebration, of which the crèche was one component. The Chief Justice found that the Constitution "affirmatively mandates" accommodation.[75] He portrayed *Marsh v. Chambers* as an example of the First Congress's "contemporaneous understanding" of the establishment clause in 1789 and a "striking example of the accommodation of religious beliefs intended by the Framers."[76] Also cited as "accommodations" to religion were *Zorach v. Clauson* (the released-time decision), "In God We Trust" on coins, "One Nation under God" in the Pledge of Allegiance, and paintings with a religious message exhibited in the National Gallery in Washington.

Whatever one's view of *Zorach*, it is hardly a firm precedent for allowing the government to display a symbol recognized as religious by the Court. As Justice Brennan observed in his dissent, acknowledgment of the deity in ceremonies and in the national motto has probably acquired a secular meaning and, in any event, lacks the element of government support for a particular religious message that the crèche connotes. And museum paintings are individual works of art, not government-sponsored religious symbols.

By viewing the crèche "in the context of the Christmas season,"[77] the Chief Justice was able to meet the three-part *Lemon* test by finding a "secular purpose" (it "depicts the historical origins of this traditional event long recognized as a National Holiday"),[78] a "primary effect" that does not benefit religion or Christianity, and no "entanglement." The Court found no "administrative entanglement," and, following *Mueller*, ruled that in the absence of a direct subsidy to a religious institution, "no inquiry into potential political divisiveness is called for."[79]

Justice O'Connor concurred in the majority opinion, but wrote "separately to suggest a clarification of our Establishment Clause doctrine." It is understandable that the newest member of the Court should attempt to clarify a confusing and controversial area of constitutional law, but her suggested approach seems no more helpful in deciding cases than the existing *Lemon* test. "The Establishment Clause," she wrote, "prohibits government from making adherence to a religion relevant in any way to a person's standing in the political community." The government violates the clause through "excessive entanglement," which she defined as "institutional entanglement" rather than "political divisiveness." The latter may be evidence of the former, or of improper endorsement of religion, but should not be an "independent ground for holding a government practice unconstitutional."[80]

Justice O'Connor would have the "purpose" and "effect" prongs relate to the endorsement of religion: "The purpose prong . . . asks whether government's actual purpose is to endorse or disapprove of religion. The effect prong asks whether, irrespective of government's actual purpose, the practice under review in fact conveys a message of endorsement or disapproval."[81] Defining "effect" this way could validate many forms of financial aid to religious schools that had been struck down (*e.g.*, the *Nyquist* or *Lemon* programs), for these might not be viewed as "communicating a message of endorsement." Moreover, it is hard to fathom how the O'Connor approach significantly clarifies "primary effect . . . that neither advances nor inhibits religion."

On the other hand, Justice O'Connor's formulation of the "secular purpose" requirement suggested a more searching evaluation of governmental intent than Chief Justice Burger had made. "That requirement is not satisfied," she pointed out, "by the mere presence of some secular purpose, however dominated by religious purposes."[82]

Applying her version of the *Lemon* test to the facts of the crèche case, Justice O'Connor reached the same result as Chief Justice Burger and for the same reason—the crèche was part of a celebration of Christmas in a holiday setting. The purpose was not to endorse religion, but to celebrate a holiday, and government celebration is "not understood to endorse the religious content of the holiday, just as government celebration of Thanksgiving is not so understood."[83] Thus, by narrowing the meaning of "effect" to encompass only endorsement or disapproval, it was easier for Justice O'Connor to conclude that cloaking a religious symbol in the trappings of a national holiday did not have a "primary effect" of advancing religion.

In the final analysis, the difference between the majority and Justice Brennan in dissent was one of sensitivity to the meaning of the nativity scene (whether standing alone or as part of the broader Christmas celebration) to Christians and non-Christians, particularly Jews, for whom the depiction of the birth of Christ as God represents a fundamental point of departure of Christianity from Judaism. The following excerpts from the two opinions speak eloquently of these different approaches to deeply felt religious beliefs:

> [Chief Justice Burger:] The crèche, like a painting, is passive; admittedly it is a reminder of the origins of Christmas. Even the traditional, purely secular displays extant at Christmas, with or without a crèche, would inevitably recall the religious nature of the Holiday. . . . It would be ironic, however, if the inclusion of a single symbol of a particular historic religious event, as part of a celebration acknowledged in the Western world for 20 centuries . . . would so "taint" the City's exhibit as to render it violative of the Establishment Clause.[84]

> [Justice Brennan:] The essence of the crèche's symbolic purpose and effect is to prompt the observer to experience a

sense of simple awe and wonder appropriate to the contemplation of one of the central elements of Christian dogma—that God sent His son into the world to be a Messiah. Contrary to the Court's suggestion, the crèche is far from a mere representation of a "particular historic religious event." It is, instead, best understood as a mystical re-creation of an event that lies at the heart of Christian faith. To suggest, as the Court does, that such a symbol is merely "traditional" and therefore no different from Santa's house or reindeer is not only offensive to those for whom the crèche has profound significance, but insulting to those who insist for religious or personal reasons that the story of Christ is in no sense a part of "history" nor an unavoidable element of our national "heritage."[85]

Though the Burger Court's interpretation of the establishment clause was not consistent, in a myriad of cases it seemed to have sounded the theme that all religious faiths are constitutionally equal and that believers and nonbelievers alike can enjoy the uniquely American experience of being neither included, nor excluded, nor insulted by government because of their religion. To those who feel excluded because to them a government-funded nativity scene is either offensive or insulting, *Lynch v. Donnelly* conveyed a sad and disappointing message.[86]

As the 1983–84 term drew to a close, only one case during the 1982–84 period, *Larkin v. Grendel's Den* (1982), evinced a strong interpretation of the establishment clause. Writing for a near-unanimous Court (only Justice Rehnquist dissented), Chief Justice Burger held that a Massachusetts statute that gave churches and schools the power to veto applications for liquor licenses at locations within five hundred feet of the church provides an actual and symbolic benefit to churches, thereby having the "primary effect" of advancing religion. The law also "enmeshes churches in the processes of government" and creates the danger of "divisiveness along religious lines," in violation of the entanglement prong.[87]

Compared with the three other cases decided during this period, the issue of whether or not a state could allow a church to veto the location of a saloon did not appear significant. These other cases—*Marsh v. Chambers, Mueller v. Allen*, and *Lynch v. Donnelly*—suggested that the shift of Justice Powell from his *Nyquist* position, and the arrival of Justice O'Connor, might create a majority prepared to reconsider the basic establishment-clause cases.

SEPARATION TO THE FORE

Both sides in the controversy over the meaning of the establishment clause worried, and hoped, as the Court deliberated during the 1984–85 term. When the Court adjourned on July 2, those who were fearful breathed a sigh of relief; those who had hoped for a sharp change in direction were bitterly disappointed. The big news was, essentially, no news: the three major decisions of the Court followed the pattern of prior precedent.

Silent Prayer: A Matter of Purpose

In 1978 Alabama enacted a law that required teachers of grades one through six to announce a period of silence "for meditation" at the start of each day's first class. A second law, enacted in 1981, provided that the teacher "may announce that a period of silence not to exceed one minute in duration shall be observed for meditation or voluntary prayer." In 1982 the Alabama legislature authorized any teacher or professor "in any public educational institution within the state of Alabama" to lead "willing students" in a prescribed prayer that recognized "Almighty God" as the "Creator and Supreme Judge of the World."[88]

All three statutes were challenged, but only the 1981 "meditation or voluntary prayer" statute was at issue in *Wallace v. Jaffree* (1985). Jaffree did not appeal the ruling of the lower federal courts upholding the 1978 "period of silence . . . for meditation" statute. The 1982 statute, with its prescribed prayer, was found by the district court to have been enacted "to encourage a religious activity." That court, nevertheless, upheld the law because, the district court concluded, the Supreme Court had misconstrued the establishment clause in its prior opinions and Alabama could establish a state-supported religion. The Eleventh Circuit Court of Appeals reversed this decision, and, acting on Alabama's appeal, the Supreme Court, in 1984, summarily and unanimously affirmed.[89] *Engel v. Vitale* was alive and well.

The district court had also upheld the 1981 law despite a finding that it, too, had been enacted for religious purposes. The Eleventh

Circuit, accepting this finding, reversed the district court, leading to Alabama's appeal.[90]

When the 1981 statute was enacted, a so-called "pure moment of silence" law already existed, and "voluntary prayer" was the only meaningful change. The new law could have only been intended to encourage religious activity, as the district and circuit courts found. Indeed, the law's sponsor had explicitly stated that the bill was intended "to return voluntary prayer" to public schools.[91] Thus, a "secular purpose" was difficult, if not impossible, to discern; if the first prong of the *Lemon* test still had life after *Lynch v. Donnelly*, the 1981 Alabama law would be difficult to sustain. By a 6–3 vote, the Supreme Court agreed, with Justices Powell and O'Connor providing the decisive "switch" votes from *Lynch v. Donnelly*.

In one sense Justice Stevens's majority opinion simply applied precedent to the peculiar history of the 1981 Alabama statute and concluded that the statute had "no secular purpose." In a broader sense, however, *Wallace v. Jaffree* was the occasion to reconsider the basic principles that had guided the Supreme Court in its interpretation of the establishment clause since 1947.

First, Justice Stevens's majority opinion reaffirmed the *Lemon v. Kurtzman* three-part test against the dissents of the Chief Justice and Justice Rehnquist, although only the first prong was actually discussed.

Second, the Court may have redefined the "purpose" prong, despite an admonition by Justice Powell that *Lemon* should be left alone. One can read the majority opinion in *Jaffree* as concluding that the Alabama law had no secular purpose at all; this was Justice Powell's interpretation.[92] But the majority opinion itself, with which Justice Powell concurred, specifically quoted Justice O'Connor's restatement of the "purpose" prong in her concurring opinion in *Lynch v. Donnelly*. "In applying the purpose test," Justice Stevens wrote, " 'it is appropriate to ask whether the government's actual purpose is to endorse or disapprove of religion.' "[93] In her concurrence in *Lynch*, Justice O'Connor had interpreted this to mean that the existence of some secular purpose would not suffice to turn away an establishment-clause challenge if the action was dominated by a religious purpose.[94] Her concurrence in *Jaffree* was based on her conclusion that Alabama intentionally endorsed the practice of prayer, not on lack of secular purpose. Justice Stevens's adoption of Justice O'Connor's formulation could be significant in future cases if there is a secular purpose that is insignificant compared with the dominant religious purpose.

Third, the majority stated clearly that it intends to apply strict constitutional standards "whenever the State itself speaks on a religious subject,"[95] thus apparently rejecting the argument, suggested with increasing frequency by the Chief Justice, that the Court should concern itself only with state practices that are "a step toward creating an established church"[96] or that are dictated by the "Archbishop of Canterbury, the Vicar of Rome, or some other powerful religious leaders."[97]

Fourth, the majority's holding rejected the "accommodation to religion" approach forcefully advanced by the Chief Justice in *Lynch* and restated in his *Jaffree* dissent, where he described the Alabama law as one that "accommodates the purely private, voluntary religious choices of the individual pupils who wish to pray while at the same time creating a time for nonreligious reflection for those who do not choose to pray,"[98] a position also argued by the United States in its *amicus* brief.[99]

Justice O'Connor's concurring opinion, which elaborated on a footnote in the majority opinion,[100] usefully analyzed how one might limit this potentially open-ended "accommodation" approach to establishment-clause issues. Drawing on the free-exercise derivation of the "accommodation" concept, she suggested that if the government "lifts a government-imposed burden on the free exercise of religion . . . then the standard Establishment Clause test should be modified accordingly. It is disingenuous to look for a purely secular purpose when the manifest objective of a statute is to facilitate the free exercise of religion by lifting a government-imposed burden."[101]

This analysis, Justice O'Connor concluded, would not save the Alabama law, because the state had imposed no burden on a child's ability to pray silently in public schools. The only burden lifted by the statute is the limitation on group silent prayer under state sponsorship. "Phrased in these terms, the burden lifted by the statute is not one imposed by the State of Alabama but by the Establishment Clause as interpreted in *Engel* and *Abington*. In my view, it is beyond the authority of the State of Alabama to remove burdens imposed by the Constitution itself."[102]

Finally, and most importantly, the majority rejected two fundamental challenges to constitutional jurisprudence in the church-state area. One section of Justice Stevens's opinion was devoted to answering what he described as the "remarkable conclusion" of the district court that the "Federal Constitution imposes no obstacle to Alabama's establishment of a state religion." Because no justice was urging the Court to read the religion clauses out of the Fourteenth Amendment's due-process clause, one suspects that the real purpose of this discussion was to answer the long and scholarly opinion of Justice Rehnquist, in which he directly challenged the historical argument, first advanced in *Everson*, that the establishment clause was intended to embody the Jefferson-Madison views of separation of church and state. His argument ran as follows:

> The Framers intended the Establishment Clause to pro-
> hibit the designation of any church as a "national" one. The
> Clause was also designed to stop the Federal Government
> from asserting a preference for one religious denomination
> or sect over others. Given the "incorporation" of the Estab-
> lishment Clause as against the States via the Fourteenth
> Amendment in *Everson*, States are prohibited as well from
> establishing a religion or discriminating between sects. As
> its history abundantly shows, however, nothing in the Es-
> tablishment Clause requires government to be strictly neu-
> tral between religion and irreligion, nor does that Clause
> prohibit Congress or the States from pursuing legitimate
> secular ends through nondiscriminatory sectarian means.[103]

The proper role of history in constitutional adjudication is a subject of considerable scholarly debate,[104] and neither conservatives nor liberals have been consistent in their uses of history. Justice Rehnquist was clearly trying to shift the direction of establishment-clause law, but so far he appears to have few if any allies on the Court. (Only Justice White expressed some support for Justice Rehnquist's position.) And though Justice Stevens acknowledged that religious freedom may have been understood "at one time" to prohibit only "the preference of one Christian sect over another," he concluded that "when the underlying principle has been examined in the crucible of litigation, the Court has unambiguously concluded that the individual freedom of conscience protected by the First Amendment embraces the right to select any religious faith or none at all."[105] He then quoted Justice Black's *Everson* dicta that the First Amendment bars "laws which aid one religion, aid all religions, or prefer one religion over another."[106]

What does *Wallace v. Jaffree* predict as to future "moment of silence" laws? A statute that merely sets aside a moment of silence, without mentioning prayer, would be sustained unless it can be shown that its legislative history demonstrated "no secular purpose" or that it was, in Justice O'Connor's words, "intended to convey a message of state encouragement of religion." Despite the reality that religion has probably been involved in "moment of silence" legislation, at least since *Engel v. Vitale*, the "secular purpose" prong may not be difficult to satisfy, even if the legislature has manifested a sectarian interest. Justice Powell, in his concurrence, stated his agreement with Justice O'Connor that "*some* moment-of-silence statutes *may* be constitutional."[107]

If the "secular purpose" requirement is met, it is unlikely that a "moment of silence" law will fail the "effect" test either. Justice Powell specifically stated that a "moment of silence" law is unlikely to have the effect of advancing religion.[108] Unless it is implemented in a sectarian manner, it would be difficult to demonstrate that a law providing for a moment of silence, enacted with secular purpose, had the effect of advancing religion.

More difficult to predict is the fate of a law providing, as did Alabama's, for a moment of silence for meditation "or silent prayer." Justice O'Connor would approve a moment-of-silence law "drafted and implemented so as to permit prayer, meditation and reflection . . . without endorsing one alternative over the others. . . ."[109] Justice Powell would have upheld the Alabama statute itself if it had a clear secular purpose.[110] He, like Justice O'Connor, would probably be satisfied if the legislative history showing a religious purpose was not so blatant as it was in Alabama. The majority opinion, moreover, stated that the intent of the Alabama law was not "merely [to protect] every student's right to engage in voluntary prayer during an appropriate moment of silence during the school day."[111] Different language and history might persuade the Court that there was a secular purpose and no proscribed religious effect in some "meditation or prayer" statutes.

Thus, one may conclude that a "pure" moment-of-silence law is probably valid unless, as was held in a case involving New Jersey's law,[112] the legislative history dilutes the purity. In today's political environment, with religious leaders actively involved in politics, those who see religious motives in all moment-of-silence laws will find *Jaffree* of some help. Yet it will also be helpful in overturning laws that provide for a moment of silence for meditation "or prayer,"[113] since it makes the defense of such statutes more difficult.

Overlooked in the several *Jaffree* opinions is an important religious consideration that should influence the constitutional result. "Silent prayer," like vocal prayer, can never be nondenominational. When the state encourages silent prayer, it endorses a practice that is unacceptable to those whose faith requires that they pray only in a place of worship or before some religious symbol. Some faiths may forbid praying with members of another faith or with the opposite sex; some require believers to stand, or face a certain direction, or sit down, or wear certain apparel, or be led by ordained spiritual leaders—the variables reflect the infinite capacity of the human spirit to worship God in different ways. Any formalized encouragement of prayer destroys the neutral position of the state, divides us along religious lines, and singles out those who choose not to pray silently in public because of either belief or nonbelief. The Constitution should reflect these differences among our people and not magnify them. Silent prayer must be an expression of individual choice by the student. All prescribed moments of silence are highly suspect.

Day Off for Sabbath: Accommodation Contained

In 1963, in *Sherbert v. Verner*,[114] the Supreme Court held that South Carolina had violated the free-exercise rights of a Seventh Day Adventist who was denied unemployment-insurance benefits because she was unable to accept a job that required her to work on Saturdays, which would have violated her religious scruples. *Sherbert* was followed by *Thomas v. Indiana Employment Security Division Review Board* (1981),[115] which concerned a factory worker who was denied unemployment compensation after he had left a job with a weapons manufacturer because of his religious convictions. *Sherbert* and *Thomas* are frequently cited as examples of permissible accommodations to religion because a state, if it enacted the exception required by the Court's decisions, would be alleviating a state-imposed burden on free exercise.

Different considerations are posed when a state compels private employers to lift the burdens that their conditions of employment impose on the religious beliefs and practices of employees. Title VII, which forbids religious discrimination in employment, requires employers to make "reasonable accommodations" to an employee's religious practices. In *TWA v. Hardison* (1977),[116] the Court interpreted Title VII to require employers to incur only minimal burdens.

Statutes that require employers to accommodate to the religious practices of employees can raise establishment-clause problems, which may be one reason why the Court in *Hardison* imposed so slight an obligation on employers. Religious belief can dictate a wide range of employee practices, and state laws requiring accommodation by employers could, at some point, confer such broad benefits on religious observers as to be considered establishments of religion.

The Connecticut statute at the center of *Thornton v. Caldor, Inc.* (1985)[117] was enacted in 1977 after the state revised its Sunday closing laws to permit certain classes of businesses to remain open. It provides:

> No person who states that a particular day of the week is observed as his Sabbath may be required by his employer to work on such day. An employee's refusal to work on his Sabbath shall not constitute grounds for his dismissal.[118]

Thornton held a management position in one of the stores of a retail chain. He refused to work on Sunday because it was his Sabbath. He also refused a transfer to a management position in a store in Massachusetts that closed on Sunday and to a nonsupervisory position in Connecticut at a lower salary. After being transferred to the latter position, he resigned, and a state administrative agency found that he had been discharged in violation of the statute.

In a rare display of consensus, the Supreme Court, with only Justice Rehnquist dissenting, found the Connecticut statute had a "primary effect that impermissibly advances a particular religion's practice."[119] Chief Justice Burger's majority opinion accepted what the Court believed to be the Connecticut Supreme Court's interpretation that the Connecticut statute, unlike the "reasonable accommodation" requirement of the federal law, "imposes on employers and employees an absolute duty to conform their business practices to the particular religious practices of the employee by enforcing observance of the Sabbath the employee unilaterally designates."[120]

Thornton is significant because the Court declined to apply the "accommodation" approach to a government action that, in many ways, represented more of an actual accommodation than Pawtucket's construction of the crèche or New York's "released time" program in *Zorach*. Although the Connecticut statute relieved only a private burden, the government action in the Pawtucket and New York cases relieved no burdens. Chief Justice Burger had been a proponent of "accommodation," and the Connecticut law presented him with an opportunity to extend the concept in a situation that would have been seen as benefiting freedom of worship. On the other hand, if the concept of "accommodation" is limited to relieving state-imposed burdens on free exercise, it can coexist with a robust establishment clause.

Public-School Teachers in Religious Schools: Meek v. Pittenger *Revisited*

Probably the most important church-state decisions of the 1984–85 term were announced on the next-to-last day—*Grand Rapids v. Ball* and *Aguilar v. Felton*.[121] Both involved the same principle that had narrowly divided the Court in *Meek v. Pittenger*—whether "remedial" courses could be taught by public-school teachers in private schools. Both programs were held unconstitutional by narrow (5–4) majorities—Grand Rapids' because its effect was to advance religion, and the New York program in *Aguilar* because of excessive entanglements. One aspect of the Grand Rapids program was struck down by a 7–2 majority.[122]

The Grand Rapids, Michigan, School District had developed a two-part program—Shared Time and Community Education. Justice Brennan, in his majority opinion, concisely described both parts, and the facts are highly significant:

> The Shared Time program offers classes during the regular school day that are intended to be supplementary to the "core curriculum" courses that the State of Michigan requires as a part of an accredited school program. Among the subjects offered are "remedial" and "enrichment" mathematics, "remedial" and "enrichment" reading, art, music, and physical education. A typical nonpublic school student attends these classes for one or two class periods per week; approximately "ten percent of any given nonpublic school

student's time during the academic year would consist of Shared Time instruction." Although Shared Time itself is a program offered only in the nonpublic schools, there was testimony that the courses included in that program are offered, albeit perhaps in a somewhat different form, in the public schools as well. All of the classes that are the subject of this case are taught in elementary schools, with the exception of Math Topics, a remedial math course taught in the secondary schools.

The Shared Time teachers are full-time employees of the public schools, who often move from classroom to classroom during the course of the school day. A "significant portion" of the teachers (approximately 10%) "previously taught in nonpublic schools, and many of those had been assigned to the same nonpublic school where they were previously employed." The School District of Grand Rapids hires Shared Time teachers in accordance with its ordinary hiring procedures. The public school system apparently provides all of the supplies, materials, and equipment used in connection with Shared Time instruction.[123]

The Community Education Program featured voluntary courses such as drama, home economics, and gymnastics. They were taught primarily by instructors from the private schools at which the courses were offered. The instructors were hired as part-time public school employees.

Although the Court relied on *Meek v. Pittenger* and other school-aid cases, it was clear that Justice Brennan was addressing the issue of aid to religious schools in a broader context. Perhaps because the Grand Rapids program, if upheld, would have virtually wiped away any significant constitutional barriers to government funding of religious schools, he addressed the core issue: whether the Grand Rapids program had the "effect" of advancing religion. For three reasons the majority concluded that it did.

First, there was a substantial risk of state-sponsored indoctrination of religion. Forty of the forty-one private schools where the "part-time public schools" were located were "identifiably religious."[124] Shared Time and Community Education teachers were performing important educational functions as an integral part of schools whose essential mission was sectarian. Their courses were part of the schools' core program, unlike diagnostic services or state-prepared standardized tests. The Community Education program suffered from the additional defect that virtually all of its courses were taught by teachers otherwise employed full-time by the same religious school at which the program was already located; this resulted in a 7–2 vote against it. No effort was made in either program to monitor the courses for religious content. Instead of relying on the "entanglement" prong, as the Court had done in *Lemon* and *Meek*, the majority concluded that "in the pervasively sectarian environment of a religious school, a teacher may unknowingly tailor the content of the course to fit the school's announced goals."[125] Thus, the danger came not only from the necessity of administrative entanglement to prevent such tailoring, but also from the substantial risk that such supervision would nonetheless fail to prevent the teaching of religion.

Second, the Grand Rapids program created a "symbolic union of government and religion in one sectarian enterprise."[126] Here was a new factor not emphasized in earlier cases but one that properly focused on what the "effects" and "entanglement" tests were trying to accomplish—avoiding the promotion of religion through "a close identification of the powers and responsibilities [of government] with those of any—or all—religious denominations."[127] Echoing a theme developed by Justice O'Connor in her *Lynch v. Donnelly* concurrence, the majority argued that schoolchildren would not easily perceive the difference between public-school and religious-school classes, and that the program would be viewed as a government endorsement of some faiths and rejection of others. The Court quoted the following excerpt from Judge Henry Friendly's extensive and masterful Second Circuit opinion in the companion *Aguilar* case (involving a far less ambitious program):

> Under the City's plan public school teachers are, so far as appearance is concerned, a regular adjunct of the religious school. They pace the same halls, use classrooms in the same building, teach the same students, and confer with the teachers hired by the religious schools, many of them members of religious orders. The religious school appears to the public as a joint enterprise staffed with some teachers paid by its religious sponsor and others by the public.[128]

The third "effect" was that providing teachers themselves, as distinguished from previously approved textbooks, for instructional (not diagnostic) purposes is the "kind of direct aid to the educational function of the religious school [that] is indistinguishable from the provision of a direct subsidy to the religious school that is most clearly prohibited under the Establishment Clause."[129] The majority rejected the argument that the courses were "supplemental." The line between regular and supplemental courses is very thin and could lead to public schools gradually taking over the entire secular curriculum of religious schools.

> To let the genie out of the bottle in this case would be to permit ever larger segments of the religious school curriculum to be turned over to the public school system, thus violating the cardinal principle that the State may not in effect become the prime supporter of the religious school system.[130]

Unlike the Grand Rapids program, which went beyond *Meek* in providing educational services through government-employed personnel, the New York program in *Aguilar* was limited to a narrow range of remedial programs funded by a federal statute enacted in 1965 to assist lower-income children in public and private schools. Enacted during President Johnson's administration,[131] Title I, as it became known, opened the prospect of federal funding to religious schools, an essential ingredient of the legislative compromise that overcame congressional objections to federal funding of public schools.

The Second Circuit Court of Appeals, striking down the program, had described it as having "done so much good and little, if any, harm."[132] It nevertheless found excessive "entanglement" and its decision was affirmed on that ground by the Supreme Court. New York, unlike Grand Rapids, had adopted a system for monitoring the religious content of government-funded classes, but the Court found that this supervision itself created a danger of excessive entanglement. As in *Meek v. Pittenger*, the fact that the instruction was provided by teachers (not books) on the premises of a pervasively sectarian school would give rise to constant visits and inspections over the continuous life of the program.[133]

The two programs, and the two opinions of the Court, demonstrated anew the importance of the distinction between programs conducted on and off the premises of the religious schools. An extensive program such as that of Grand Rapids involves the government, as Justice Brennan argued, in a financially and administratively joint educational venture. Although the overall impact of a narrower program, such as the one in *Aguilar*, may have less of a "symbolic" and fiscal effect of aiding religion, it still risks uniting church and state in the critical government function of education. The dangers of government-sponsored teaching of religion, of a union of government and religion in the operation of schools, of excessive day-to-day entanglement, and of government subsidy of a major portion of the religious schools' curriculum, are far greater if programs are conducted on religious-school premises.

Grand Rapids could have been based on entanglement alone, but the Court was right to recognize that when the state program actually moves close to the point of achieving the very evil that the prophylactic "entanglement" rule was designed to prevent, then the "effect" is, as the Court said, impermissibly to advance the cause of religion.

It is possible that in some areas of the United States religious and government authorities will try to work together to relieve religious schools of the task of secular education, with pupils in parochial schools attending public schools for instruction in secular subjects— the reverse of "released time." Whether such programs are valid is one issue on the horizon. But religious schools may find this alternative inherently unattractive; moreover, it would involve extensive cooperation between public and religious school systems over scheduling, transportation, and teaching materials. The resulting entanglement, both political and administrative, and the message of endorsement that such cooperation would involve, might result in the same impermissible "effect" or "entanglement" that proved fatal to the programs in Grand Rapids and New York.

CONCLUSION

The continued pressure to enlist government support for religion guarantees a steady flow of establishment-clause cases in the years ahead, although the pace may not be quite so hectic. On the horizon is the question of whether the *Widmar* principle of "equal access" for religious clubs in public universities should be extended to public high schools, and whether Congress's recent action bestowing such access is constitutional.[134] There will be more silent-prayer cases,[135] challenges to religious symbols in public places,[136] and to the crèche standing alone without Christmas decorations. If the past is prologue to the future, *Grand Rapids* and *Aguilar* will not resolve the issue of financial aid but will instead trigger new forms of government funding for religious schools. Laws such as that upheld in *Mueller v. Allen*[137] may be enacted at the state or national level, and sectarian schools may try to work out extensive arrangements with public-school authorities for their pupils to spend much of their school day taking secular courses in public schools.

The view that the establishment clause should be interpreted to emphasize the separation of church and state still commands a majority on the Court, even with the departure of Chief Justice Burger and the appointment of Justice Scalia. Five of the remaining Justices restated that view most forcefully during the 1984–85 term, and a sixth (Justice O'Connor) joined that group in *Jaffree*. Her interpretation of the establishment clause may be less demanding in practice than that of some of her colleagues, but Justice O'Connor has clearly not abandoned the effort to define the clause within the separationist model.

The new Chief Justice's views have been clearly and forcefully stated, particularly in his *Jaffree* dissent. Chief Justice Rehnquist is a sharp critic of the *Lemon* three-part test (although he joined the majority in the original opinion), and he has adopted the historical position that the establishment clause was intended only to prevent the establishment of a national religion and the favoring of one religious sect over another. He is clearly prepared to abandon the Madison-Jefferson version that has formed the basis of the Court's establishment-clause jurisprudence. Justice White appears ready to join him.

Chief Justice Burger left the Court having compiled a contradictory record in the area of church-state relations. He never adopted the Rehnquist position, even though he moved sharply toward a position of government accommodation of religion, particularly in *Lynch v. Donnelly, Aguilar v. Felton,* and *Grand Rapids v. Ball.* Nevertheless, he repeatedly reaffirmed the leading cases supporting a strong separationist position, even while writing opinions that significantly undermined them. And it should not be forgotten that he wrote the majority opinion in *Lemon, Larkin v. Grendel's Den,* and *Thornton v. Caldor.* He may have charted a path that veered sharply from Justice Black's views in *Everson,* and his own in *Lemon,* but he never completely abandoned them.

When Warren Burger was appointed in 1969, the Court had attempted in a handful of cases to define the broad contours of establishment-clause law. For seventeen years the Burger Court responded to the intense pressure for government financial support for religious schools and to the growing political power of the Religious Right during the Reagan years. While the path has been irregular, and the results far from coherent, a slender majority still appears to cling to constitutional principles that were first articulated by the Court nearly four decades ago. But the close division on the Court, uncertainties about a new justice, the untested capacity of a new chief justice to influence a divided Court toward a radical restructuring of the relationship between government and religion, and the vagaries of presidential politics remind us that the establishment clause, like Jefferson's wall, is not built of stone.

· III ·

EQUALITY

·6·

The Activism Is Not Affirmative

HAYWOOD BURNS

One day in the summer of 1968 I stood on the steps of the United States Supreme Court building and watched as throngs of people advanced from the Mall below. They were part of the encampment around the Washington Monument known as Resurrection City—a conglomeration of tents, wooden shacks, and lean-tos that were temporary homes for representatives of the Poor People's Campaign, the Reverend Martin Luther King, Jr.,'s last major project. King was dead. Robert Kennedy's assassination was but a few weeks past. I had just inherited the position of chief legal counsel for the campaign.

As they approached, I saw Native Americans in full headdress and regalia, Southern blacks wearing bib overalls and full Afros, muscled, moustachioed Chicanos from the Southwest, gaunt, pinch-faced whites from Appalachia, a sprinkling of Asian and Pacific peoples. Nothing in my Yale Law School training had prepared me to deal with this. The people were angered by a recent Court decision that had undermined the treaty rights of Native Americans, and they had come to register their grievance. As I watched them near the steps, my peripheral vision took in hundreds of D.C.'s finest, truncheons ready. As I rushed forward to advise King's successor, the Reverend Ralph Abernathy, and my other clients of their legal rights, I heard behind me a loud rumbling sound, and turned in amazement to witness the massive bronze doors of the Court tremble and groan as they slowly closed, and then banged shut.

In retrospect that scene has become terribly emblematic, a fore-shadowing of the Burger Court's response to racial minorities and poor people who come to it seeking justice. The counterrevolution predicted by many has yet to occur, at least in the form expected. While the Burger Court did not go so far as to revoke the Thirteenth Amendment, it drastically reduced civil rights litigants' access to the courts. Through recasting procedural devices and erecting technical barriers, usually without specific reference to race, it placed obstacles in the way of those who turn to the legal system to redress racial wrongs.

Specifically, the Burger Court set more stringent criteria for determining "standing" in civil rights cases—that is, who has a sufficient interest in the case to be permitted to bring it before the Court—than its predecessors did. This narrower view of standing means that fewer cases reach adjudication on the merits. By the same token, the Court took a much more restricted view of class actions and what constitutes a class for purposes of bringing a suit on behalf of persons similarly situated. Thus it became more difficult for members of a group to put forth their claims under the umbrella of a single lawsuit. They were left with piecemeal justice through multiple litigation, which, given the paucity of most such plaintiffs' resources, meant no justice at all.[1]

The ability of victims of discrimination to sue the state was further reduced by the Burger Court's doctrines of sovereign, judicial, and prosecutorial immunity.[2] Just as an increasingly conservative post–Civil War Supreme Court interpreted the Civil War constitutional amendments and the postwar civil rights statutes so narrowly as to dilute their strength and effectiveness, the Burger Court, through interpretation and fiat, stripped the legal tools from the hands of legal advocates fighting for racial justice.

Even where access might be obtained by alleging violation of civil rights "under color of law," the Burger Court made it more difficult to obtain full relief in racial cases, both by limiting the scope of the remedies available in federal courts and by imposing a more onerous burden of proof on plaintiffs. In the first instance, it curtailed the powers of federal judges to fashion what they deem to be adequate and appropriate remedial measures upon a finding of discrimination. In the second, it held that plaintiffs may not simply demonstrate that harmful discrimination has occurred; they must also prove that there was an intention to discriminate.[3]

Some of these decisions ostensibly had nothing to do with race. Considering the nation's racist legacy, however, its ongoing bigotry, and its inequitable social and economic structure, it is not surprising that decisions that strike against the politically dissident, the impoverished, the criminally accused, or the incarcerated have had a disproportionately negative impact on blacks, Hispanics, and Native Americans. In rejecting the pleas of the poor for equitable school financing, of suspects for time-honored constitutional guarantees, and of prisoners for recognition of their basic needs, including life itself (as discussed elsewhere in this symposium), the Supreme Court has had an awesomely detrimental effect on the nation's nonwhite communities.

Of course, we must not speak of the Burger Court as a monolithic tribunal that reacted with predictable philosophic singlemindedness. Gradations and shading of views among the justices resulted in shifting combinations of votes on the various issues that came before them. There was no unalterable alignment of "pro–civil rights" and "anti–civil rights" justices, though some seemed consistently to identify themselves more with one view than with the other.

Nevertheless, certain patterns and trends were visible. There really was a *Burger Court* in the sense that its dominant tone was set by the Chief Justice, a hard core of his fellow Nixon appointees, and Reagan appointee Sandra Day O'Connor. It is accurate to say that after Warren Burger became chief justice, this tone was one of conservatism or reaction on civil rights and civil liberties issues.

SCHOOL DESEGREGATION

In general, where questions of race were explicitly at stake, the Court proceeded cautiously.[4] Its record in these cases is subtle and also complicated. For the Warren Court, *Brown v. Board of Education* (1954)[5] was the zenith of its civil rights decision-making, at once a watershed opinion on education and a historic line of demarcation between an older, Jim Crow America and a newer, desegregating one. Although the Burger Court often failed to move forward in complete harmony with the spirit of *Brown*, it did systematically oppose segregation that resulted from past official educational policies.

In *Swann v. Charlotte-Mecklenburg Board of Education* (1971),[6] the Court affirmed a lower court's ruling striking down the neighborhood school policy in Charlotte, North Carolina, and ordering a change of school zones and pupil transportation to achieve a racial mix throughout the district. The opinion was written by Chief Justice Burger. It was the Burger Court's first major school desegregation decision and its last unanimous one.

As the litigation moved into northern school districts, the lines between *de jure* and *de facto* segregation blurred, and the question of how far the Court was prepared to go in unearthing past official discrimination became a source of disagreement, as did the question of how far it was willing to go in fashioning remedies for school segregation. In 1973, in *Keyes v. Denver School District No. 1*,[7] the Court was faced with a defendant that had never legally ordained school segregation. Nonetheless, a majority of the Court found for the plaintiffs, noting that though there may not have been statutory segregation, it was clear that the school board was responsible for segregation throughout the school district because of its placement of schools and drawing of district lines. Of the Nixon appointees, only Justice Harry Blackmun joined the majority opinion. Burger concurred in the results, Justice Lewis Powell dissented in part and concurred in part, and Justice William Rehnquist dissented. The Court's unity on school desegregation was disintegrating as philosophical differences surfaced.

Keyes highlighted the issue of how *de jure* and *de facto* segregation should be defined. The Court was agreed that intentional segregation was unlawful, but how remote and indirect could the evidence establishing official intent be? Further, the case focused on the question of remedy. If the Court finds unequal education in one part of a system, should it order that the whole system be revamped? The majority in *Keyes* said the entire Denver school system would have to be desegregated unless the city could accomplish the almost impossible task of demonstrating that education in the rest of the system had not been influenced by the segregation found to exist in a substantial part of it.

Tensions within the Court came to a head later with *Milliken v. Bradley* (1974),[8] a case involving the Detroit school system. It seemed irrefutable that white flight to the suburbs was largely responsible for the segregated nature of the Detroit public schools and that a Detroit-only remedy would be futile. Nonetheless, the Court balked at the trial court's metropolitan desegregation plan, which included the suburbs and had been approved by the court of appeals. Chief Justice Burger, writing for a 5–4 majority, reasoned that since the suburban communities had not been involved in intentional segregation, they should not be required to participate in an areawide solution.

In the *Milliken* opinion the Court betrayed its bias in favor of local control of schools. Just how far it is willing to carry that bias in the face of increasingly segregated inner-city school systems remains to be seen. The effect of *Milliken* has been to encourage segregation in metropolitan areas, not just in education but also in housing.

Though the Court in *Milliken* steadfastly refused to follow a *Keyes* approach and make presumptions about how a finding of racial segregation in a given community would affect contiguous areas, *Milliken* does not reflect adversely on the overall viability of *Keyes* in Supreme Court jurisprudence concerning school desegregation. There was ample basis in *Milliken* for the Court to link the inner-city Detroit school segregation with the ring of white suburban schools around the city. The reason it was unprepared to go that far seems less a retreat from *Keyes* than a profound belief in the almost sacrosanct nature of the integrity of city boundaries and local school control. The Court just would not go outside the city limits of Detroit to find the spillover effects of segregation in the metropolitan region as a whole. However, as long as the issue is segregation within a community, *Keyes* apparently continues to be viable, making the plaintiff's burden in proving discrimination decidedly less onerous than one might otherwise expect after reading *Milliken*.

Nowhere is this better demonstrated, perhaps, than in the *Keyes* approach taken by the Court several years after *Milliken* in the two Ohio cases, *Columbus Board of Education v. Penick* and *Dayton Board of Education v. Brinkman* (1979).[9] Although there had been no history of modern *de jure* segregation in these Ohio communities, the Court found that at the time of the *Brown* decision there had been intentional segregation in parts of the Columbus and Dayton school systems and that local authorities had taken insufficient action to correct the effects of past intentional segregation since that time. On these findings, the majority ruled for the plaintiffs. Since a link to intentional segregation can be found in most American communities' past, the *Keyes-Columbus-Dayton* trilogy has given school-desegregation plaintiffs at least some measure of hope when faced with the difficult problem of proof.

Even with this elasticity, however, the *de facto–de jure* distinction was not eliminated, as *Milliken* so amply demonstrated. There remains considerable sentiment on the Court in favor of extremely stringent proof standards in school-desegregation cases, biased in favor of local neighborhood schools and against busing to end racial segregation.

THE INTENT REQUIREMENT

While not openly trying to reinstate the separate-but-equal doctrine set down in *Plessy v. Ferguson* (1896),[10] on the whole, the Burger Court was far less effective on the question of civil rights than the Warren Court. It was especially conservative about what constitutes intentional segregation, grossly unimaginative in reaching out and fashioning solutions to racial-discrimination problems, and much too deferential to local decision-makers where the rights of racial minorities are concerned. This Court would not have attempted to reverse the tide of legal history by upholding the right of Jackson, Mississippi, to have segregated swimming facilities in *Palmer v. Thompson* (1971),[11] but it found nothing constitutionally objectionable in the city's decision to close down all the pools rather than integrate them.

Although the discriminatory intent behind Jackson's action in closing the pools did not seem to bother the Court in *Palmer*, the unifying principle of its decisions in many civil rights cases is that the Constitution is not offended by invidious racial treatment unless there is an intention to discriminate. On the other hand, if the claim of discrimination is based on a *statute*, the Court generally grants relief from the discrimination solely on the basis of a showing that the challenged activity produced effects disproportionately adverse to the plaintiffs. In *Griggs v. Duke Power Company* (1971),[12] the Court, relying on Title VII of the Civil Rights Act of 1964, invalidated an examination that the company had administered to employees who were being considered for transfer to more desirable departments. Writing for the majority, Chief Justice Burger explained that the test was not related to the job in question and its administration had effectively excluded black workers from the job category. Five years later, in *Washington v. Davis*,[13] however, the same Court upheld the

Washington, D.C., police-force entrance exam in the face of a constitutional challenge, ruling that no intent to discriminate had been proved, even though a disproportionate number of black applicants failed the test.

The same duality of approach appeared in other contexts. On April 22, 1980, in *Rome v. United States*,[14] the Court held that a proposed annexation in Rome, Georgia, which would have diluted black voting strength, violated the Voting Rights Act of 1965 even though there was no proof of a discriminatory intent. That same day, in *Mobile v. Bolden*,[15] however, the Court refused to strike down a system of at-large elections that had been challenged in Mobile, Alabama, under the Fifteenth Amendment, stating there was no proof of intent to reduce black people's political power.

On the face of it, it may thus appear that the issue is simply a matter of whether there is a statute involved, in which case an impact test will be applied without regard to a showing of discriminatory intent, or whether the challenge is raised under the Fourteenth or Fifteenth Amendment, in which case there is a requirement of showing intent. These neat lines were more than a little blurred, however, in the voting-rights area by the Court's holding in 1982 in *Rogers v. Lodge*.[16] There it sustained an attack on an at-large system of voting in Burke County, Georgia, on the ground that it diluted the voting power of black citizens. There was no real showing that discrimination was intended when the election system was introduced, but the overwhelming evidence supported a finding that this system was maintained for discriminatory purposes, and the Court had no trouble finding an intent to discriminate. The decision seemed to reflect a view that in Fifteenth Amendment cases the Court will continue to use the language of "intent" but will rest its decision on effects if they clearly signal purposive discrimination.

After much public debate and national clamor, the problems of proof and the rigors of the "intent" standard in voting cases were somewhat ameliorated by the 1982 changes in and extension of the Voting Rights Act. Thus the Court obtained a firmer statutory foundation for dealing with voting issues, and the difficulties of proving intent under a constitutional standard were obviated.[17]

The stringency of the Burger Court's intent requirement in Fourteenth and Fifteenth Amendment cases often makes it very difficult to prove discrimination. Surely a less rigid and less formidable approach could have been developed even if the intent requirement had been retained. Another Court might have taken at least some of the burden off the minority plaintiffs, once a disparate impact was shown, and demanded that the alleged discriminators show they were not, in fact, discriminating. After all, the latter have the best access to the evidence.

AFFIRMATIVE ACTION

A central issue in American life continues to be how white people will respond to the historic wrongs visited on Americans of African descent. As in the past, with *Dred Scott v. Sandford* (1857),[18] with *Plessy* and *Brown*, the nation has turned to its courts for resolution of raging racial debates. During the past decades the Supreme Court has had to devise legal standards against which to measure efforts to redress injuries suffered by an entire group of people; this presented the justices with one of their most vexing problems. The Burger Court's solution was somewhat garbled, but the direction seemed obvious to those who had hopes that the legal system responsible for much of their degradation might have the capacity to repair some of the damage. Much of their hope had rested on affirmative-action programs.

The case of *Regents of the University of California v. Bakke* (1978)[19] presented the Court with a major opportunity to make a clear statement on these programs. The University of California Medical School at Davis had set aside sixteen places for minority students under a special admissions program. A white student, Alan Bakke, challenged the program after being denied admission. Those on both sides of the question had hoped the *Bakke* case would provide definitive legal guidance. It was a vain hope, for the Court ended up speaking in many tongues. With four justices upholding the plan, four opposed, and Powell somewhere in the middle, it turned out to be something of a $4\frac{1}{2}$–$4\frac{1}{2}$ decision. Justice Powell's view was that on the one hand it was permissible for Davis to take race into account in shaping its admissions policy, while, on the other, the school could not lawfully maintain its admissions quota based on race. *Bakke* was decidedly unhelpful in resolving the dilemma, except insofar as it provided insight into the attitudes of the individual justices toward affirmative action.

The issue was pressed further and presented in a somewhat different light the following year in *United Steelworkers of America v. Weber* (1979).[20] Brian Weber, a white worker, challenged a craft-training program designed to accommodate blacks and whites in equal numbers until the proportion of black craft workers at the plant was equal to that in the local labor force. When he was not accepted for the program, Weber attacked it as a racial quota system in violation of Title VII of the Civil Rights Act of 1964. Five justices disagreed, pointing out that the plan was a private agreement entered into by the employer and the union, one of limited scope and duration, and remedial in character, and that in fact its aim was to correct the great racial imbalance in this particular workplace. The majority also found that the arrangement was consistent with the legislative intent of Title VII. Burger and Rehnquist dissented. Powell and John Paul Stevens did not participate, Blackmun being the only Nixon appointee to side with the majority.

The issue came before the Court in yet another form the next year. The Public Works Employment Act of 1977 declares that at least 10 percent of federal funds for public-works projects must be used to procure the services of business enterprises run by members of minority groups. In 1980, in *Fullilove v. Klutznick*,[21] the Supreme Court addressed the constitutionality of the 10 percent minority set-aside and upheld the statute, 6–3. There was no majority opinion. The Chief Justice's opinion, which Justices Powell and Byron White joined, argued that Congress could take such action using racial criteria if it judged it necessary as a remedial measure, especially where it was limited, properly tailored, and did not impose too great a burden on "innocent" parties. In the view of Justices Thurgood Marshall, William J. Brennan, and Blackmun, the law passed constitutional muster because of the substantial government interest in overcoming past discrimination and providing opportunity within the society across racial lines. Justices Rehnquist, Stevens, and Potter Stewart dissented.

Although a pattern of decision-making on affirmative action is not easy to discern, it does appear that if Congress has recognized the need for official agencies to take remedial action, and if the claimants are direct victims of racial discrimination, a majority of the Court will support the affirmative action. Similarly, certain voluntary, private arrangements will win approval by a narrow majority. But the Court does not give any assurance that it is in tune with a philosophy that would generally provide group remedies for group wrongs. With the exception of Justices Marshall and Brennan, and sometimes Blackmun, the justices do not seem to appreciate the historic injury done to nonwhites and to women in American society, or the persistence of institutional and structural racism. Little weight is accorded the vital interest a supposedly modern, democratic, pluralistic state has in doing simple justice for its racial minorities. Too much weight is given to the putative interests of so-called innocent parties. Although it is proper for the Court to show concern for all affected parties, it is difficult to see how even the most ordinary and inoffensive white workers, who often got their jobs as a result of a biased job market, are entirely innocent; although they are not directly responsible for the favoritism built into the system, they directly benefit from it.

The canons of interpretation by which affirmative-action issues will be decided are still being established in the Supreme Court, but the extent to which the Burger Court was prepared to allow the interests of racial minorities to give way to other compelling interests was sadly revealed in 1984 in *Firefighters v. Stotts*.[22] A 6–3 majority struck down a court order designed to prevent the layoff of black firefighters hired under a court-approved affirmative-action plan, in favor of a preexisting seniority system. In a head-on clash between the seniority system of a workplace with a history of gross racial exclusion and an affirmative-action plan designed to correct that injustice, the seniority system won easily. The message was loud and clear: black job rights take low priority.

Lest too many labor under the misapprehension that *Stotts* provided the definitive blueprint for the future direction of Supreme Court affirmative-action jurisprudence, the Court issued three decisions in the last days of the Burger Court, which reflect the complexity of the legal issues involved and the continuing doctrinal development in the area.

Wygant v. Jackson (Mich.) Bd. of Education[23] involved a collective bargaining agreement under which seniority determined which teachers would be retained should layoffs become necessary, except that at no time would a greater percentage of minority teachers be laid off than the percentage of such teachers employed at the time of the layoff. The school district had a history of racial discrimination in its hiring and educational practices, and an appreciable number of minority faculty had been hired only in recent times.

As a result of the exception to seniority, some white teachers were laid off who were senior to some black teachers. The whites sued under the equal protection clause of the Fourteenth Amendment, and the Justice Department, seeing an opportunity to advance its position against any race-based preferences, supported the white teachers.

By a 5–4 vote, the Supreme Court threw out the exception to seniority. In an opinion by Justice Powell, joined by Chief Justice Burger and Justices Rehnquist and O'Connor, Powell said he found no compelling state interest to justify the racial classifications made by the Board of Education. He went on to say that in any event, the plan was not "narrowly drawn" because it burdened innocent whites too much; other less intrusive means like hiring goals are preferable. Justice White joined in the judgment.

The narrow victory in *Wygant* heartened the Justice Department and its allies, who vigorously renewed their efforts to dismantle affirmative action. Assistant Attorney General William Bradford Reynolds continued his pressure, initiated after *Stotts*, to get fifty-one state and municipal jurisdictions to undo affirmative action plans arrived at through consent decrees and to do away with numerical goals in the promotion and hiring of minorities and women. Within the administration there was stepped-up activity to eliminate Executive Order No. 11246 (1965), which requires federal contractors to pursue numerical goals in the hiring of minorities and women.

This headlong rush was abruptly interrupted by the companion affirmative-action cases that came down on July 2, 1986. Victories for affirmative action in these two important cases underscore the legal complexities as well as the continuing evolution of constitutional doctrine.

In *Local 93, International Association of Firefighters v. City of Cleveland*,[24] by a 6–3 vote the Supreme Court upheld a race-based promotion plan for black and Hispanic firefighters in a consent decree that was not limited to actual victims of past discrimination. The Justice Department and Local 93, an overwhelmingly white union, challenged the plan, arguing that Section 706(g) of Title VII of the 1964 Civil Rights Act prohibits consent decrees that contain relief for nonvictims. Justice Brennan, writing for the Court, disagreed, declaring that if the parties agreed to such relief because of a history of racial discrimination, Section 706(g) did not stop them.

In *Local 28, Sheet Metal Workers International Association v.*

EEOC,[25] six justices, including Justice White in dissent, agreed that Section 706(g) does not prevent a court from ordering race-conscious relief for persons who are nonvictims. Justice Brennan writing for a plurality of four (Justices Blackmun, Marshall, Stevens, and himself) reviewed the legislative history of 706(g) and concluded that Congress did not intend to tie the hands of the courts through any strict limitation on the relief that could be fashioned in racial discrimination cases of this kind, and certainly did not intend to limit relief to only the proven, identifiable direct victims of racial discrimination. In an "appropriate" case, such as where there is "particularly longstanding or egregious discrimination," a court may order race-based relief. Justice Rehnquist, joined in dissent by Chief Justice Burger, remained adamant that relief can go *only* to the actual victims of racial discrimination.

Local 93 and *Sheet Metal Workers* immediately slowed some of the administration's efforts to destroy affirmative action. In August of 1986 Assistant Attorney General Reynolds announced that the Justice Department was giving up its efforts to have the fifty-one state and municipal jurisdictions dismantle their affirmative-action plans. Plans to eliminate or seriously modify Executive Order 11246 were also put on hold.

The long-range prognosis in Supreme Court affirmative-action jurisprudence is still uncertain. The law is still being developed and refined, the limits delineated. Changes in the Court, not the least of which is the elevation of Justice Rehnquist to chief justice, will influence the future direction of this law. His sturdy dissents in both *Local 93* and *Sheet Metal Workers*, consistent with his overall record, are the most extreme expressions on the Court of opposition to affirmative action. How much his newly achieved status of chief will permit him to sway his colleagues remains to be seen. The process of extending his influence may of course be greatly aided by other changes in the Court membership. The addition of jurists like Antonin Scalia will obviously fortify the forces against affirmative action.

THE FUTURE

The constricted vision of the Burger Court where the rights of racial minorities are concerned has resulted in a narrower concept of what these rights are, and a restricted ability on the part of minorities to enforce them. There are many chilling adumbrations. In *Grove City College v. Bell* (1984),[26] the Court recognized that Title IX of the 1972 Education Amendment prohibited gender discrimination in colleges that receive even indirect federal assistance. However, the prohibition was held to apply only to the specific program involved and *not* to the institution as a whole. Thus, a college with a discriminatory program could continue to receive federal aid as long as the offending unit did not get further assistance.

Though *Grove City* is not a race case, there is a direct analogy to Title VI of the Civil Rights Act of 1964, which forbids federal assistance to institutions that engage in racial discrimination. *Grove City* is thus disturbing not only in its own right, but as a foreshadowing of what the Court might do when faced with a similar issue involving Title VI. A similar approach would result in Supreme Court approval of federal funding for institutions with racially discriminatory programs. There are overwhelmingly large majorities in Congress to overturn the *Grove City* decision, which would apply to both Title IX and Title VI, but the issue became entangled in the abortion controversy, and the bill died in the 98th and 99th Congresses.

The problem of acknowledging the existence of a right but preventing its enforcement or enjoyment is not limited to speculation based upon the Court's performance in analogous areas. In *Bob Jones University v. U.S.* (1983),[27] the Court upheld the IRS policy of denying tax-exempt status to private schools that are racially discriminatory. However, the very next year in *Allen v. Wright,*[28] the Court told black parents in a community with racially segregated private schools that they had no "standing" to use the courts to have the IRS enforce a set of IRS rules denying tax-exempt status to such schools. The Court said that the parents had not been sufficiently affected because their own children had not been denied admission to these schools on racial grounds. Chief Justice Rehnquist and the newly appointed Justice Scalia are both hostile to judicial protection for minorities. For racial minorities the future thus augurs a diminished concept of rights and, even where those rights are present, a diminished capacity to enforce them. The doors slam shut.

The Burger Court did not launch a full-scale, frontal attack on the civil rights gains made under the Warren Court. That would have been unlikely. So conservative an institution, even when it is up to no good, does not move in such a manner. The ground lost during

Burger's tenure was lost through erosion, through tinkering with procedural devices, cutting off access, constricting remedy. Even though no direct racial animus was revealed, the Court's narrowness of vision, lack of social sensitivity, and lack of commitment to racial justice mean that it failed to play a constructive role in providing justice to the nation's racial minorities. Of course it was sitting at a time when the entire administration and the Justice Department unashamedly sought to turn back the civil rights clock. By and large the Burger Court demonstrated a measure of independence. But if the Court's resolve weakens in the years to come, it will be in even greater jeopardy if the political climate grows more reactionary and more justices like Rehnquist and Scalia join the Court.

·7·

Sex Discrimination: Closing the Law's Gender Gap

WENDY W. WILLIAMS

Nineteenth-century laws that classified by sex were based on an all-encompassing duality sometimes called the "separate-spheres ideology." Its chief characteristics were segregation and complementarity. Men were assigned to the lifelong functions of breadwinner, head of household, and representative in the social state; women, to those of child-bearer and -rearer, and keeper of the home. These roles were considered to be dictated by nature: the physical, mental, psychological, and moral attributes of the sexes designed them for distinct life courses. Masculine and feminine characteristics were expressed as complementaries: strong-weak, intellectual-emotional, self-sufficient-dependent, aggressive-passive, sexual-asexual, dominant-subordinate, protector-protected. Laws merely reflected nature's and God's allocation of earthly tasks.

This role allocation required a trade-off between the sexes, at the core of which was the husband's undertaking to support and protect his wife in return for her services to him and his children. An elaborate legal edifice was constructed, prescribing, first, reciprocal rights and duties within marriage, giving the husband ownership or management of property, prerogatives about sex, discipline, and family location, and rights concerning custody and control of children; second, civil status, curtailing the wife's power to contract, to sue and be sued, and to earn a living; and third, relationships to government, making the husband the family's representative, who alone could vote, hold office, and participate in the justice system. Men, of course, also went to war to protect home and country while women stayed behind to "keep the home fires burning."

Despite the hierarchical character of this arrangement, the separate-sphere ideologists proclaimed that the spheres were of equal dignity and importance. Sex-based classifications in law were essential, they argued, to provide women, who were inherently unequal to men, with "true equality" and to protect them. Thus, laws that treated women differently from men were viewed as essentially compensatory, accommodations to women's innate differences and, as the Supreme Court reiterated over the years, to women's special burdens of child-bearing and -rearing.

In 1969, when Warren Burger became Chief Justice, law students were taught that in deciding discrimination cases under the equal protection clause of the Constitution, the Supreme Court employed a two-tiered standard of review. In suits challenging classifications based on race and national origin, the Court applied "upper-tier" review. (It did the same for classifications based on "fundamental rights," but that is another story.) Those classifications were considered "suspect," were scrutinized "strictly," and were presumed invalid unless the government could show that they were "necessary to a compelling state interest" and that there were no alternative ways to achieve the state's objective. The "lower tier" included all other legislative classifications. Challenges to the constitutionality of one of those would fail if the Court found any conceivable rational basis for the classification. In practice the standard worked like an electrical switch: if the classification made it into the upper tier, the legislation would be struck down; if not, it would be upheld. Needless to say, classifications based on gender were assigned to the lower tier.

Shortly after Chief Justice Burger joined the Court, the legal representatives of a reborn feminist movement set out to hoist gender-based legislation into the upper tier. The first sign of progress appeared in 1971. In *Reed v. Reed*,[1] in an opinion written by the new chief justice, a unanimous Court struck down a law preferring men to women as estate administrators. For the first time in its history, the Court invalidated sex-based legislation under the equal protection clause. Sex classifications, the Court said, were "subject to scrutiny" and must "bear a fair and substantial relation to the object of the legislation," a standard with noticeably more bite than the "any conceivable rational basis" approach of the lower tier.

Two years later, in *Frontiero v. Richardson*,[2] the Court struck down a statute that granted male members of the armed forces greater benefits for their families than female members. Four Justices went further and voted to treat sex classifications like race classifications. The fifth justice needed to deliver a majority for the strict standard of review failed to materialize, however, and over the next few years, Justice William Brennan, author of the plurality opinion in *Frontiero*, developed an alternative strategy for gender cases. Picking up on the stronger formulation suggested in *Reed*, he wrote in *Craig v. Boren* (1976) that "classifications by gender must serve important governmental objectives and must be substantially related to achievement of those objectives."[3] Since then, the Court has frequently used Brennan's *Craig* standard to strike down sex-based legislation.

In *Craig*, Justice Brennan identified two government interests that would not be considered "important" for sex discrimination cases. One was administrative convenience, such as saving money or simplifying procedures. The second was more radical. "Fostering 'old notions' of role typing" was no longer a constitutionally adequate government purpose. "No longer is the female destined solely for the home and the rearing of the family, and only the male for the marketplace and the world of ideas." This was a breathtaking stroke. Traditional role assignments had been the basis of most family law doctrine and an organizing principle for government benefit schemes as diverse as Social Security, welfare, and workers' compensation. And the point is not that such policies are, as Justice Brennan said, "unimportant"—the wisdom of adopting such policies is debatable but their importance is not. What he should have said, because it was surely what he meant, is that they are constitutionally unacceptable.

The doctrine Justice Brennan announced struck directly at the separate-spheres ideology. With *Craig* it became apparent that the Court was engaged in nothing less than the dismantling of the breadwinner-homemaker dichotomy. The Burger Court insisted that female wage earners under military, Social Security, and welfare and workers' compensation programs receive the same benefits for their families as men do; that when their spouses die men receive the same child-care allowance as women do; that the daughters of divorce be entitled to support for the same length of time as the sons; that the duty of support through alimony not be visited exclusively on husbands; that wives as well as husbands participate in the management of community property; and that wives as well as husbands be eligible to administer deceased relatives' estates.[4]

This transformation required the justices to see the world in a different way. Whereas earlier Supreme Courts reflected society's conviction that distinct fundamental physical and mental qualities destined the sexes for different functions throughout their lives, the Burger Court, with some important qualifications, saw the sexes as leading essentially similar lives. The view was expressed as a presumption that a sex-based law is unconstitutional and will be struck down unless a heavy burden of justification is met. When the Court applied the *Craig* standard and made the defender of sex-based legislation justify it, that legislation usually fell.

But Justice Brennan's approach is only precariously anchored in Supreme Court jurisprudence. While Justices Thurgood Marshall and Byron White can be counted on to apply the *Craig* standard, other justices—indeed, from time to time a majority—do not approach gender classifications so rigorously. Chief Justice William Rehnquist, the Court's most conservative member during the Burger Court era, and Justice Potter Stewart (before his replacement in September 1981 by Sandra Day O'Connor) fashioned a significantly less stringent standard of review, reflecting their predisposition to see clear differences between the sexes and a lackadaisical attitude as to whether those sex differences were relevant to the case before the Court. Justices Harry Blackmun and Lewis Powell swung one way or the other, moved by the facts of a case rather than a consistent philosophy, while Justice John Paul Stevens worked out an idiosyncratic approach that usually, but not always, aligned him with the Brennan group. The former Chief Justice was a frequent adherent to the Rehnquist-Stewart axis. In gender cases, his replacement on the Court, Antonin Scalia, is likely to prove an even more reliable ally for the new Chief Justice.

And what about the Burger Court's junior member, Sandra Day O'Connor? Despite her otherwise impeccably conservative voting record, she emerged as the Court's most liberal member on the standard of review in gender cases. In *Mississippi University for Women v. Hogan* (1982),[5] she out-Brennaned Justice Brennan, writing that when the purpose of a statute is to "exclude or 'protect' members of one gender because they are presumed to suffer from an inherent handicap or to be innately inferior, the objective itself is illegitimate." In footnote 9, she even suggested that the strongest standard of review—that used in race cases—might be the proper one. This raised to four the number of justices who faithfully adhered to a tough review standard in gender cases.

The Rehnquist-Stewart line prevailed in cases concerning sexuality and reproduction. In those cases, a much diminished but persistent concept of "real" difference between the sexes survived the abolition of the separate-spheres ideology. Because legislation bearing on reproduction and male-female sexuality conjures up the distinctive reproductive anatomy of the sexes and the image of difference and complementarity that comes with it, in cases involving such legislation apparent differences blinded the Burger Court to what the sexes have in common and made social hierarchies seem dictated by nature.

In *Dothard v. Rawlinson* (1977), for example, the Court upheld the exclusion of women from the position of guard in a male maximum-security prison. "The likelihood that inmates would assault a woman because she was a woman would pose a real threat . . . to the basic control of the penitentiary and protection of its inmates and the other security personnel," declared Justice Stewart, writing for the majority, even though the only evidence in the record was to the contrary. Woman's "very womanhood," he concluded, renders her ineligible for the job.[6]

Dothard's reliance on the stereotype of man as sexual aggressor and woman as sexually passive object provided the underpinnings of the Rehnquist opinion in *Michael M. v. Superior Court* (1981),[7] in which the Court upheld the statutory-rape conviction of a seventeen-year-old man under a California law that punished men for consensual sexual intercourse with women under eighteen years of age but did not punish the women. The case was an especially rich candidate for confusion because a majority of the Court viewed it as dealing with reproductive as well as sexual differences. It seemed obvious to the Court's majority that the statute was founded on a "real difference" between men and women. Since young women can become pregnant, thus suffering untoward consequences of teen-age sex to a far greater extent than young men, a criminal penalty for men provides an artificial deterrent to match women's natural deterrent. A statutory-rape provision limited to males thus equalizes the otherwise unequal positions of the sexes. There was no evidence whatsoever that the statutory-rape provision deterred a single California teen-ager from having intercourse, nor did the Court seem to care that venerable statutory-rape laws originated in the desire to protect "young girls" from loss of virginity, and thus diminished marriageability, rather than to prevent pregnancies.

Interestingly, the final months of the Burger Court produced a decision involving women and sexuality unique both in the degree of consensus reached by the justices and in its commitment to gender equality. Perhaps most remarkable of all was the identity of the author— William Rehnquist—who just a few days before the decision was announced had become Chief Justice-Designate. The case, *Meritor Savings Bank v. Vinson*,[8] brought under Title VII of the Civil Rights Act of 1964, rather than under the Constitution, held that, under the act, sexual harassment constitutes sex discrimination. Not only does the act prohibit sexual imposition that is made a *quid pro quo* for hiring or promotion, said the Court, but it also reaches those situations where harassment has created an abusive work environment. In so holding, the High Court put its imprimatur on views that had been expressed by most federal appeals courts for more than a decade.[9]

Two aspects of the Court's opinion are noteworthy. First, the Court rejected the proposition urged by the defendant and accepted by the district court that the plaintiff could not prevail where her participation in the sexual conduct was "voluntary," announcing that "the correct inquiry is whether respondent by her conduct indicated that the alleged sexual advances were unwelcome, not whether her actual participation in sexual intercourse was voluntary."[10] Second, the Court rejected the court of appeals ruling that testimony about the plaintiff's dress and personal fantasies should be excluded from evidence. Such evidence, said the Court, was "obviously relevant." While the trial court should carefully weigh the relevance of such evidence against the potential for unfair prejudice, "there is no per se rule against admissibility."[11]

The first ruling reveals a commendable sensitivity to the psychological position of an employee sexually importuned by one who has authority over the incidents of her employment, the second a too facile assumption that general fantasy and dress evidence is relevant to whether the advances of a particular supervisor are "welcome." This second ruling leaves it within trial judges' discretion to permit sexual harassment trials to become explorations of the plaintiff's sexual psyche rather than a look at whether the defendant's sexual advances were welcomed by her. It is reminiscent of the days when a woman's sexual history, long deemed "obviously relevant" to whether or not she consented to sexual intercourse with an accused rapist, made her sex life, rather than the particular interaction between her and the rape defendant, the focus of rape trials.

It is when the Supreme Court considers legislative classifications based explicitly on pregnancy that the issue of "real" differences takes its most dramatic turn. In *Geduldig v. Aiello* (1974),[12] Justice Stewart wrote for the Court that a classification that excluded pregnancy-related disabilities from California's comprehensive disability insurance program was not sex discrimination because it sorted out people by whether they were pregnant or not, not by whether they were men or women; that is, it simply removed a type of physical disability—that connected with pregnancy—from the list of compensated disabilities. This, said the Court, was not sex discrimination. Two years later, in *General Electric Co. v. Gilbert*,[13] Justice Rehnquist added the *coup de grace:* pregnancy, he said, was an *extra* characteristic of women that men did not share; to compensate women for pregnancy-related disabilities might well discriminate against men.

Thus, for the Burger Court, man was the benchmark. Since the unique reproductive anatomy of women was considered simply an add-on to the basic male model, coverage of pregnancy would give women more than men got. The conclusion is remarkable when one considers the practical consequence of this exclusion: men who for physical reasons were rendered temporarily unable to work—whatever the cause—received partial wage replacement under the California program, while women temporarily unable to work did so only so long as the work disability was unrelated to pregnancy; rather than avoiding reimbursing women for an "extra," the program gave men total coverage and women partial coverage for temporary physical disabilities.[14]

To some extent, the Burger Court grasped the centrality of reproductive issues to women's lives, but only in cases brought under the due process rather than the equal protection clause. In *Roe v. Wade* (1973),[15] the most significant of those, it recognized a woman's right to choose whether or not to have an abortion.[16] *Roe* announced a fundamental right on the part of women to choose abortion free of government interference, unless the government could establish that its interest in regulating abortion was a compelling one and that the regulation chosen was closely tailored to that compelling interest. Purporting to eschew the moral and religious disputes swirling around abortion, the Court sought refuge in the apparent neutrality of medicine and technology. While recognizing that women's interests make the right to choose fundamental, the choice is a medical one, said the Court, to be made by a woman in consultation with her physician.

Medicalization of abortion offered the Court a compromise between the polar positions of the advocates before it, who proclaimed on the one hand that human life deserves protection from the moment of conception and on the other that the choice is the pregnant woman's until childbirth. In the medical circumstances of pregnancy, the Court identified State interests, conveniently located at the beginning of the second and third trimesters of pregnancy, that might outweigh the woman's constitutional right. The State's interest in maternal health becomes compelling at the beginning of the second trimester, said the Court, because abortion by that point in the pregnancy is more dangerous than childbirth; the State also has an interest in fetal life that becomes compelling at the point at which a fetus can sustain life outside the womb—becomes "viable"—an event that naturally occurs roughly at the beginning of the third trimester but which, according to the Court, can be affected by the availability of artificial life-support systems. Thus, concluded the Court, regulation of abortion procedures aimed at women's health is constitutionally acceptable after the first trimester. Outlawing abortion in the interest of fetal life is permissible at the outset of the third trimester, except where abortion is necessary to preserve the life or health of the pregnant woman.

The practical meaning of *Roe* was that women could obtain safe and legal abortions in the first two trimesters of pregnancy. Yet the Court's resolution of the issue was unreservedly acclaimed by no one. Legal scholars of all stripes make a sport of picking apart the opinion on doctrinal grounds. Abortion foes, continuing to assert the primacy of fetal life at every stage of gestation, commenced and have sustained a massive effort to move state and federal governments to an antiabortion stance in every context in which government deals with procreation issues. Feminists and pro-choice advocates, hailing the opinion as the cornerstone of procreative choice, balk at the power given to medicine to estabish conditions under which abortion must be performed. Eyeing the possibility that technological and medical advances will move the viability of fetuses from the current twenty-four to twenty-eight weeks of gestation to earlier points, they assert that women's autonomy rather than medical privacy is the more secure and appropriate basis for the constitutional right to choose abortion.

In the years after *Roe* the Burger Court defended the abortion right against a series of potential limitations. For example, it prohibited states from granting husbands[17] or parents of pregnant minors[18] an absolute veto over a woman's choice to obtain an abortion, but upheld state statutes requiring parental consent or notification so long as the minor can, in the alternative, obtain judicial approval without parental consent.[19] And in 1983, one decade after *Roe*, the Court took the occasion in *City of Akron v. Akron Center for Reproductive Health*[20] explicitly to reaffirm, by a 6–3 majority, a woman's fundamental right to decide whether or not to terminate her pregnancy, and tightened the reins on state efforts to make abortion more expensive and inaccessible in the name of medical safety. The Burger Court's final abortion case, *Thornburgh v. American College of Obstetricians and Gynecologists* (1986), similarly reaffirmed *Roe*.[21]

But while the basic abortion right remains intact, it is, in important ways, both compromised and precarious. First and most immediately, in a series of decisions, culminating in *Harris v. McRae* (1980),[22] the Court upheld the excision of funding for virtually all abortions from otherwise comprehensive state and federal health programs for the poor, explaining, "The financial restraints that restrict an indigent woman's ability to enjoy the full range of constitutionally protected freedom of choice are the product not of governmental restrictions on access to abortions, but rather on her indigency."

Second, the Court's concession to a state interest in maternal health—problematical because it was never apparent why the Court concluded that general standards applicable to other medical procedures would not suffice for abortions—has proved its mischievous potential.[23] Some state legislatures, chafing at their inability to outlaw abortions, passed laws regulating the abortion procedure, which in some way made it difficult to get an abortion, sometimes with the obvious intent to discourage women from obtaining one. Some of these, such as the requirement of a second physician for abortions of viable fetuses performed to preserve the life or health of the pregnant woman, have been upheld by the Court.[24] Many—including laws directing that second-trimester abortions be performed in hospitals, establishing a twenty-four-hour waiting period after a woman consents to abortion, and requiring that doctors inform a woman seeking an abortion that "the unborn child is a human life from the moment of conception" and provide her with a detailed description of "the anatomical and physiological characteristics of the particular unborn child"[25]—have been struck down. The Court's majority reserved its strongest language for *Thornburgh*, in which it invalidated a whole range of provisions including a statutory list of information that must be given a woman considering abortion before she consents to the procedure. The Court's majority, after declaring its fealty to *Roe*, stated: "The states are not free, under the guise of protecting maternal health or potential life, to intimidate women into continuing pregnancies. . . . Close analysis [of the provisions before the Court] shows that they wholly subordinate constitutional privacy interests and concerns with maternal health in an effort to deter a woman from making a decision that, with her physician, is hers to make."[26]

Third, while claims that advances in neonatal technology have moved the viability line significantly since *Roe* was decided are incorrect[27] (more infants born at twenty-four weeks are sustained today, but the prospect of dropping below that point would take a major technological breakthrough), it is possible that the constitutional right will eventually contract because its medical marker, viability, might occur earlier. If the Court abandons the marker and persists with the second-trimester line, another, and thus far submerged, issue will be confronted: is the abortion right the right only to terminate the pregnancy—producing, against the woman's will, a premature infant or perhaps transplantable embryo—or is it the right to terminate both pregnancy and fetal life, notwithstanding the technological capacity to sustain fetal life outside a woman's womb?

In *Thornburgh*, the Court ruled upon an issue bearing on the ultimate resolution of this question. The issue was whether the state can require, in certain circumstances, the use of the abortion technique that enhances the possibility of fetal survival. The state statute required that the abortion technique employed in postviability abortions be that which would "provide the best opportunity for the unborn child to be aborted alive" unless the technique would present a "significantly greater" medical risk to the life or health of the pregnant woman. The statute also required physicians performing post-viability abortions to exercise that degree of care "which such person would be required to exercise in order to preserve the life and health of any unborn child intended to be born and not aborted." The statute made violation of the standard a felony, subjecting the violator to the possibility of fine or imprisonment. The Court struck down both requirements, agreeing with the Court of Appeals that the provisions were unconstitutional because they "required a 'trade-off' between the woman's health and fetal survival and failed to require that maternal health be the physician's paramount consideration."[28] A contrary holding would have made it clear by implication that the abortion right is only a right to terminate the pregnancy; the Court's holding in *Thornburgh* left the underlying question of termination of fetal life undiscussed and unanswered.

Finally, even though a majority of the American people continues to support the right to choose abortion, at least in the early stages of pregnancy, the federal government opposes it. Less than two years after the Court's reaffirmation of *Roe* in the *Akron* case, the Solicitor General submitted a brief on behalf of the government in the *Thornburgh* case asking for the reversal of *Roe*.[29] And President Reagan, hostile to the abortion right, took the opportunity to select a second justice, Antonin Scalia, who, like his first, Sandra Day O'Connor, is opposed to the *Roe v. Wade* decision.

The *Roe* decision, by its terms, protects the right of a woman to decide whether *or not* to terminate her pregnancy. The central meaning of the case is that the Constitution protects from state interference a person's reproductive choice. The protected choice to become pregnant and carry that pregnancy to term is the basis for challenges to the more extreme state policies that affect pregnant employed women. Thus, building on *Roe, Cleveland Board of Education v. LaFleur* (1974),[30] invalidated a school-board policy requiring pregnant school-teachers to take an unpaid leave of absence beginning in the fourth or fifth month of pregnancy. In *LaFleur*, the Court declared that the due process clause protected against undue state meddling an individual's right to choose whether or not to bear or beget children. The *LaFleur* approach has not substantially mitigated the effect of the Court's holdings in cases like *Geduldig v. Aiello* that pregnancy discrimination is not sex discrimination.[31] The equal protection approach to pregnancy had power to reach practices that the due process clause does not. Nonetheless, while the approach to reproductive issues taken in *Roe* and in *LaFleur* is not directly attuned to the issue of equality, its prohibitions against some restrictions on women's choices concerning contraception, abortion, and pregnancy undeniably enhance women's status by giving them more control over the timing and frequency of childbearing, and limiting penalties on maternity.

Justice Blackmun, the author of the Burger Court's first and last abortion cases, *Roe* and *Thornburgh*, concluded *Thornburgh* with a statement of the importance of choice to women: "Few decisions are more personal and intimate, more properly private, or more basic to individual dignity and autonomy, than a woman's decision—with the guidance of her physician and within the limits specified in *Roe*—whether to end her pregnancy. A woman's right to make that choice freely is fundamental. Any other result, in our view, would protect inadequately a central part of the sphere of liberty that our law guarantees equally to all."[32]

One additional line of cases, whose implicit relationship to issues of sexuality and reproduction makes it a problem for the Court, deserves mention here. The Burger Court showed a deep ambivalence about the equality of fathers and mothers in cases involving the parental rights of unwed parents. On the one hand, it was willing to extend to the father the right accorded the mother to veto the adoption of children in those cases in which the children had lived with and been supported by him in a family setting, as it demonstrated in *Caban v. Mohammed* (1979);[33] on the other hand, in *Lehr v. Robertson* (1983), decided a few years later, it dismissed the claim of an unwed father to object to the adoption of his child by the child's stepfather where he had not in fact supported or had a personal relationship with his daughter, even though, as the dissenting opinion pointed out, the reason for his failure to do so despite his considerable effort was the mother's deliberate concealment from him of her and the child's whereabouts.[34] And when an unwed father, who did have daily contact with and supported his son, sued for his wrongful death after the child and his mother had been killed in an automobile accident, the Court, in *Parham v. Hughes* (1979), upheld a statute that foreclosed the unwed father but not the unwed mother from suing for wrongful death unless the father had "legitimated" the child.[35]

Two themes in the Burger Court's discussion of these cases provide some explanation of the outcomes. First, there is a moral and social judgment that unwed parenthood is bad for the child and that legitimation of the child or, better yet, its inclusion into a "normal" two-parent household should be the goal. The father who failed to legitimate his child, even though he maintained a relationship with him and supported him, was punished for his sexual irresponsibility by denial of his right to sue when his child was killed. Second, the Court seemed to be influenced by what it took to be inherent distinctions between mothers and fathers of young children. Justice Stevens, who wrote for the majority in *Lehr*, dissented in *Caban*, citing "natural differences" between unmarried fathers and mothers that included both physical differences (i.e., gestation, mother-infant "bonding," difficulties with ascertaining fathers' identities) and, oddly, legal differences (i.e., the mother's ability to marry a different man before the birth of the child and thereby confer legitimacy on the child; the father's ability to deny legitimacy by marrying someone other than the mother). This line of cases has had the important effect of consolidating the unwed mother's decision-making power, which is warranted in the average case where a child is born out of wedlock, but does so at the expense of the exceptional unwed fathers before the Court, whose commitments to their children were demonstrated. Because lack of commitment and nonsupport by fathers is a major social problem, one might question the wisdom (quite aside from the constitutional appropriateness) of ratifying disincentives to paternal responsibility in situations where fathers do try in good faith to carry out parental commitments.

A final Burger Court decision, seemingly unrelated to reproductive and sexual issues but really determined by them, is *Rostker v. Goldberg* (1981).[36] In an opinion by Justice Rehnquist, the Court upheld the male-only draft-registration law. The majority reasoned that since the primary purpose of the draft is to raise combat troops, there is no point in registering women, who are excluded from combat. Even the dissenting justices did not question the combat exclusion. Rather, they quarreled with the majority's conclusion that the draft was aimed only at combat-eligible persons. The Court thus failed to confront the explosive issues lurking just beneath the surface of the registration law. Congress had been more forthcoming. The legislative debate on the law revealed that such considerations as the effect of drafting women on the national will to fight and the specter of mothers being sent off to war while fathers stayed home with the children were very much on the lawmakers' minds when they decided to exclude women from registration.[37] The challenge to society's most basic assumptions about maleness and femaleness, alluded to by Congress and posed by *Rostker*, was met with deafening judicial silence.

The Burger Court's holdings on gender and affirmative action were a botched job. Affirmative action is compatible with equality when its purpose is to "bring up to the starting line" groups held back by discrimination. By definition, it is a temporary measure to permit artificially restricted groups to achieve equality, rather than a permanent accommodation to inherent difference or inferiority. Characteristically, affirmative action focuses on access to training, education, trades, and professions rather than after-the-fact compensation for discriminatory lack of access. The Court, unfortunately, was prone to mistake sex-based legislation designed as a permanent accommodation to women's traditional role for affirmative action, and uphold it.

To pick the most striking example, in *Kahn v. Shevin* (1974)[38] the Court refused to strike down a modest property-tax exemption for Florida widows that was enacted before the turn of the century. All widows, rich or poor, as distinguished from widowers no matter what their economic status, were presumed destitute after the death of their spouse. The Court preserved a negligible economic benefit that failed to address the underlying causes of women's persistently inferior economic status. History is replete with laws that merely reinforced stereotypes while purporting to compensate for the disadvantages of life in the separate sphere. When the Court defines affirmative action in the sloppy way it did in *Kahn*, it does women no favor.[39]

An equally serious problem is raised by legislation that does not, on its face, mandate different treatment of men and women but that has a substantially disparate effect on the sexes. The Burger Court tended to take a statute's neutrality at face value unless the challenger could establish that the legislature *intended* that it discriminate against one sex or the other. It was not enough that the impact is foreseeable and inevitable; legislators must have passed the law "because of, not merely in spite of" its effect on women.

The case that spelled this out, *Personnel Administrator of Massachusetts v. Feeney* (1979),[40] upheld an absolute lifetime preference for war veterans in state civil service jobs, even though that preference resulted in an exclusively male work force at the higher levels of civil service employment in Massachusetts. The legislature's intention appeared to be a neutral one: to reward veterans for their service to the country. The devastating effect such a rule would have on women, however, was obvious, given the 2 percent quota (lifted only recently) on women's participation in the military. The legislators, intent on rewarding the peculiarly male role of warrior by securing public benefits for the duration of a soldier's lifetime, were indifferent to this foreseeable effect. That they regarded a civil service that was male at the top and female at the bottom as part of the natural order of things was apparent from the veterans preference provisions themselves: the legislature exempted traditional low-paying "women's jobs" from the preference.

The Burger Court's strict intent approach in equal protection cases was too limited to address the range of gender arrangements in society. Apparently neutral legislation is often embedded in social structures and driven by cultural assumptions that arrange, just as potently as overt gender and race classifications, the divisions that keep women and members of minority groups in their traditional places. A test focusing on effect was successfully used in enforcing Title VII of the Civil Rights Act of 1964, which bars racial and sex-based discrimination in employment.[41] Surely a similarly workable standard might be fashioned under the equal protection clause.

In the seventeen years during which Warren Burger was chief justice, equal protection doctrine in sex discrimination cases underwent a modest revolution. The "middle-tier" standard crafted by Justice Brennan gave an impetus for overturning numerous laws that pigeonholed women as dependent homemakers and men as breadwinners. That change is obviously important, but it mainly signifies a recognition that the law must catch up with a changed world in which women have joined the work force in unprecedented numbers.

The most deeply embedded gender dichotomies retain their hold on the Supreme Court. Women may go to work and participate in the political process, but the Court draws the line at combat, the ultimate male preserve. Moreover, the powerful image of the duality of male and female sexuality, and the gender hierarchy that is part of it, gives a "reason" for upholding sex-based legislation touching on sexuality. Pregnancy puts women outside the equality principle altogether, beyond judicial scrutiny, a result only partly, although importantly, mitigated by the doctrines of reproductive choice that have emerged during the Burger years under the due process clause.

By the time Warren Burger left the Supreme Court, the major equality issues were decided: the earlier flood of decisions had diminished to a trickle. The addition of Antonin Scalia to the Court and the elevation of William Rehnquist to chief justice weakens, but does not radically change, the Court's commitment to gender equality. If given the opportunity by the death or retirement of any of the liberal justices, however, President Reagan will almost certainly transfigure the Court and end its already declining activism on the issue. In any case, the equality the Court's revolution has brought has not fundamentally improved the economic status of women. Commentators have noted with alarm the "feminization of poverty," a result of the wage gap[42] and a soaring divorce rate coupled with inadequate spousal and child-support awards indifferently enforced.[43] Such disparities, driven by profound social change, are for the most part beyond the narrow purview of even an activist judiciary. As reformers turn away from the courts, social reform will again be the province of legislatures that, for the first time in history, will feel the influence, in ways we cannot foresee, of the growing ranks of women members.

·8·

Activism without Equality

NORMAN S. ROSENBERG

The movement to bring mentally disabled people under the protection of our nation's laws began at about the same time that Warren E. Burger became Chief Justice of the United States.* The Burger Court's response to this movement was mixed. In various contexts, the Court affirmed the existence of constitutional rights not previously recognized. At the same time, it sanctioned ineffectual procedures to vindicate those rights, imposed severe restrictions on the availability of remedies, and made access to the courts more difficult for mentally disabled people. In the final analysis, the Burger Court's jurisprudential goal was to limit the federal courts' power to intervene in the system by which we take care of mentally disabled people. It achieved this goal and in the process ignored their needs.

CIVIL COMMITMENT AND INSTITUTIONS

State-operated institutions were disability advocates' first target for reform in the early 1970s. Most were dismal places—human warehouses—where neglect, abuse, idleness, and regression were facts of everyday life. Despite the media's periodic disclosures of their intol-

*I use the terms "mentally disabled" and "disabled" to denote people who are mentally ill or mentally retarded or have been so labeled.

erable conditions and a body of literature that supported the view that large institutions were inherently bad,[1] political pressure failed to bring about reform. The courts were the last resort.

Litigation followed several distinct but related paths. The first sought to establish substantive standards as to when people could be involuntarily confined in a mental institution, along with procedural safeguards in the commitment process.[2] The second, exemplified by widely heralded federal-court cases in the early 1970's such as *Wyatt v. Stickney*[3] and *New York State Association for Retarded Children v. Rockefeller*[4] (the "Willowbrook" case), attempted to improve conditions in state institutions by establishing their residents' right to treatment and habilitation. A third argued that institutions in general were incapable of providing the sort of care and treatment that satisfy humanitarian or constitutional imperatives; these cases tried to release patients and to scale down or close institutions.

Civil Commitment

For psychiatry, the first half of the nineteenth century was an era of great optimism.[5] The belief developed that biological and environmental factors helped to determine human behavior and that they could be influenced by psychiatric intervention.[6] Reportedly high rates of cure of mental illness stimulated a movement to draw distinctions between mentally ill people and criminals: the former were deemed worthy of and amenable to treatment; the latter were not. This change led over time to the development of a civil-commitment system that purported to treat and cure those who would not or could not help themselves. It also dramatically expanded the authority of medical professionals, as courts increasingly abdicated their decision-making to psychiatrists.[7] By the mid-1950s, more than 500,000 people in the United States were civilly committed to state psychiatric hospitals.[8]

Despite some promising early litigation to establish adequate safeguards in the civil-commitment system,[9] most of the recent battles over this issue have been in state legislatures. However, the Burger Court decided two important civil-commitment cases. Although both addressed relatively narrow issues, they illustrate political and doctrinal themes that characterize the Court's decision-making in this area.

The first was *Addington v. Texas* (1979),[10] in which the Supreme Court was asked to decide how strong the proof must be before someone may be involuntarily committed. Rejecting both "preponderance of the evidence," the standard applied in most civil cases, which requires little more than a probability, and "proof beyond a reasonable doubt," the very demanding standard applied in criminal prosecutions, the Court held unanimously that the Constitution required a midlevel standard of "clear and convincing evidence." Chief Justice Warren Burger first distinguished civil commitment from criminal proceedings. The former is designed to further the state's legitimate interest in treating people who are "suffering from a debilitating mental illness,"[11] not to punish. The Court also noted that the civilly committed person, unlike the convicted criminal, has continuous opportunities after admission to correct erroneous commitment decisions.

Perhaps more important for Burger, the subtleties and nuances of psychiatric diagnosis raised serious questions as to whether or not a state could ever prove beyond a reasonable doubt that someone is mentally ill and dangerous. Psychiatric diagnosis is to a large extent based on medical "impressions," drawn from subjective analyses and filtered through the experience of the diagnostician. This process, the Chief Justice wrote, makes it difficult to offer definite conclusions about any particular patient.[12]

Although Chief Justice Burger's critique of the fallibility of psychiatric diagnosis may have been correct, he seemed to have forgotten it less than two months later when he wrote for the Court in *Parham v. J.R.*[13] In *Parham* and a companion case, *Secretary of Public Welfare of Pennsylvania v. Institutionalized Juveniles*,[14] the Court reviewed preadmission procedures for minors proposed for commitment to state institutions by their parents or, in the case of children who are wards of the state, by state agencies. At issue was whether or not the due process clause of the Constitution required a hearing before commitment and, if it did, what sort of hearing it should be. In its decision, the Court established for the first time that children have a constitutionally protected interest in avoiding inappropriate or unnecessary institutionalization and could not be confined without some precommitment review. The Court ruled, however, that the child's interests could be adequately protected by a "neutral factfinder," such as the admitting psychiatrist. The same psychiatrists who in *Addington* were described by the Chief Justice as unable to offer definite conclusions about any patient were now made the instrument for protecting children against erroneous commitment decisions.

On its face, these differing attitudes toward psychiatrists defy logic.

But they are readily understood when considered in light of the Court's goal of limiting judicial intervention in the mental-health system and, generally, in the protection of individual rights. When, as in *Addington*, skepticism serves this overarching end, the Court is openly critical of psychiatrists, the accuracy of diagnosis, and the quality of treatment; when skepticism does not serve that purpose, the Court's criticism is muted. Accordingly, while the *Parham* Court stopped short of disavowing the *Addington* critique of psychiatry (Chief Justice Burger did acknowledge that psychiatric judgments are not error-free), its analysis focused instead on psychiatrists as unbiased healers. This premise enabled the Court to make them gatekeepers and thus eliminate the need for judicial review of admissions decisions.

The Court's analysis was flawed and its remedy ineffectual. By virtue of their training and experience, psychiatrists think in terms of psychopathology. They develop confidence in the benefits of treatment and tend to err on the side of caution when faced with the difficult choice of recommending compulsory confinement or release. In short, many institutional psychiatrists are predisposed to commitment.[15] For this reason, an underlying objective of many system-changing cases has been to impose legal and regulatory controls on psychiatric authority.

The Right to Treatment

Kenneth Donaldson had been involuntarily confined at the Florida State Hospital for fourteen years, since 1957, when he sued, alleging that his psychiatrists had intentionally deprived him of his right to liberty and that, in any event, the hospital was not treating his supposed illness. The jury awarded Donaldson compensatory and punitive damages. The psychiatrists appealed to the Supreme Court, contending that the Constitution does not guarantee to involuntarily committed persons a right to treatment. The Court explicitly declined to decide whether Donaldson had such a right, but ruled instead that if the state failed to treat a nondangerous person capable of living in freedom, he or she could not be involuntarily confined. Accordingly, Donaldson had been denied his right to liberty.[16]

Chief Justice Burger agreed with the holding but wrote a lengthy concurring opinion in which he rejected the premise underlying the right-to-treatment principle, which stated that due process requires the provision of adequate treatment as the *quid pro quo* for involuntary confinement on therapeutic grounds.[17]

Chief Justice Burger's critique notwithstanding, several years later, in *Youngberg v. Romeo* (1982)[18] the Court ruled for the first time that institutionalized mentally retarded people do have a right to treatment that at least guarantees them a safe environment and freedom from undue bodily restraint.[19] These are fundamental liberty interests protected by the due process clause and survive criminal conviction and incarceration; surely they must survive involuntary commitment.[20]

The victory was a narrow one. The Court ignored the growing body of lower-court decisions exposing the deplorable conditions and lack of purposeful activity in so many institutions, and declined to decide whether involuntary commitment itself creates a general right to treatment or habilitation.[21] Somewhat surprisingly, three justices representing diverse ideological perspectives (Harry Blackmun, William Brennan, and Sandra Day O'Connor) in a concurring opinion suggested that if the state commits a mentally retarded person for care and treatment, it may have bound itself to provide treatment. Further, there may be an independent claim, grounded in the due process clause, to habilitation or training to preserve skills. While the state may not have a duty to improve or cure people in its care, it may at least be obligated to prevent their regression or deterioration.[22]

Chief Justice Burger did not agree. Refusing to sign either the majority or concurring opinion, he characterized as "obviously frivolous"[23] the idea that people have a substantive constitutional right to treatment or habilitation. Although he had endorsed the holding in *Donaldson* that the absence of treatment could not justify continued confinement of a nondangerous person, he was not prepared to say that the Constitution requires the state to do anything for people to improve or maintain the condition for which they are confined. For him, the state's obligation to mentally retarded people is no greater than it is to pretrial jail detainees:[24] the provision of food, shelter, medical care, and safe living conditions.[25]

The *Youngberg* decision left unresolved many questions about what an inmate's right to treatment is in state institutions. Although there have been comparatively few right-to-treatment cases since *Youngberg*, these decisions suggest that the range of violations for which relief can be sought is still broad when the claims relate to basic humane care and treatment. (For example, when evidence has shown that residents were living in unsanitary and crowded conditions, when little or no training was taking place and when the absence of training meant that the residents' health deteriorated, when there were serious staffing shortages and when treatment plans and recordkeeping were inadequate, courts have issued detailed orders mandating improvements.[26]) To the extent that courts have addressed the general right to treatment or whether there is a right to be in the least restrictive environment, however, they either have avoided deciding whether such rights are required by the Constitution[27] or, in light of *Youngberg*, have decided they are not.[28]

Whatever *Youngberg* stands for in terms of the rights of institutionalized retarded people to care and treatment, the Supreme Court tightly circumscribed those rights by submitting them to the judgment of professionals. Putting aside reservations about the quality of psychiatric decision-making, in *Youngberg* the Court again emphasized the deference that must be paid to qualified professionals. Interference with the internal operations of institutions should be minimized. Professional decisions are "presumptively valid." Accordingly, they should stand unless the professional's conduct is "such a substantial departure from accepted professional judgment . . . as to demonstrate that the person responsible actually did not base the decision on such a judgment"[29]—a standard for professional judgment even lower than that applied in malpractice cases. In imposing it, the Court restricted litigants' access to the courts and limited liability to only the most outrageous cases—those that evince an utter absence of professional judgment.

Deinstitutionalization

Mental institutions are inherently coercive. They breed violence, neglect, and abuse. They offer little to their residents that cannot be provided in the more normal surroundings of home and community.[30] From the outset of the disability rights movement, therefore, there were persistent calls from progressive professionals, former patients, and advocates who all demanded that they be depopulated or closed. Yet while the path toward deinstitutionalization was paved by federal legislative initiatives,[31] the resources needed to develop a system of community care never materialized. *Pennhurst State School & Hos-*

pital v. Halderman (1981)[32] held out the hope of generating such resources.

Halderman was filed in 1974 to compel Pennsylvania to create alternative, less restrictive settings for the mentally retarded residents of the Pennhurst State School and Hospital, a large, remote institution outside Philadelphia. Having found conditions at Pennhurst deplorable, the district court ordered it closed and appointed a special master to develop a plan for providing community services for its residents. The decision was a major victory for proponents of deinstitutionalization. It raised the question of whether Pennhurst or, indeed, any similar institution could ever be improved to the point of meeting minimal constitutional standards of adequacy.

The appeals court affirmed the liability determination but did so based on a legal theory that had not been decided by the trial court: that under the Developmentally Disabled Assistance and Bill of Rights Act (the DD Act), the plaintiffs had a right to treatment in the least restrictive setting.[33] The DD Act, passed by Congress in 1975,[34] provided to cooperating states funds to provide services for developmentally disabled people.

The Supreme Court agreed to consider whether the DD Act created substantive rights that were judicially enforceable on behalf of the plaintiff class. Writing for the six-member majority, Justice William Rehnquist said that Congress had not specified in the act that funds were conditional on the provision of adequate services. Therefore, it could not be said that Congress intended to require states to assume the high cost of community alternatives—despite congressional findings incorporated in the act's bill-of-rights section that "developmentally disabled people have a right to treatment, services and habilitation for such disabilities which should be provided in settings that are least restrictive of the person's liberty."[35]

Technically, *Pennhurst* was a narrow decision. The Court had eliminated only one section of the DD Act as a standard for compelling states to promote community-based treatment. But the majority painted with a broad brush, with Rehnquist repeatedly suggesting that the act as a whole did nothing more than express a congressional preference for certain kinds of treatment; it did not create a right to treatment in the community.[36]

Moreover, the decision revealed a troubling consensus that the appellate court had gone too far when it "assumed the task of managing Pennhurst or [deciding] in the first instance which patients should remain and which should be removed."[37] The Court was sending a signal, which it made explicit a year later in *Youngberg*, that lower courts should not interfere in the daily operations of public institutions, even if those institutions are unable to provide the care for which confinement was ordered.

The Court's admonition was reinforced by constitutional doctrine in the second chapter of the Pennhurst litigation. In 1984, a 5–4 majority concluded in *Pennhurst* II[38] that the Eleventh Amendment to the Constitution (or the doctrine of sovereign immunity it is said to reflect) takes away from the federal courts the authority to order state officials to obey state law.

Pennhurst II imposed a formidable barrier to the federal courts for mentally disabled and other civil rights litigants. For example, a mentally disabled person challenging substandard institutional conditions under both federal and state law will now be forced either to bring both claims in state court—a forum generally viewed as less sympathetic than federal court to cases intended to change the system—or to sue in federal court without being able to raise the state-law violations. Yet many of the claims made by residents of institutions against state officials involve violations of both federal and state law; to protest both, litigants will have to either give up going to federal court or file two separate, time-consuming, and complex lawsuits.

The doctrine of sovereign immunity is at war with the principle that government must be accountable to the people through the courts. In *Pennhurst* II, by treating the doctrine with a degree of respect approaching "awe,"[39] the Court took a giant step toward reducing that accountability.

DISABLED PEOPLE IN THE COMMUNITY

In the last twenty-five years, with little or no support from the Supreme Court, there has been a shift in taking care of disabled people, a shift from hospital to community-based settings. Yet dollars to pay for the care have not shifted. Today, for example, community programs receive on average only 25 percent of states' mental-health funds, although the vast majority of people served by the public mental-health system depend on these programs.[40]

Persistent shortages in social support, housing, education, and job training and rehabilitation programs, exacerbated by deep-rooted discriminatory attitudes toward mentally disabled people, have reinforced the second-class status of these people in society. Congress has tried to improve their plight through enactment of laws such as section 504 of the Rehabilitation Act of 1973 and the Education for All Handicapped Children Act of 1975.[41] Primarily, however, the Burger Court's decisions interpreting these laws, and its rulings regarding the protection of individual rights under the Fourteenth Amendment, have been of only marginal value in integrating mentally disabled people into the mainstream of American life.

Housing

Community-living opportunities are a crucial need for mentally disabled people. The chronic shortage of well-supervised and affordable housing has left thousands of people needlessly confined in institutions; countless others have been dumped into welfare hotels, board-and-care homes, or the city streets.

Community objections to having mentally disabled people as neighbors have slowed the creation of group homes, halfway houses, supervised apartments, and other residential facilities. This discrimination has been expressed through zoning ordinances, restrictive covenants, and special-use permit requirements—weapons less dramatic than cross-burnings and fire bombings but nevertheless quite effective.

In 1985, the Supreme Court ruled in *City of Cleburne, Texas v. Cleburne Living Center*[42] that the City of Cleburne could not refuse a permit to operate a group home for thirteen mentally retarded adults. While this ruling allowed a group home to be set up in Cleburne, the Court's analysis of the rights of mentally retarded people under the equal protection clause of the Constitution—the centerpiece of the decision—shows a serious lack of appreciation for the plight of disabled people and an implicit admonition against relying on the Court to achieve basic equality.

The majority opinion, written by Justice Byron White, rejected the lower court's conclusion that mental retardation should be a "quasi-suspect classification" requiring that social or economic laws or official actions relating to mentally retarded people be justified by a showing that the harsher treatment of the retarded is necessary in order to achieve an important governmental objective—what lawyers call "close" or "heightened judicial scrutiny." This is a heavier burden than social legislation usually has, for such legislation will normally stand up if there is merely some rational basis, some merely plausible reason for it.

The Court acknowledged that mentally retarded people have been victimized by invidious discrimination, a traditional basis for a higher burden of justification, but it refused to treat discrimination against the mentally retarded the way it treats other groups with a similar history, for whom heightened judicial scrutiny has been applied—women and illegitimate children, for example. Rather it ruled that differential treatment of the retarded should not necessarily be considered suspect, given the range of their abilities and the state's legitimate interest in dealing with and providing for them.[43]

Justice White was, of course, correct; retarded people are not all cut from the same pattern. And some mentally retarded people do have serious disabilities that may be taken into account by lawmakers. But that is also true of some women, illegitimate children, or aliens, yet official actions concerning these groups are granted the extra judicial scrutiny involved in the heavier burden of justification. Individual differences within each group may sometimes justify different legislative treatment in certain circumstances. But because those circumstances may in certain instances be relevant does not mean they are always relevant, especially if there is good reason—manifest community prejudice, for example—to suspect that they are not.

The Court's perception of the current status of retarded people in American society is similarly flawed. While acknowledging the history of discrimination against them, it trivialized this dark past by pointing to recent laws passed on their behalf without referring to the countless local ordinances that still effectively block retarded people from entering community life. Instead, the Court pointed to beneficial legislative responses, such as the Developmentally Disabled Assistance and Bill of Rights Act, and argued that these showed that lawmakers had addressed the difficulties mentally retarded people face, so much so that one could not claim they were still politically powerless.[44]

Even if irrational fear and prejudice did not continue to motivate some legislative actions toward retarded people, a rigorous standard of justification would still be appropriate. The Court found improvement in legislative attitudes and yet it imposed heightened scrutiny on official actions using gender classifications.[45] Moreover, as Justice Thurgood Marshall pointed out in a dissent, even when judicial action has catalyzed legislative change, suspect classifications became no less suspect.[46]

On the positive side, while rejecting heightened scrutiny for mentally retarded people,[47] the Burger Court may have breathed new life into the rational-basis test by probing Cleburne's motivation for singling out retarded people for differential treatment. The Court determined that the city's proposed justifications were either unacceptable (neighbors' fears) or not believable (concern for residents' safety).[48]

The Court's limited decision raises other problems, however. Instead of invalidating the entire ordinance, which required special-use permits for group homes for retarded people, the Court declared only that this particular permit application was wrongly denied. Why? The majority offered a simple but unsupported explanation: limiting its decision to this particular situation is the "preferred course of adjudication."[49] It is hard to imagine why. Surely the Court had not lost its zeal for judicial economy. But by its failure to elucidate any principles by which the ordinance might be validly applied, the decision seemed to invite further litigation. The answer probably lies in the Court's analysis of the heightened scrutiny issue: the Court had refused to require a heavier burden of justification than in other social welfare cases, because some retarded people may have special disabilities that legislation may take into account. So, too, a zoning ordinance like Cleburne's may be appropriate in some situations involving mentally retarded people under certain (unidentified) circumstances. The cause of constitutional adjudication and equality for disabled people could have been better served.

Employment and Access to Other Services

A major achievement for disabled people was the congressional passage of section 504 of the Rehabilitation Act of 1973, which provides that "[n]o otherwise qualified handicapped individual in the United States . . . shall solely by reason of his handicap, be excluded from participation in, be denied the benefits of, or be subjected to discrimination under any program or activity receiving Federal financial assistance." The history of its enactment shows that Congress has recognized the potential of disabled people and the conditions required to allow them to participate in American society.[50] It was hoped that section 504, patterned after Title VI of the Civil Rights Act of 1964, would be a key weapon in combating discrimination based on handicap.

The Burger Court's section 504 decisions were only of limited value, however. While it has been suggested that they went well beyond society's commitment to the disabled,[51] they nevertheless showed a lack of appreciation of the structural and institutional discrimination that has confronted this group and of what is needed to overcome it.

Section 504 established a broad ban on discrimination based on handicap. The statute covers both mentally and physically disabled people. Indeed, most of the litigation brought under section 504 has involved physically handicapped people. As a matter of judicial doctrine, however, these rulings apply to mentally disabled people as well.

The Court's first section 504 decision was *Southeastern Community College v. Davis* (1979),[52] in which a unanimous Court reversed a lower-court decision declaring that Southeastern's nursing school must modify its training program for registered nurses to accommodate a severely hearing-impaired student. The Court held that if a handicapped person is unable to meet qualifying standards without program modifications that would create "undue financial and administrative burdens," he or she is not an "otherwise qualified handicapped individual" and may be denied access to such program.

Davis was a difficult case. A nurse who cannot hear her patients and whose lip-reading skill is useless in settings where surgical masks are worn, raised the likelihood of causing harm to patients. But the tone of the decision seemed to suggest that recipients of federal aid have only a limited obligation to meet the needs of handicapped people. For example, the Court noted that other sections of the Rehabilitation Act—sections 501 (nondiscrimination in federal employment) and 503 (nondiscrimination in federal contractors' employment)—require affirmative action, but section 504 does not. By erroneously equating affirmative action, which is a remedial policy for the victims of past discrimination, with "reasonable accommodation," which eliminates existing obstacles, the Court seemed to say that Section 504 might not require any significant modification of facilities to accommodate the handicapped.

More recently, in *Alexander v. Choate* (1985),[53] a case involving the reduction of health-care services to Medicaid recipients, a unanimous Court explicitly ruled that claims under section 504 must be resolved by balancing "the statutory rights of the handicapped to be integrated into society and the legitimate interests of the federal grantees in preserving the integrity of their programs." Any interpretation of section 504, wrote Justice Marshall, must balance two countervailing considerations—the need to give effect to the objectives of section 504, and the desire to keep it within manageable bounds.[54]

Although these cases suggest that the Supreme Court grants relief to victims of discrimination quite narrowly, they have at least allowed litigants access to the courts and a realistic opportunity to prove their claims. In *Consolidated Rail Corporation v. Darrone* (1984),[55] the Court ruled for the first time that handicapped employees had a private right of action under section 504 to file suits for intentional discrimination. And in the *Alexander* case mentioned earlier, the Court rejected the state's argument that section 504 applies only to intentional discrimination. Thus, if governmental action has an unjustifiably disparate impact on the handicapped—even if it is not intended—a section 504 violation may be proved.

Education

Until only a few years ago, the parents of a handicapped child often faced a painful choice: keep the child at home, without access to appropriate treatment or habilitation, education or vocational services; or place the child in an institution, possibly for lifelong confinement. Thousands of handicapped children were systematically excluded from the public schools. Those who were permitted to enroll were, typically, taught in makeshift basement classrooms or in segregated special schools whose resources were inadequate and where they of course had no chance to learn from and interact with their nonhandicapped peers.

Following litigation in the early 1970s to establish a constitutional right to an appropriate education,[56] Congress enacted the Education for All Handicapped Children Act of 1975 (EAHCA) (P.L. 94-142),[57] which mandates that all physically and mentally handicapped children, regardless of the severity of their condition, must be provided with a free appropriate public education, including special education and related services consistent with the unique needs of each child.

P.L. 94-142 has dominated cases about education for the handicapped ever since its enactment. And it has emerged more or less intact from this litigation; indeed, enhanced benefits have been achieved in selected areas.[58] While the Burger Court's EAHCA decisions broke no new ground, the Court adopted a fairly straightforward view of the child's and parents' substantive rights under the act. Its first and most important decision was *Board of Education of the Hendrick Hudson School District v. Rowley* (1982).[59]

In *Rowley*, the Court was asked to determine the meaning of a "free appropriate public education." In a 6–3 decision, Justice Rehnquist wrote that a "free appropriate" education requires school districts to provide individualized instruction with adequate support services to ensure that every child receives "educational benefit" from the program.[60] This means the child's program must meet state standards, approximate the grade levels used in regular public-school classes, and reflect a systematic planning process that includes consultation between parents and professionals. The Court rejected as unworkable a proposal that school districts provide services that would maximize the potential of the child. At a minimum, however, each child must receive services that will afford him "meaningful" access to an education.

The *Rowley* decision affirmed the existence of rights that had not been previously passed on by the Supreme Court. But, as it had done in *Romeo* and *Parham*, the Court imposed restrictions on the remedy available to vindicate those rights. The restrictions in *Rowley*, however, reflect a somewhat fairer balancing of the competing individual and state interests than in those other cases. In *Rowley*, the Court held that the act's provisions for judicial review of the administrative decisions regarding the child's program did not require, as had been proposed by disability advocates, entirely new hearings in federal court. At the same time, judicial proceedings were not limited to review of the state's compliance with the procedural requirements of the act. Instead, a court may determine whether the substance of the child's educational program is reasonably calculated to enable the child to receive educational benefit.[61]

The Court decided one other case dealing with the programmatic requirements of EAHCA. In *Irving Independent School District v. Tatro* (1984),[62] a unanimous Court ruled that a public-school district must provide a child who suffers from spina bifida with clean intermittent catheterization (CIC), a procedure that enables the child to void her bladder during the school day. In reaching this result, the Court was called upon to interpret the meaning of the act's "related services" provision.[63] "Related services" are generally defined as developmental, corrective, and other support services, except medical care, required to enable the child to benefit from special education.

The Court first concluded that CIC was a related service because without it the child could not attend school and would, therefore, be prevented from receiving any educational benefits. Next the Court determined that because CIC could be administered by a school nurse or other qualified person, CIC was a "school health service," which must be provided under the act, rather than a "medical service," which need not be. Only services that must be administered by a licensed physician constitute "medical services," which are exempt under 94-142.

Although the *Tatro* holding applies to a very small group of children, its reach may ultimately be far broader. One of the most controversial issues regarding EAHCA is the obligation of school districts to provide the high-cost therapies and supportive services often required by severely handicapped children. *Tatro* supports those who argue that if such services will make the difference between whether or not a child attends school, school districts must provide them.

CONCLUSION

The Burger Court decided some thirty cases affecting rights of and services for mentally disabled people. In relation to other minority groups, mentally disabled people fared reasonably well. But in light of the dismal conditions that exist in many public institutions and the virulent discrimination against disabled people that persists in nearly every community, the Burger Court was not helpful.

It is tempting to accuse the Court of callousness and insensitivity, but handicapped people are obviously not the Court's target. The target is judicial oversight, an oversight that tries to check the arbitrariness of state governments and state bureaucracies. Unfortunately, the Supreme Court's insistence on judicial passivity left the legitimate and urgent claims of mentally disabled people at the mercy of those who prefer them to be out of sight and out of mind.

·IV·

CRIMINAL JUSTICE

·9·

The "Police Practice" Phases of the Criminal Process and the Three Phases of the Burger Court

YALE KAMISAR

When we talk about the Burger Court, we are talking about a fluid process, a Court that was always moving but not always in a straight line—and sometimes not even in the same direction. There were many predictions about the Court's future course when Judge Warren Burger ascended to the chief justiceship. And there was no shortage of predictions when Justice William Rehnquist was named to replace him. But as Professor Laurence Tribe has observed: "A word of caution for any [who would predict where the Court is going]. Whoever lives by the crystal ball soon learns to eat ground glass."[1]

Writing about the Burger Court only a few years ago, I was so bold as to say that there seemed to be *two* Burger Courts.[2] The first one, the Court of the early and middle 1970s, seemed to have mounted the expected attack on the Warren Court's criminal procedure cases. Thus, with two quick, heavy blows, it crippled the lineup rulings[3] (which sought to establish fair pretrial identification procedures for suspects);[4] appeared to be stalking the Fourth Amendment exclusionary rule (which bars the government's use of evidence obtained in violation of the protection against unreasonable search and seizure); and seemed to be laying the groundwork to overrule *Miranda v. Arizona* (1966)[5] (the landmark confession case that applied the Fifth Amendment privilege against compelled self-incrimination to the informal compulsion exerted by the police when they question a person they have taken into custody). Except for the lineup cases, however, the fears (or hopes) that the Warren Court's work would be dismantled did not materialize.

Instead, starting in 1977 (about the time Justice John Paul Stevens was appointed to the Court), a significantly less police-oriented Court emerged. During this second phase the Court's hostility to its predecessor's police-practice decisions subsided appreciably, or so it seemed to me.[6] The Court rejected a goodly number of government contentions in various search-and-seizure cases,[7] reinvigorated *Miranda* in some respects, and revivified—even expanded—the *Massiah* doctrine[8] (a rule, supplementing *Miranda*, that prohibits the government from "deliberately eliciting" statements from a suspect once adversary judicial proceedings have begun), making that doctrine a more potent force than it had ever been before.

Writing in 1982, I therefore concluded that Warren Court supporters had reason to be encouraged.[9] Although the Burger Court had at first treated its predecessor's landmark criminal-procedures decisions unkindly, admirers of the Warren Court could fairly say that more recently the new Court was holding firm on some search-and-seizure issues and even advancing on others, and that its performance concerning confessions was an especially pleasant surprise. The Court's abandonment of its efforts to provide meaningful judicial regulation of police interrogation had been "confidently forecasted by a number of commentators throughout the 1970's."[10] But the Court's ungrudging interpretation of *Miranda* in two important cases[11] and its even more generous treatment of the *Massiah* doctrine from 1977 to 1981 seemed to demonstrate its determination to control police efforts to induce incriminating statements and to do so by rules that look beyond the reliability of the resulting statements and the abusiveness of the tactics used to obtain them.

No sooner had I written this rather cheery report (again viewed from the perspective of a Warren Court supporter), than a third Burger Court began to take shape, one perhaps associated with the retirement of the late Justice Potter Stewart and his replacement by Justice Sandra Day O'Connor in the summer of 1981. In the main, this third Burger Court—the one operating when Chief Justice Burger stepped down—picked up where the first had left off in the mid-1970s.

For example, perhaps because the Court had become convinced that more law-enforcement tools were needed to combat drug traffic, during the 1982–83 term the government gained complete or partial victory in all nine search-and-seizure cases decided that term (all involving drugs).[12] As Professor Wayne LaFave, the nation's leading authority on the law of search and seizure, observed, more significant than the government's impressive won-lost record was "the tenor and style of [these] decisions; it is almost as if a majority of the Court was hell-bent to seize any available opportunity to define more expansively the constitutional authority of law enforcement officials."[13] The following term, in *United States v. Leon* (1984),[14] after having hinted for a decade that it would do so, the Court finally adopted a "good faith" (actually a "reasonable mistake") exception to the Fourth Amendment exclusionary rule in its central application: the prosecution's case against the direct victim of a Fourth Amendment violation.[15]

Nor did *Miranda* fare well during the last phase of the Burger Court's work. In *New York v. Quarles* (1984),[16] in the course of establishing a "public safety" exception to the *Miranda* warnings—an exception of unknown dimensions that may make the *Miranda* requirements much more difficult to understand—the Court viewed the now-familiar warnings as merely nonconstitutional "prophylactic rules." And a year later, in *Oregon v. Elstad*,[17] while admitting into evidence a "second confession" that had been preceded by an incriminating statement obtained in violation of *Miranda*, the Court distinguished between what might be called *real* constitutional violations and *mere Miranda* violations—sharply contrasting statements that are *actually* "coerced" or "compelled" from those that are *only* obtained in violation of *Miranda*'s "procedural safeguards" or "prophylactic rules."

Thus, Chief Justice Burger announced his retirement just when the so-called Burger Court seemed to have hit its pro-police stride at last, just when he and his colleagues were demonstrating, after a number of years in which the government had experienced only mixed success, that criminal procedure is indeed "the part of the Court's work most susceptible to swings of the pendulum after a change of personnel."[18]

PRETRIAL IDENTIFICATION

Although mistaken identification has probably been the single greatest cause of conviction of the innocent,[19] the Supreme Court did not come to grips with this problem until surprisingly late in the day. When it finally did, in a 1967 trilogy of cases, *United States v. Wade, Gilbert v. California*, and *Stovall v. Denno*,[20] it seemed bent on making up for lost time. It leapfrogged a case-by-case analysis of various identification situations and applied the right to counsel to pretrial identifications in one swoop. "Since it appears that there is grave potential for prejudice [in] the pretrial lineup, which [absent counsel's presence] may not be capable of reconstruction at trial," the Court deemed counsel's presence essential to "avert prejudice and assure a meaningful confrontation at trial."[21]

The pretrial identification in *Wade* and *Gilbert* did take place after the defendants had been indicted, and the Court mentioned this fact. But nothing in the Court's reasoning suggested that a lineup or showup held before formal judicial proceedings begin—which is usually the case—is less riddled with dangers or less difficult for a suspect to reconstruct at trial than one occurring after that point.

Nevertheless, in *Kirby v. Illinois* (1972),[22] the Burger Court announced a "post-indictment" rule, one that enables law-enforcement officials to manipulate the applicability of the right to counsel by conducting identification procedures before formal charges are filed. Such a rule is not in keeping with a judicial system that deals with realities of the criminal process rather than labels. Moreover, a ruling such as *Kirby* could not but encourage the lower courts (many of which were unhappy with the recent "revolution" in criminal procedure and watching for new signals from the Supreme Court) to commence, or to intensify, efforts to "contain" the lineup decisions in other respects, or for that matter to give other Warren Court decisions similar treatment. The Burger Court showed them how.

A year after *Kirby*, the Burger Court struck the *Wade-Gilbert* rule another blow. Unmoved by the argument (which I find persuasive) that the availability of the photographs at trial provides no protection against the suggestive manner in which they may have been originally displayed to the witness or the comments or gestures that may have accompanied the display, the Court ruled in *United States v. Ash* (1973)[23] that photographic identification may take place without the defense counsel's participation, whether conducted before or after the filing of formal charges, and even though the suspect could have appeared in person at a lineup.

Although *Kirby* and *Ash* crippled the original lineup decisions, abuses in photographic displays and in preindictment lineups are not, in theory at least, beyond the reach of the Constitution: a defendant may still convince a court that the circumstances surrounding his identification present so "substantial" a "likelihood of misidentification" as to violate due process.[24] But the Burger Court made this quite difficult to achieve. An "unnecessarily suggestive" identification is not enough (although it ought to be)—the "totality of circumstances" may still allow identification evidence if, despite the unnecessary "suggestiveness," "the out-of-court identification possesses certain features of reliability."[25] This is an elusive, unpredictable case-by-case standard that was unlikely, and has not turned out, to be any more manageable for appellate courts or any more illuminating for law-enforcement officers than the "totality of the circumstances" test for admitting confessions that proved so unsuccessful in the thirty years before *Miranda*.

The Burger Court's decisions concerning pretrial identification may well be the saddest chapter in modern American criminal procedure. This is not so much because the retreat from the 1967 lineup decisions was so extensive, but because these decisions, unlike the Warren Court's most publicized criminal-procedure rulings, had been so explicitly designed to protect the innocent from wrongful conviction.[26] Various commentators have pointed out that the Burger Court appeared to be far more impressed than its predecessor with "the importance of being guilty."[27] But the Burger Court's unkind treatment of the 1967 lineup decisions suggests that even the reliability of the guilt-determining process can be subordinated to the demands for speed and finality.

When the Burger Court handed down the *Kirby* and *Ash* decisions in the early 1970s it demonstrated how quickly and easily it could cripple landmark Warren Court decisions without flatly overruling them. But its decisions concerning search and seizure and confessions proved to be a good deal more mixed.

POLICE INTERROGATION AND CONFESSIONS

Miranda, a Much Misunderstood Case

Miranda is probably the most highly publicized criminal procedure case in our history. It is also probably the most maligned and most misunderstood one. Although it has been called "the high-water mark of the due process revolution,"[28] I think it reflects considerable moderation and compromise.

Miranda applied the privilege against compelled self-incrimination to the informal compulsion exerted by the police in the interrogation room and in other kinds of "in-custody questioning," where previously the privilege had applied only to judicial or other formal proceedings. The Miranda Court concluded that in the "interrogation environment" the suspect typically assumed (erroneously), or was led to believe, that he had to answer questions or that it would be so much the worse for him. Thus, unless "adequate protective devices" were used to dispel the coercion inherent in custodial police interrogation, no statement obtained from the suspect could truly be the product of his free choice. The "adequate protective devices" deemed necessary (unless the government adopted other fully effective means) were, of course, the now-familiar warnings—for example: "You have the right to remain silent" and "Anything you say can be used against you."

Although most people think—and the media has led them to believe—that a suspect must be given the Miranda warnings immediately upon arrest or before being questioned, this is not so. Neither custody alone nor questioning alone, if one is not under arrest, requires the warnings. It is the impact on the suspect of the combination of interrogation and custody—each condition reinforcing the pressures and anxieties produced by the other—that, as the Miranda Court correctly discerned, makes "custodial police interrogation" so intimidating that the neutralizing warnings are required.

On the eve of Miranda, not a few commentators warned that law enforcement would suffer a grievous blow if the Court was to allow defense counsel in the police station. As it turned out, however, Miranda did so only in a very limited way. The ruling does not require that a prime suspect or a person taken into custody first consult with a lawyer or actually have a lawyer present in order for his waiver of constitutional rights to be deemed valid. Miranda's great weakness (or saving grace, depending upon one's viewpoint) is that it permits someone subjected to the inherent pressures of arrest and detention to "waive" his rights without actually getting the guidance of counsel.

Miranda even permits the police to obtain waivers of a person's constitutional rights without the presence of any disinterested observer and without any tape recording or other objective recording of the "waiver" transaction, even when such a recording is feasible. Thus it may be forcefully argued that *Miranda* does not go far enough.[29]

A system that allows police to obtain waivers of a person's constitutional rights without the presence of any disinterested observer, or any other objective record of the proceedings, is an inherently weak procedural safeguard. I say this not because a police officer is more dishonest than the rest of us but because we are entitled to assume he is no less human—no less inclined to remember, reconstruct, and interpret past events in a light favorable to himself.

Whether suspects are continuing to confess because they do not fully grasp the significance of the *Miranda* warnings or whether the police, aware that their version of how they gave the warnings is likely to prevail, too often mumble or undermine the warnings or whether the promptings of conscience (and the desire to get the matter over with) override the impact of the warnings, it is plain that for the past twenty years suspects have continued to make incriminating statements with great frequency. This might not have been the case if a tape recording of the police warnings and the suspect's response was required whenever feasible. There is no doubt that it would not have been the case if *Miranda* really had projected defense counsel into the police station—had required that a suspect *first* consult with a lawyer or *actually have a lawyer present* in order for his waiver of constitutional rights to be effective.

Recently, recognition that *Miranda* was not, as is widely believed, designed to do everything possible to prevent a suspect from talking to the police, but was instead an attempt to strike a proper balance between law-enforcement needs and a suspect's needs, came from— of all places—the Burger Court.

In *Moran v. Burbine* (1986),[30] the Court held that a confession preceded by an otherwise valid waiver of *Miranda* rights should not be excluded "either because the police misinformed an inquiring attorney about their plans [they told the attorney that they were 'through' with the suspect for the night, but then proceeded to question him] or because they failed to inform the suspect of the attorney's efforts to reach him."[31] In the course of reaching this conclusion six justices— none of whom (up to this point at least) could be called friends or admirers of *Miranda*[32]—joined an opinion that observed:

> [B]ecause we think that [*Miranda*] as written strikes the
> proper balance between society's legitimate law-enforce-

ment interests and the protection of the defendant's Fifth Amendment rights, we decline [to] further extend Miranda's reach. . . .

Declining to adopt the more extreme position that the actual presence of a lawyer was necessary to dispel the coercion inherent in custodial interrogation, [the Miranda Court] found that the suspect's Fifth Amendment rights could be adequately protected by less intrusive means . . . [R]ather than proceeding from the premise that the rights and needs of the defendant are paramount to all others, [Miranda] embodies a carefully crafted balance designed to fully protect both the defendants' and society's interests.[33]

This is the way Miranda's defenders—not its critics—have talked about the case for the past twenty years. Although it is too early to tell, the Court's view of Miranda as a serious effort to strike a proper "balance" between, or to "reconcile," competing interests may turn out to be more important than its specific ruling.[34]

The "Miranda Impeachment" Cases

The first blows the Burger Court struck against Miranda were two cases involving use of a Miranda-violative statement for cross-examination.

Harris v. New York (1971)[35] held that statements preceded by incomplete Miranda warnings, and thus inadmissible for the purpose of establishing the prosecution's case, could nevertheless be used as part of the prosecution's cross-examination to impeach the defendant's credibility if he chose to take the stand in his own defense. The Court recognized that some comments in the Miranda opinion could be read as barring the use of statements obtained in violation of Miranda for any purpose, but it seemed unperturbed by this.

With Harris on the books, the Burger Court had little difficulty going a step further a few years later in Oregon v. Hass (1975).[36] Although Harris was the more highly publicized decision, the second "impeachment" case, Hass, dealt Miranda a harder blow. Harris might have been explained—and contained—on the ground that permitting impeachment use of statements acquired without proper or complete warnings would not much encourage the police to violate Miranda by giving defective or incomplete warnings. Many suspects confess even when given adequate Miranda warnings. Thus, the somewhat increased probability of obtaining statements by failing to give a full set of warnings, one might argue, would not give the police much incentive to engage in such a practice. Why would the police do something to prevent the use of any resulting statement in the presentation of the prosecution's case, when they are likely to obtain statements usable for all purposes even if they give complete warnings?

In *Hass*, however, after being advised of his rights, the suspect *asserted* them. Thus he made plain that he was the unusual suspect who was not going to make any statement—if the police complied with *Miranda*. But the police refused to honor his request for a lawyer and continued to question him. That such a flagrant violation should yield evidence that may be used for impeachment purposes is especially troublesome, for under these circumstances, unlike those in *Harris*, the police have nothing to lose and everything to gain by disregarding the suspect's assertion of his rights. If they honor the assertion, they get nothing, but if they disregard it, they at least get the impeachment use, with the added possibility that this might induce the defendant not to take the stand for fear of having the prior statement revealed.

The *Hass* majority took cognizance of this argument, but shrugged it off: "[T]he balance was struck in *Harris*, and we are not disposed to change it now."[37] The Court did not seem to grasp that it was striking a very different balance—one tilted much more in favor of the government.[38]

The Tucker-Elstad Way of Thinking About Miranda

Although supporters of *Miranda* were troubled by the "impeachment" cases, they were troubled still more by Justice Rehnquist's opinion for the Court in *Michigan v. Tucker* (1974).[39]

Twenty years ago the late Judge Henry Friendly complained that the Warren Court should not make extreme cases occasions to expand the rights of the accused, but handle them on an individualized basis.[40] But in the 1970s it became the turn of the defense-minded to complain that the Burger Court should not make a mild case the occasion for contracting the rights of the accused but handle such cases on an individualized basis.

Tucker was a mild case of police misconduct—a very attractive case from the prosecution's point of view. First of all, the police questioning occurred before *Miranda* was decided, although the defendant's trial took place afterward. Thus, *Miranda* was just barely applicable. Second, *Tucker* dealt with the admissibility not of the defendant's own statements—they had been excluded—but only the testimony of a witness whose identity had been discovered by questioning the suspect without giving him the full set of *Miranda* warnings.

Under the circumstances, the Court held that the witness's testimony was admissible. The case can be read very narrowly, but Justice Rehnquist's opinion for the Court contains a good deal of mischievous broad language.

As the Court, per Justice O'Connor, was to do eleven years later in *Oregon v. Elstad*, the 1974 *Tucker* Court, per Justice Rehnquist, seemed to equate the "compulsion" barred by the privilege against self-incrimination with "coercion" or "involuntariness" under the pre-*Miranda* "totality of circumstances" test.[41] This is quite misleading. Much more oppressive police interrogation methods were needed to render a confession "coerced" or "involuntary" under the pre-*Miranda* test than are necessary to make a confession "compelled" within the meaning of the self-incrimination clause. That, at least, is the premise of *Miranda*. That was why the old test was abandoned in favor of *Miranda*. And that was why law-enforcement officials so fiercely resisted the application of the self-incrimination clause to police interrogation.

In the 1940s or 1950s Ernest Miranda's confession would have plainly been admissible under the then-prevailing "totality of the circumstances" test. For his questioning had been mild compared with the offensive police methods that had rendered a resulting confession "involuntary" or "coerced" in past cases: for example, stripping off a suspect's clothes and keeping him naked for several hours; subjecting a suspect to some thirty-six hours of almost continuous questioning; pretending to "bring in" a suspect's ailing wife for questioning if he persisted in his denial of guilt; or threatening to take a female suspect's infant children away from her if she failed to "cooperate" with the police.[42] As the 1966 Court observed, however:

> [In *Miranda* and its three companion cases as well], we might
> not find the defendant's statements to have been *involun-*
> *tary in traditional terms*. Our concern for adequate safe-

guards to protect precious Fifth Amendment rights is, of course, not lessened in the slightest. [Although] the records do not evince overt physical coercion or patented psychological ploys, [in] none of these cases did the officers undertake to afford appropriate safeguards [to] insure that the statements were truly the product of free choice. [The "interrogation environment" to which each defendant was subjected] is at odds with one of our Nation's most cherished principles—that the individual may not be compelled to incriminate himself.[43]

By lumping together self-incrimination "compulsion" and pre-*Miranda* "involuntariness" or "coercion," and then declaring that a *Miranda* violation is not necessarily a violation of the self-incrimination clause—it is only if the confession was "involuntary" under traditional standards[44]—the *Tucker* majority rejected the core premise of *Miranda*.[45] If this view of *Miranda* were correct, then that landmark decision would not have accomplished anything by applying the privilege against self-incrimination to the proceedings in the police station.

There is another troubling aspect to *Tucker* and its recent progeny, *Elstad*. In his opinion for the Court in *Tucker*, Justice Rehnquist claimed that *Miranda* "recognized" that the now-familiar warnings "were not themselves rights protected by the Constitution."[46] No, not quite.

Miranda recognized that protective measures other than the warnings[47] might suffice to dispel the "compulsion inherent in custodial surroundings." But *"unless other fully effective means are adopted* to notify the person of [his rights and to assure that their exercise] will be scrupulously honored"[48] the warnings *are* required by the Constitution.

Neither in the *Tucker* case nor in two more recent cases, *Quarles* and *Elstad*, was there any claim or suggestion that procedural safeguards or protective devices other than the warnings had been utilized. Without other "fully effective means" to ensure the privilege against self-incrimination, the *Miranda* warnings *are* rights protected by the Constitution.

I had hoped that the language in Justice Rehnquist's *Tucker* opinion would just go away—even that it had gone away. For in the early 1980s *Miranda* seemed to enjoy a "second honeymoon."

First, the Court gave the key term "interrogation" a fairly generous reading in *Rhode Island v. Innis* (1980).[49] The Court might have taken a mechanical approach to "interrogation" and limited it, as some lower courts had, to situations where the police directly address a suspect. It did not do so. It might have limited interrogation to situations where the record establishes that the police *intended* to elicit a response, an obviously difficult standard. It did not do this either. Instead, the Court held that *Miranda* safeguards are triggered whenever a person is subjected either to express questioning or its "functional equivalent"—"interrogation" includes "any words or actions on the part of the police (other than those normally attendant to arrest and custody) that the police should know are reasonably likely to elicit an incriminating response from the suspect."[50] Although the *Innis* case involved police "speech," the Court's definition embraces police tactics that do not. Thus, the Court seemed to repudiate the position taken by a number of lower courts that confronting a suspect with physical evidence or with an accomplice who has confessed is not "interrogation" within the meaning of *Miranda* because it does not entail *verbal conduct* on the part of the police.[51]

The following year, in *Edwards v. Arizona* (1981),[52] the Court reinvigorated *Miranda* in another important respect by holding that when a suspect asserts his right to *counsel* (as opposed to his right to remain silent), the police cannot "try again."[53] Under these circumstances, a suspect cannot be questioned anew "*until* counsel has been made available to him, *unless* [he] himself *initiates* further communication, exchanges or conversations with the police."[54]

But then Justice Rehnquist's way of thinking about *Miranda* reappeared—first in *New York v. Quarles* (1984) (recognizing a "public safety" exception to *Miranda*) and then, more prominently, in Justice O'Connor's opinion for the Court in *Oregon v. Elstad* (1985). *Elstad* is worth discussing at some length.

Mr. Elstad was implicated in a burglary. The police went to his home. Without advising him of his rights, an officer expressed the belief that Elstad was "involved" in the crime. Elstad replied, "Yes, I was there." He was taken to the police station. This time an officer did read him his rights. He waived them and made a full confession.

Elstad argued that his second confession, although immediately preceded by *Miranda* warnings, was nevertheless the "tainted fruit" of the statement that he had made in his own home, which, it was conceded, was obtained in violation of *Miranda*. The Court disagreed. Elstad's "fruit of the poisonous tree" argument assumed the existence of a constitutional right, but, observed Justice O'Connor for the Court, a failure to give the *Miranda* warnings, when called for, is not in itself a violation of the Fifth Amendment.[55] "[A]bsent deliberately coercive or improper tactics in obtaining the initial statement," wrote O'Connor, "the mere fact that a suspect has made an unwarned admission does not warrant a presumption of compulsion."[56]

I am flabbergasted by this way of looking at *Miranda*. And I make so bold as to say that the author of the *Miranda* opinion would be equally taken aback. Whether Elstad was "in custody" (a precondition to triggering a suspect's *Miranda* rights) when he talked to a police officer in his own living room is questionable. But the state conceded that he was (perhaps because it was eager to reach the question of whether evidence derived from illegally obtained evidence is admissible) and the Court assumed he was. Therefore, the police did violate *Miranda* when they questioned Elstad in his own home. Isn't a violation of *Miranda* itself an "improper tactic"? As for the need to establish actual coercion, *Miranda* assumes that subjecting someone to custodial interrogation without giving him the requisite warnings *necessarily* undermines his ability to express his free will, and amounts to compulsion—and that there is no distinction, for constitutional purposes, between such inherent or presumed compulsion on the one hand and actual compulsion on the other.[57]

I am well aware that it is difficult to get agitated about the particular facts of this case. But *Elstad* is not going to be limited to suspects who make barely incriminating statements (and a four-word statement at that) when they are barely in custody, sitting in their own living rooms at midday. The case is going to apply to situations where the suspect made an unwarned, fairly lengthy, quite detailed confession sitting in the backroom of a police station late at night. And as Justice William J. Brennan (joined by Justice Thurgood Marshall) pointed out in his dissent, the interrogation manuals describe the point of the first admission as the "breakthrough" and the "beachhead."[58]

Derivative Use

Elstad can, of course, be read very narrowly,[59] but I think a supporter of *Miranda* would have to engage in wishful thinking to do so. I once read the *Tucker* case narrowly, but it has become clear that that was wishful thinking. One thing is plain—the *Elstad* majority did not read *Tucker* narrowly.

This is especially clear in Justice O'Connor's treatment of physical or other evidence discovered from a *Miranda*-violative statement. "Since there was no actual infringement of the suspect's constitutional rights [in *Tucker*]," Justice O'Connor tells us in *Elstad*, "the case was not controlled" by the "fruit of the poisonous tree" doctrine.[60] Of course, if you believe *that*, you are not going to apply the doctrine to physical evidence discovered as a result of a *Miranda* violation, any more than you are going to apply it to *any other* "fruit." We *know* that Justice O'Connor herself would not apply the "fruit" doctrine to physical evidence turned up as a result of a *Miranda* violation, for she made that clear in her concurring opinion in the *Quarles* case.[61]

In *Elstad* Justice O'Connor states that the reasoning in *Tucker* "applies with equal force when the alleged 'fruit' of a noncoercive *Miranda* violation is neither a witness nor an article of evidence, but the accused's [second confession]."[62] Notice how that sentence is written—as if the Court had *already held* that the "fruit of the poisonous tree" doctrine does not apply to "fruits" of *Miranda* violations that are live witnesses or articles of evidence and is now simply extending that approach to "second confessions."

Nietzsche once said that the commonest stupidity consists in forgetting what one is trying to do. What the *Miranda* Court was trying to do was take away the police's incentive to exploit people's anxiety, confusion, and ignorance when they interrogate suspects in a way that implies that they have a right to an answer, or at least implies that it will be so much the worse for the suspect if he does not answer. How can we expect the police to comply with *Miranda* when we prohibit only the confessions obtained in violation of that doctrine, but permit the use of everything these confessions bring to light? Police experts themselves acknowledge how often confessions lead to other evidence and how useful that other evidence often is. Indeed, when the police resort to forbidden means to obtain confessions, not infrequently they may do so more for the purpose of discovering clues than for using the confessions themselves.

Permitting the police to make derivative uses of *Miranda* violations would deal that landmark case a heavy blow, but that is not the worst (or, depending upon one's viewpoint, the best) that can be said for the *Tucker-Elstad* way of thinking about *Miranda*. Since the Supreme Court has no supervisory power over *state* criminal justice but can only apply constitutional limitations, if an "ordinary" violation of *Miranda* does not, or at least does not usually, violate the Constitution, where did the Court get the authority to impose *Miranda* on the fifty states?

By disparaging the *Miranda* warnings, by viewing them as only "second-class" prophylactic safeguards and *Miranda* violations as only "second-class" wrongs (if they are "wrongs" at all), language in *Tucker* and the more recent *Quarles* and *Elstad* cases may have prepared the way for the overruling of *Miranda* itself.

ARREST, SEARCH AND SEIZURE

The late Justice Stewart pointed out[63] that there are *two* principal ways to reduce the impact of the rule that evidence seized in violation of the Fourth Amendment may not be used against the victim of the violation: by shrinking the scope of the amendment itself, thereby giving the police more leeway to investigate crime; and by restricting the circumstances in which evidence obtained in violation of the amendment may be kept out of the government's case. Although the Burger Court's rulings on the search-and-seizure field have been somewhat mixed, especially during its "middle phase," overall the Court has significantly reduced the effect of the exclusionary rule in both respects.

Reducing the Scope of the Protections Afforded by the Fourth Amendment Itself

The Fourth Amendment protects "the right of the people to be secure . . . against unreasonable searches and seizures"—i.e., against searches and seizures without probable cause or reasonable grounds to believe that criminal activity is afoot. Perhaps the first thing that strikes one who has observed the Court in recent years is the grudging view the Court has taken of what consitutes a "search" or "seizure" within the meaning of the Fourth Amendment.[64] Consider these recent rulings.

WHAT IS A "SEARCH"?

The totality of bank records provides a kind of current biography of an individual. Nevertheless, *U.S. v. Miller* (1976)[65] tells us that a depositor has no "legitimate expectation of privacy" as to the checks and deposit slips he "voluntarily" conveys to the banks and exposes to their employees in the ordinary course of business. The depositor "assumes the risk," in revealing his affairs to the bank, that they will be conveyed to the government.

A list of numbers dialed from a private phone could also reveal intimate details of a person's life. Yet *Smith v. Maryland* (1979)[66] holds that police use of a pen register (a device that records all numbers dialed from a given phone and the times the numbers were dialed, but does not overhear oral communications) does not constitute a "search" either. Thus, the police need no warrant to use such a device (nor, presumably, "probable cause" or any cause whatsoever). No less than one who opens a bank account, reasoned the Court, one who uses the phone "assumes the risk" that the telephone company will reveal the numbers he dialed to the police.

Continuing further down this path, the Burger Court told us in *United States v. Knotts* (1983)[67] that the monitoring of a suspect for many miles by means of a "beeper" (an electronic tracking device) until his car stopped at a certain cabin in a secluded area amounts to neither a "search" nor a "seizure." Justice Rehnquist's opinion for the Court contains the remarkable statement that "[n]othing in the Fourth Amendment prohibited the police from augmenting the sensory facilities bestowed upon them at birth with such enhancement as science and technology afforded them in this case."[68] I call this a "remarkable statement" because, as pointed out by concurring Justice Stevens,[69] such an assertion seems to conflict directly with the view taken by the Court in the landmark case of *Katz v. U.S.* (1967).[70]

EXCEPTIONS TO THE WARRANT REQUIREMENTS

That an officer is armed with probable cause to believe that criminal activity is afoot may not be enough to satisfy the Fourth Amendment. As a general principle, at least whenever it is practical to do so, the police must obtain permission from a judicial officer—a warrant—in order to conduct a lawful search under the amendment. But a number of exceptions to the search-warrant requirement have developed. The Burger Court's treatment of the two major exceptions—(1) the search incident to a lawful arrest and (2) the *Carroll* doctrine, often called the "automobile exception"[71]—also illustrates how it has cut down the protections provided by the Fourth Amendment.

In a series of cases starting in 1914, the Court carved out an exception to the warrant requirement when the police arrest someone (for which they need no warrant): in making the arrest the police may search the area within the control of the person arrested without a warrant. Limiting this kind of warrantless search to the area within the arrestee's "grabbing distance" would seem to confine the police to a fairly small area. In *New York v. Belton* (1981),[72] however, the Court held that, whether or not there is any reason to believe a car contains evidence of crime, so long as there are adequate grounds to make a lawful custodial arrest of the car's occupants the police may conduct a warrantless search of the entire interior or passenger compartment of the car, including closed containers found within that zone—even after the occupants have been removed from the car and are in handcuffs and surrounded by police officers. This is a massive broadening of the "search incident" exception. As a result, warned concurring Justice Stevens, an arresting officer may find reason to take a minor traffic offender into custody "whenever he sees an interesting looking briefcase or package in a vehicle that has been stopped for a traffic violation."[73]

The *Carroll* doctrine, a judicially created exception to the warrant requirement, permits a warrantless search of the entire vehicle, including the car trunk. As it was originally understood when it was created in 1925, and for most of its life, the doctrine allowed police to search a car without a warrant only when there were both (1) probable cause to believe the car contained evidence of crime and (2) "exigent circumstances," making it impractical to obtain a search warrant.[74] In the 1970s, however, the Burger Court virtually eliminated the exigent-circumstances requirement. Thus, in essence, the doctrine became simply a "probable cause" exception to the warrant requirement for automobiles. Even cars that had been removed to a police station could be subjected to warrantless searches.[75] In the 1982 *Ross* case,[76] the Court further extended the *Carroll* doctrine, using it to sustain the warrantless search of a "movable container" found in a locked car trunk.

PROBABLE CAUSE

The heart of the Fourth Amendment is "probable cause": the police may not restrict a person's liberty or invade his privacy on a hunch or mere suspicion; they must have "probable cause"—i.e., good cause or substantial reasons to believe that a person has committed, or is committing, a crime.

The Burger Court's treatment of the "probable cause" standard merits attention. In *Illinois v. Gates* (1983),[77] the Court abandoned the existing probable-cause structure in favor of a "totality of the circumstances" test. The *Gates* Court stressed that "probable cause" is a "practical, common-sense" concept, a "fluid concept . . . not readily, or even usefully, reduced to a neat set of legal rules."[78] The Court made it fairly clear, I think, that "probable cause" is *something less* than "more-probable-than-not" (although how much less is anything but clear). Indeed, at one point the Court told us that "probable cause requires only a probability or *substantial chance* of criminal activity."[79]

After *Gates*, it does not require very much to issue a warrant, but it takes even less to uphold one on review. All that is needed is a "substantial basis" for a "fair probability"—or "substantial chance"— "that contraband or evidence of a crime will be found in a particular place."[80]

CONSENT

A final example should suffice to illustrate how the Burger Court diminished Fourth Amendment protections.

The simplest way for the police to avoid Fourth Amendment problems is to obtain a "consent" to what otherwise would be an unconstitutional search or seizure. Thus, the scope of the Fourth Amendment will vary greatly depending on how easy it is for the police to establish "consent." *Schneckloth v. Bustamonte* (1973)[81] made it all too easy. According to the *Schneckloth* majority, a person may effectively consent to a search even though he was never informed—and the government has failed to demonstrate that he was aware—that he had the right to refuse the officer's "request." After *Schneckloth*, the criminal-justice system, in one important respect at least, can (to borrow a phrase from the 1964 *Escobedo* case) "depend for its continued effectiveness on the citizens' abdication through unawareness of their constitutional rights."[82]

Narrowing the Thrust of the Exclusionary Rule

It is a truism that rights are only as meaningful as the remedies for their violation. The Burger Court not only contracted our rights to be free of excessive police intrusions of our privacy, but weakened the remedies for proven violation of them.

The primary remedy for violation of the Fourth Amendment is the exclusion of evidence illegally obtained. In a recent case, Justice Stevens thought that the Court should expressly address the question of whether the exclusionary rule operated in juvenile delinquency proceedings to bar evidence unlawfully seized by school officials. For him the answer was clear: "[T]he application of the exclusionary rule is a simple corollary of the principle that 'all evidence obtained by searches and seizures in violation of the Constitution is, by that same authority, inadmissible in a state court' " (quoting from *Mapp v. Ohio* [1961]).[83]

Unfortunately, it is no longer so simple. It no longer can be said that all evidence obtained in violation of the Constitution "is, by that same authority, inadmissible." Now, there must be a "balancing of competing interests," and a "cost-benefit analysis" still has to be worked out.

COST-BENEFIT

Although one would gain little inkling of this from recent majority opinions of the Burger Court, originally and for much of its life the federal exclusionary rule, first promulgated in the famous 1914 *Weeks* case,[84] rested not on an empirical proposition that it actually deterred the police from unconstitutional searches by denying them the fruits of their illegality but on what might be called a "principled basis."[85] That principle was to avoid "sanctioning" or "ratifying" the unconstitutional police conduct that produced the proffered evidence, to keep the judicial process from being contaminated by partnership in police misconduct, to prevent the government whose agents violated the Constitution from being in any better position than the government whose agents obeyed it, and ultimately, to assure the police and the public alike that the Court took constitutional rights seriously.[86] I believe this is the proper way to think about, and to apply, the exclusionary rule.

The framers of the exclusionary rule may have expected, or at least hoped, to influence police behavior, but there is no suggestion in any of the early cases that the rule's survival was to depend on proof that it significantly influences police behavior.

What might be called the "original understanding" of the exclusionary rule is, I believe, the correct one. Although I am convinced that the exclusionary rule does significantly affect police conduct,[87] I do not think that the rule must be justified by, or applied on the basis of, its deterrent effect on police officials.

But ways of thinking about the exclusionary rule have changed. The "deterrence" rationale, and its concomitant "interest balancing," bloomed in *U.S. v. Calandra* (1974),[88] the most important exclusionary-rule case to be decided in the 1970s. In ruling that a grand jury witness may not refuse to answer questions on the ground that they are based on the fruits of an unlawful search, the Court characterized the exclusionary rule—one might say *disparaged* it—as a "judicially created remedy designed to safeguard Fourth Amendment rights generally through its deterrent effect" rather than "a personal constitutional right of the party aggrieved."

Thus, whether the exclusionary rule should be applied "presents a question, not of rights but of remedies"—a question to be answered by weighing the "likely 'costs' " of the rule against its "likely 'benefits.' "[89]

The exclusionary rule lost in *Calandra*; in *Stone v. Powell* (1976),[90] greatly limiting a state prisoner's ability to get habeas corpus relief on search-and-seizure grounds; in *United States v. Janis* (1976),[91] holding that the rule's deterrent purpose would not be served by barring evidence obtained illegally by state police from federal civil tax proceedings; and it lost in the 1984 *Leon* and *Sheppard* cases,[92] adopting a "reasonable, good faith" modification of the exclusionary rule, at least in search-warrant cases. By "deconstitutionalizing" it— by "shift[ing] the scope of the debate from arguments about constitutional law and judicial integrity (where they had lost) to arguments about the empirical data"[93]—the critics of the exclusionary rule won some important victories. This is hardly surprising.

The costs of the exclusionary rule are immediately apparent—the "freeing" of a "plainly guilty" heroin dealer—but the benefits of the rule are only conjectural. It is never easy to prove a negative, and police compliance with the exclusionary rule produces a nonevent that is not directly observable—it consists of *not* carrying out an illegal search. Moreover, if one is supposed to "balance" the "competing interests" before deciding whether to apply the exclusionary rule, how does one do so without measuring imponderables or comparing incommensurables? How does one "balance" "privacy" (or "individual liberty" or "personal dignity") against the interest in suppressing crime, or "law and order" or the "general welfare"?

Since "privacy" or "liberty" and "police efficiency" in combatting crime are different kinds of interests, how can they be compared quantitatively, unless the judge has some standard independent of both to which they can be referred? If the standard is not to be the Fourth Amendment, which embodies the judgment that securing all citizens "in their persons, houses, papers, and effects, against unreasonable searches and seizures" outweighs society's interest in combatting crime, then what is it to be?

It is difficult to read the Burger Court's search-and-seizure cases without coming away with the feeling that it did its "balancing" in an empirical fog, by "intuition," or, still worse, by "predisposition." It is hard not to conclude that the cost-benefit analysis—although it sounds objective, even "scientific"—simply gives one back whatever values or assumptions one feeds into it. Thus, if, as the Burger Court did, one calls the benefits of the exclusionary rule "speculative" or "uncertain at best," and characterizes the rule's social costs as "well known" and "long recognized," the outcome is quite predictable.

Yet is not all the talk about "the substantial costs of *the exclusionary rule*" misleading? Is it not the Fourth Amendment itself, rather than the exclusionary rule, that imposes these costs? The "substantial costs" said to be exacted by the exclusionary rule[94] would also be exacted by any other means of eliminating significant incentives for making illegal searches—by any other means of enforcing the Fourth Amendment that worked. A society whose officials obey the Fourth Amendment in the first place (because of effective self-discipline or an effective tort remedy) "pays the same 'price' " as the society whose officials cannot use the evidence they obtained because they obtained it in violation of the Fourth Amendment: both societies convict fewer criminals.

If a society relies on the exclusionary rule to enforce the Fourth Amendment, the convictions of some "guilty" defendants will indeed be overturned. If a society relies on an alternative means of enforcing the Fourth Amendment, one that critics of the exclusionary rule have assured us would be at least equally effective, then " 'guilty' defendants will not be set free—but only because they will not be arrested [unlawfully] in the first place."[95] The only time the Fourth Amendment would not impose "substantial societal costs," as defined by the Burger Court, would be if it was converted into "an unenforced honor code that the police could follow in their discretion."[96]

"GOOD FAITH"

The "deterrence" rationale (and its concomitant cost-benefit analysis) dominated the Burger Court's way of thinking about the exclusionary rule for more than a decade. Yet until July 1984, when the Court handed down *U.S. v. Leon* and *Massachusetts v. Sheppard*, one could still say that the Burger Court's "deconstitutionalization" of the exclusionary rule had only narrowed the rule's thrust in "peripheral" or "collateral" settings, such as grand jury proceedings, civil tax proceedings, and the use of illegally obtained evidence for impeachment purposes. The rule had not been affected in its central application: the prosecution's case against a victim of a Fourth Amendment violation. Indeed, earlier Burger Court cases gave reason to think that at least in its central application the exclusionary rule would be spared the ordeal of being subjected to "interest-balancing" or "cost-benefit" analysis, of having to "pay its way." But this was not to be.

In *Leon* the Burger Court culminated its "cost-benefit" or "balancing" approach to the Fourth Amendment exclusionary rule by "conclud[ing] that the marginal or nonexistent benefits produced by suppressing evidence obtained in objectively reasonable [but mistaken] reliance on a subsequently invalidated search warrant cannot justify the substantial cost of exclusion."[97] Although the *Leon* opinion may appear to be little more than a routine application of the "cost-benefit" approach utilized in earlier cases, this appearance is misleading. The earlier cases were based on the assumption that the exclusionary rule—fully applicable in a criminal prosecution against the direct victim of a Fourth Amendment violation—need not also be applied in certain "collateral" or "peripheral" contexts because no significant *additional* increment of deterrence was considered likely.

Even if, as a majority of the Court apparently believed, the police were hobbled by rigid and technical warrant procedures prior to the 1982–83 term, the Court seems to have engaged in "overkill" or "doublekill" from that point on. By diluting the "probable cause" standard in *Gates* and, a year later, establishing a "reasonable mistake" or "good faith" exception to the exclusionary rule (at least in search-warrant cases), the Court "killed one bird with two stones."

There is much to be said for confining the "reasonable good faith" exception to the warrant setting, and some of the *Leon* opinion supports this view.[98] But *Leon* must be read against the backdrop of the previous decade, when the Court expressed growing hostility to the exclusionary rule, and when the Court, and individual justices in separate opinions, voiced growing doubts that "the extreme sanction of exclusion," as the Court twice called it in *Leon*,[99] is appropriate or can "pay its way" in any setting, let alone a setting where the Fourth Amendment violations are neither deliberate nor "substantial."

The majority opinion in *Leon* explicitly stated that the cost-benefit balancing in which the Court had engaged for years "forcefully suggests"[100] and "provides strong support"[101] for the result it reached in *Leon*. In the future, I fear, the Rehnquist Court may say that that same cost-benefit balancing supports a "good faith" exception across the board. After years and years of talk about a "good faith" or "reasonable mistake" exception to the exclusionary rule, it is hard to believe that the Court finally reached out to adopt such an exception only to limit it to the tiny percentage of police searches conducted pursuant to warrants.

On the same day the *Leon* opinion was handed down, its author, Justice Byron White, this time dissenting in *Lopez-Mendoza*,[102] described *Leon* as follows: "In *United States v. Leon* we have held that the exclusionary rule is not applicable when officers are acting in objective good faith. Thus, if the [Immigration and Naturalization Service] agents neither knew nor should have known that they were acting contrary to the dictates of the Fourth Amendment, evidence will not be suppressed even if it is held that their conduct was illegal."[103] The *Lopez-Mendoza* majority held that the exclusionary rule should not be applied at all in civil deportation proceedings; dissenting Justice White maintained that it should be applied, just as it should be in "ordinary criminal proceedings," "when evidence has been obtained by deliberate violations of the Fourth Amendment or by conduct a reasonably competent officer would know is contrary to the Fourth Amendment."[104]

True, Justice Stevens, who filed a separate dissent in *Lopez-Mendoza*, pointed out that "the Court has not yet held that the rule of *United States v. Leon* has any application to warrantless searches"[105] (and thus did not join the portion of Justice White's opinion relying on that case), but Stevens was the only member of the Court to make this point in *Lopez-Mendoza*. Justice Stevens may want to limit *Leon* to search-warrant cases, but I do not think he has four other votes. I am afraid that Justice White does.

A word more about *Lopez-Mendoza*. In some respects this case is more ominous for proponents of the exclusionary rule than *Leon* or *Sheppard*. Although Justice O'Connor, writing for the majority, acknowledged that "the arresting officer's primary objective, in practice, will be to use evidence in the civil deportation proceeding" and that "the agency officials who effect the unlawful arrest are the same officials who subsequently bring the deportation action,"[106] she concluded nevertheless that the exclusionary rule was inapplicable to deportation proceedings.

The opinion pointed to a number of factors that "significantly reduce the likely deterrent value of the exclusionary rule in a civil deportation proceeding,"[107] but these factors apply to ordinary criminal prosecutions as well. Even if the evidence produced by illegal arrests was excluded, observed Justice O'Connor, deportation proceedings would still be possible if lawful evidence was sufficient to support deportation. But it is also true that even if the fruits of illegal police action were suppressed, criminal convictions would still be possible if the remaining lawful evidence sufficed to support a guilty verdict. The Court noted, too, that the great majority of illegal aliens agree to voluntary deportation without a hearing. But again, the great majority of criminal defendants plead guilty without going to trial.

"Perhaps most important," observed the *Lopez-Mendoza* opinion, "the INS has its own comprehensive scheme for deterring Fourth Amendment violations by its officers," "has developed rules restricting stop, interrogation, and arrest practices," and "has in place a procedure for investigating and punishing immigration officers who commit Fourth Amendment violations."[108] Yet the Court did not cite a single instance in which the scheme has been invoked. And the FBI and every major police department also have their "own schemes" for deterring Fourth Amendment violations, as well as rules governing, and restricting, arrest and search-and-seizure practices. Moreover, each major police department also has in place—at least on paper— a procedure for investigating and punishing its transgressing officers. If, as the Burger Court told us in *Lopez-Mendoza*, the INS's "own scheme" for complying with the Fourth Amendment reduces the deterrent value of the exclusionary rule in deportation proceedings,[109] why doesn't the existence of a police department's "own scheme" for dealing with Fourth Amendment violations similarly weaken the case for the exclusionary rule in ordinary criminal proceedings?

THE FUTURE OF *MIRANDA* AND THE FOURTH AMENDMENT EXCLUSIONARY RULE

The reasoning the Burger Court used in Fourth Amendment and confession cases outruns the results it reached. If, as the Court has repeatedly told us, a mere violation of *Miranda* is not a violation of the Constitution, then the Supreme Court must have gone awry in the *Miranda* case itself when it imposed the new confession doctrine on the states. For if a confession obtained without giving a suspect the *Miranda* warnings does not infringe on the self-incrimination clause *unless it is accompanied by actual coercion*, then why are the state courts not free to admit all confessions not the product of actual coercion? Moreover, if, as the Court told us, any rule that excludes probative and reliable evidence must "pay its way" by deterring official lawlessness[110] and if, as it also told us, the deterrent effect of the exclusionary rule has never been established (to the satisfaction of the Burger Court, at any rate),[111] then why stop with only a modification of the exclusionary rule? Why not abolish the rule altogether?

If law were entirely a syllogism, it would follow that the Rehnquist Court will soon finish off both *Miranda* and the Fourth Amendment exclusionary rule. Nevertheless, I do not think that at the present time (the fall of 1986), a majority of the Court is prepared to overrule *Miranda* or get rid of the exclusionary rule altogether. While Chief Justice Rehnquist, and perhaps Justice Antonin Scalia as well, might welcome such results, those members of the Court who may be called the "swing justices"—Justices White, Harry Blackmun, and Lewis Powell—I think would not. The powerful intellect and considerable persuasiveness of Rehnquist and Scalia may have an important impact on unknown future justices, but not, I think, on such independent-minded and battle-scarred veterans as White, Blackmun, and Powell.

In various Burger Court opinions, these "swing justices" may have gone along with the reasoning that, taken to its logical conclusion, would seem to lead to the demise of *Miranda* and the exclusionary rule, but I doubt very much that they will allow this reasoning to be applied "to the limits of its logic."[112] I think rather that these justices are prepared to "live with" what they would probably call a "pruned" exclusionary rule and a "workable" Fourth Amendment (and what I would call a "battered" exclusionary rule and a "shrunken" Fourth Amendment). I believe these pivotal justices are even more willing to put up with the *Miranda* doctrine now that it has been more or less limited to the police station or an equivalent setting[113] and subdued in other ways, especially if the Court continues to view the decision as a serious effort to strike a proper balance between the need for police questioning and the importance of protecting a suspect against impermissible compulsion.[114]

The trouble is (from the vantage point of a Warren Court admirer at any rate) that these justices, and, of course, the present Court's staunchest defenders of *Miranda* and the exclusionary rule (Justices Brennan, Marshall, and Stevens) will not be with us forever. And the Burger Court's "deconstitutionalization" of *Miranda* and the Fourth Amendment exclusionary rule will make it relatively easy for new justices to abolish *Miranda* and/or the exclusionary rule—to carry the Burger Court's characterization of these doctrines to "the limits of its logic." New, yet unnamed justices will feel more comfortable doing so, and it will be more respectable to do so, because the Court has stripped these doctrines of their constitutional bases in recent years. The reasoning of the Burger Court, whatever reservations some justices who concurred in that reasoning may have had about its ultimate reach, has a life of its own.

Now that the Fourth Amendment exclusionary rule rests on an "empirical proposition" rather than on a "principled basis," it is especially vulnerable. The fact that the Burger Court has finally carved out a "good faith" exception to the exclusionary rule in its central application, together with the cost-benefit balancing it used to reach that result, renders the rule almost defenseless against congressional efforts to repeal it, most likely by a statute that purports to replace the rule with what we shall be assured is an "effective" alternative remedy.

As Justice Brennan recently observed, "[a] doctrine that is explained as if it were an empirical proposition but for which there is only limited empirical support" is "an easy mark for critics."[115] The exclusionary rule has many critics in the Congress and the state legislatures, and these critics will be quick to assert that the legislature has far greater institutional competence to evaluate the "costs" and "benefits" of suppressing reliable physical evidence than do the courts.

If the Court's current way of thinking about the exclusionary rule is not wrong—and I believe that it *is* wrong—then I fear the rule's many critics in the legislature are right.

·10·

On Death Row,
the Wait Continues

MICHAEL MELTSNER

In the years following World War II, the number of executions of murderers in this country, as well as in Canada, Great Britain, and Western Europe, decreased steadily. One reason for the decline was a public loss of faith in the utility of the death penalty to deter murder more effectively than would a long prison sentence. Few criminals bent on killing believe they will be caught; most homicides are the product of intrafamilial passions or psychological pressures that remain unaffected by the dimly perceived prospect of a death sentence. Equally indifferent to capital punishment are professional killers and would-be terrorists. Whether in theory more frequent executions would protect human life, jurors recommend the death penalty in only about 10 percent of the cases where it is an available sentence. Thus, even a calculating killer has little reason to hesitate out of fear for his life. In the United States, in addition to skepticism about the likelihood of the death penalty, as administered, reducing the murder rate, 1960s civil rights activity provided another factor: greater sensitivity to the effects of poverty and race in capital sentencing: for the same crime, blacks stand a far greater chance than whites of receiving death sentences.

In 1972 such themes were the background for *Furman v. Georgia*,[1] in which the Supreme Court startled the legal world by holding that the procedure for selecting those condemned to die violated the Constitution. For decades, juries and judges had been given complete discretion, unfettered by legal standards, when deciding whether convicted murderers were to be executed or sentenced to prison. In contrast to the complex rules governing the determination of guilt, sentencing was literally lawless. The result was a pattern of "arbitrary" and "freakish" sentencing decisions that, according to the Court, amounted to cruel and unusual punishment in violation of the Eighth Amendment. With a stroke, *Furman* invalidated virtually all existing death-penalty laws and removed the threat of execution for more than six hundred men and a handful of women.

Those in the *Furman* majority—all had served under Chief Justice Earl Warren—could not agree on the basis of the ruling, and the four Nixon appointees (Chief Justice Warren Burger and Justices Lewis Powell, Harry Blackmun, and William Rehnquist) dissented. Justices William Brennan and Thurgood Marshall thought the death penalty unconstitutional per se, but because Justices Potter Stewart, Byron White, and William Douglas focused on the means employed to select the condemned rather than on capital punishment itself, the states remained free to enact death-sentence laws. One possible response by the states would have been to spell out the aggravating and mitigating factors that juries and judges should consider in deciding who lived and who died. Another would have been to eliminate sentencing laws that provided no guidance as to which factors merited execution, so that juries were unable to winnow out the "worst" offenders.

In July 1976, the Court decided five cases involving versions of both those schemes. In *Gregg v. Georgia*[2] and two companion cases, it ruled that "guided discretion" provided sufficient protection against arbitrary infliction of death if judges or jurors had been told the rules governing the life-death choice and had an opportunity to hear background facts about defendants and their crimes. From this affirmation of capital punishment as constitutionally permissible, only Justices Brennan and Marshall dissented. In *Woodson v. North Carolina* (1976)[3] and *Roberts v. Louisiana* (1977),[4] a different lineup rejected the designation of certain crimes as carrying mandatory death penalties. Justices Stewart, Powell, and John Paul Stevens, joined by Brennan and Marshall, concluded that "human dignity" required consideration of the "character of the individual offender and the circumstances of the particular offense" before "imposing the ultimate penalty of death." In short, seven justices thought "guided discretion" enough to legitimate the death penalty; four thought capital punishment permissible even if the death sentence followed automatically upon conviction; two rejected the death penalty regardless of the crime or the criminal.

During the next six years, the Burger Court refined the *Gregg* standards. In 1977 and 1982, it held that the death penalty may not be imposed for rape[5] or on a defendant who participated in a crime in which someone was killed but in which the defendant did not commit the murder or intend to do so.[6] Other procedural rules were mandated: mitigating factors must be considered by the sentencing judge or jury;[7] a death sentence may not be based on material not revealed to the defendant;[8] because of the prohibition of double jeopardy, the death penalty may not be imposed in a retrial if the defendant received a noncapital punishment in the first trial.[9]

But by 1983, the Burger Court majority began to lose patience with the long delays in executions and insisted that death sentences be carried out. In a particularly harsh outburst, the Chief Justice lashed out at lawyers who persisted in bringing appeals to save their clients, charging they were engaged in "calculated efforts to frustrate valid [death-penalty] judgments," and adding that "at some point there must be finality."[10] In the last three years, stays of execution have become difficult to obtain.

Although the Court continued to embrace the theory of guided discretion enunciated in *Gregg*, it steadfastly refused to consider how that theory works in practice—whether tightening procedures had eliminated the arbitrary and freakish sentences that were held unconstitutional in *Furman*. More recently, it even showed itself willing to allow a good deal of error in the sentencing process. In a 1983 case the Court approved a special summary procedure for death-penalty cases, leading Justice Marshall to complain that the Court would "afford less consideration to an appeal in which a man's life is at stake than to an appeal challenging an ordinary money judgment."[11]

The Court also declined to weigh powerful evidence that race or fortuitous circumstances such as geography determine who is sentenced to death. The justices showed a strong unwillingness to postpone execution dates and took a strict view of federal habeas corpus petitions by death-row inmates. In *Pulley v. Harris* (1984),[12] the Court decided that nothing in the Constitution requires state courts to rule out a death sentence merely because a lesser sentence had been imposed on someone similarly culpable of a similar crime. The opinion, written by Justice White, who had voted in *Furman* to declare state laws invalid because lower courts had rarely chosen the worst criminals to die, marked a retreat to yesteryear.

Why was the Burger Court unwilling to go further than it had in *Furman*, either by putting teeth in its guided-discretion standard or by abolishing capital punishment? In the mid-1960s the anti–death penalty movement suggested to the Court two possible ways toward abolition (short of a single dramatic decision ending capital punishment). One was to tighten procedures to the point where only a very few highly culpable criminals would be sentenced to die. Abolitionist lawyers believed that making such distinctions would be so difficult, cumbersome, and costly that capital punishment would eventually be abandoned. This strict-procedures approach had the virtue of not exposing the Supreme Court to the intense criticism—not to mention provoking efforts to amend the Constitution—that would surely have followed total abolition, but it left until another day the question of whether the Court would accept the new death-penalty laws the states would enact.

The other possibility was to recognize that capital punishment in the United States has always been linked to race. Lawyers presented both the Warren and Burger Courts with opportunities to make anti–capital punishment decisions on the grounds that it was impossible to eliminate race as a decisional factor in the death-sentencing process. But the Court always ducked that argument. In *Furman* only Justice Douglas emphasized the disproportionate number of death sentences handed out to blacks. When the Court ruled in *Coker v. Georgia* that the death penalty was a cruel and unusual punishment for the rape of an adult woman, it ignored evidence showing that the death penalty for rape had been given almost exclusively to blacks who had raped whites. Sentencing discretion may have been narrowed under post-*Furman* statutes, but despite a new set of rules, judges and jurors still reach discriminatory results by valuing the life of black and white victims differently.

One characteristic of recent death-penalty litigation is the indifference of the courts to social-science evidence showing that sentencing guidelines, separate sentencing hearings, and appellate review of death sentences have failed to prevent arbitrariness. In Georgia, for example, the state is nine times more likely to send to death the killer of a white than the killer of a black. Murders that take place in the bedroom suburbs are more likely to result in capital punishment than killings that take place in urban areas. Forty-nine of the fifty-four executions that took place between 1977 and March 1986 occurred in southern states. Race is a more significant prediction of the death penalty than the use of a handgun, the relationship between murderer and victim, or the age of the victim or defendant. Even though a higher proportion of blacks than whites are murdered, it is whites, not blacks, who receive such protection as proponents claim for the death penalty. Since 1976, Louisiana has executed more people per capita than any other state: a computer analysis of 504 Louisiana death cases led the *New Orleans Times-Picayune* to conclude that "Race, locale and luck often play a larger role in determining a criminal's fate than the facts of a crime or the character of the criminal."

Researchers have found a similar pattern in other states. The discretion that abides at key points in the trial process—what to charge, whether to plea-bargain, whether to convict of a lesser crime or sentence to prison—is still employed, consciously or unconsciously, to favor whites. But a ruling on this ground—saying, essentially, that the judicial system (including thousands of jurors) has been guilty of institutional racism—was unpalatable to the justices of the Burger Court.

The Burger Court chose in *Furman* to exercise one of what the late constitutional expert Alexander Bickel called the "passive virtues," attempting to honor both principle and prudence by wiping the statute books clean of death laws but allowing the political process to restore them in revised form if there was a popular will to do so. Its approach mediated, in Bickel's phrase, between the "ultimates of legitimation and invalidation." The Warren Court had done as much with the famous "deliberate speed" formula in the school segregation cases. Nothing was the same after *Brown v. Board of Education* (1954)[13] because, hesitant and partial as the Court's support was, powerful forces rallied to reject racial bias in education, employment, and other areas.

Things turned out differently for the death penalty. Several justices reportedly believed capital punishment would wither away after *Furman* and welcomed removal of the burden of making life-and-death decisions. But by choosing to avoid the racial issue in favor of a ruling based on criminal procedure, the Court stimulated a public debate over deterrence and just deserts rather than discrimination. Abolitionists lost the debate. Soon after *Furman*, California voters amended the state constitution to overrule an abolition decision of the state supreme court; Massachusetts later followed California's lead; and more than thirty-seven states soon enacted new death-penalty laws. Over 1,650 men and women now wait on death row. Anywhere from fifty to one hundred of them may be executed in the next two years.

In a century of world wars, genocide, and terrorism, of Hiroshima and political murder, in a country where homicide is commonplace, efforts to abolish one form of killing through the courts seem almost romantic. If violence is everywhere, why should judges in particular stand against the crowd? Execution is one end of a bureaucratic process that fragments responsibility. The fear of crime is widespread and the value of a killer's life debased. Of what great cost is it to add a few more bodies to death's already bloated count?

The Burger Court's record, however, is no less disappointing for being an understandable reaction to world events and national values. What other government institution with comparable power can be expected to inquire calmly into the relationship between crime and race, punishment and conduct, private and state-inflicted violence? Where else in public life are we likely to find a measured view of human nature that permits rejection of execution despite outrage at violence, despite identification with victims, past and future—a moral calculus that does not confuse understandable feelings of revenge with a need to behave monstrously?

Such attitudes are hard to find in legislative chambers and executive offices, especially when the voices of tiny constituencies favoring abolition are overwhelmed by polls that make it all too clear where most voters stand. The quality of legislative debate over capital punishment runs from lackluster and uninformed to knee-jerk and demagogic. But courts are supposed to be different. Judges are protected from the electorate; it is their job to consider matters of principle and equity, to take the longer view, even if that means opposing the popular will. And many judges have enough experience in the operation of criminal law to know that the uselessness of the death penalty as a crime-prevention device is matched only by its capacity to weave racial and class distinctions into the fabric of the law. Can one have faith in the reliability of any capital sentencing selection process?

Alas, the Burger years were characterized not only by a reluctance to resist public pressure but by a lack of interest in reviewing the implications of trying to electrocute or gas away the problem of violence. Warren-era justices attempted to facilitate the elimination of a penalty that under modern conditions has more sacrificial and psychological than penological consequences. They began a process that could have confined capital punishment to an exceedingly small set of cases. The Burger Court first halted and then reversed that process.

The latest example is the Court's ruling in *Lockhart v. McCree* (1986)[14] upholding the constitutionality of a procedure known as "death qualification," by which prospective jurors who state that they will not consider a death penalty are excused from service—not just from the phase of a capital trial that deals with sentencing but from the determination of guilt as well, even if they state they can be impartial determining guilt or innocence. In *McCree* the defendant argued that a jury purged of death-penalty opponents is a biased jury, that the jurors who remain favor the prosecution. In 1968, the Supreme Court refused to rule on this question, because the evidence then available about the attitudes of jurors was too slim to establish that the purged jury was more likely to convict. In part because of the attention received by the Court's decision in what is known as the *Witherspoon* case,[15] a number of investigators directed their attention to the question. Lawyers challenging the impartiality of "death qualified" juries have put before the courts a half-dozen empirical studies supporting their argument. These studies range from opinion polls to interviews with jurors to responses based on video-taped reenactments of murder trials. In one study, for example, 288 eligible jurors watched a video reenactment of a murder trial. "Death qualified" jurors voted to convict 25 percent more often than those who refused to consider the death penalty and also voted significantly heavier degrees of guilt (murder as opposed to manslaughter). Rejection of the significance of these studies by the Court in *Lockhart* may mark the last chance for a constitutional argument that will limit the scope of the new death-penalty laws.

The extent to which the criminal-justice system ought to tolerate partiality arising from preexisting attitudes was the specific question in the *Lockhart* case, but of even greater importance for the future of capital punishment is the extent to which the Supreme Court will be responsive to empirical research. Will the Court ever monitor the actual behavior of the states under the death laws passed in response to its 1976 decisions approving limited capital sentencing? The Burger

Court rejected efforts to abolish the death penalty on human-rights grounds while still asserting that high standards of reliability and fairness must govern the death-case process. The only resource left to death-row inmates is to prove that the reliability and fairness of the new law is more theoretical than real. The next round will probably be fought more with statistics than appeals to the sanctity of life—one of the first cases the new Supreme Court will hear involves a claim that the death penalty is imposed more frequently when the victim of the crime is white than when the victim is black, even though a higher percentage of blacks are murdered.[16]

It is acceptable that the Supreme Court show itself to be pragmatic and even, in a sense, political. When life is on the scale, however, we have a right to expect something more. With respect to capital punishment, "something more" means confronting the actual results of post-*Furman* death sentencing and requiring that the states either give up racial and other arbitrary selection of the condemned or give up the death penalty. This agenda awaits another Supreme Court, perhaps another century.

· 11 ·

The Burger Court and the Prisoner

HERMAN SCHWARTZ

The Burger Court's treatment of the rights of prisoners was of a piece with the rest of its record: much good, much bad, and on balance, probably beneficial.

This last judgment will probably come as a surprise to current prisoner-rights activists, who are staggering from a series of recent decisions that seem to shut the courthouse door to prisoner complaints about our seemingly unchangeable dungeons. But to see where we are, we must remember where we were.

It may be difficult to recall just how appalling America's prisons used to be. Though still dreadful by any civilized standard, they are better than they were. In Arkansas, a federal court in 1965 found that prisoners had been forced to work beyond their capacity, often in freezing weather wearing only light clothing and sometimes without shoes; they were whipped with a strap on bare skin; armed "trusty" prisoners were in charge of security, and meted out punishment to other prisoners; torture was rife—trusties at the Tucker prison attached telephone wires to other prisoners' genitals and administered electric shocks (the "Tucker telephone"); homosexual rape, stabbings, and deadly fights were commonplace; there was widespread, open consumption of liquor and drugs; isolation cells were filthy and dangerously unsanitary; medical care was negligible; the kitchens were filthy.[1] In Mississippi, a federal judge in 1972 found racial segregation and discrimination, a state-condemned sanitation system that included open sewage breeding rats and vermin and that contaminated the drinking water, exposed and frayed electrical wires, inadequate heating facilities and broken windows; in one barracks, three oil drums cut in half served as washbasins for eighty men.[2]

These conditions were not peculiar to the more benighted parts of our country. A prisoner in upstate New York, one of the coldest parts of the country, was stripped naked during the winter, put in an unheated isolation cell with open windows, and left without soap, towel, toilet paper, or a toothbrush. Medical care throughout the New York system was grossly inadequate; punishments included bread-and-water diets. The report on the 1971 Attica uprising found that "for inmates, 'correction' meant daily degradation and humiliation."[3] In Rhode Island, as late as 1977, a visitor to the state prison found walkways and walls encrusted with dried excrement, maddening noise levels, fire hazards, and unhealthy plumbing. Persons awaiting trial were kept in this institution, even though they had not been found guilty of anything and were presumed innocent.[4]

The list of horrors extended to less physical matters as well. No books relating to race or psychology, or that were in any way displeasing to the largely rural mind of jail administrators were permitted. Charles Silberman's *Crisis in Black and White* was kept out of New York state prisons, as were Nikki Giovanni's poetry and an article in *The New York Times Sunday Magazine* relating to the death of George Jackson. The censors often didn't even read the books: *White Niggers of Quebec*, which dealt with Quebecois separatism, was excluded because the title misled the censor into thinking it was about black activism. Mail was read and often stopped, even mail to lawyers; one reason given prisoners in New York state prisons for this interference was, "You did not stick to your subject." Harmless religious practices were forbidden. Family visits had to be conducted through a wire or glass screen, allowing no physical contact, with communication possible only through a voice-powered phone; they were often preceded and followed by humiliating strip searches of the inmate that investigated "mouth, ears, hair, the bottom of his feet, under his arms, around the testicles and in the rectum"[5] and, for female inmates, the vagina. In one particularly bizarre case, a blanket hand-knitted by a prisoner's fiancée could not be given to him because it contained a blue square design—"blue is the guards' color," a prison guard told me; in another of my cases, an inmate lost thirty days' "good time" and was put in solitary confinement for writing in a personal diary—which he did not circulate—that the deputy warden was a "cigar-chomping S.O.B." and that the inmate would like to "ball the nurse." Other state and local jails were as bad or worse. Everything, no matter how trivial or innocuous, was justified in the name of "security."

Few people knew or cared. Prisons were deliberately placed in distant rural areas, where decent folks could forget about them and their troublesome inhabitants. This usually helped the local economy, but created fertile ground for enmity between an overwhelmingly white rural guard corps and an increasingly black and urban prison population.

The federal courts were particularly indifferent, and adopted a "hands-off policy"—they didn't want to mix into prison administration and especially not in state prisons. Judicial attitudes had not changed much since a Virginia judge ruled in 1871 that a prisoner was "a slave of the state," although sometimes a court did purport to recognize more.[6]

During the Warren years, the Supreme Court did little to advance prisoners' rights—whatever action there was occurred mostly in the lower courts—though it also did nothing to curtail them. In 1968, for example, the Court summarily upheld a lower-court decision that struck down statutorily imposed racial segregation in prisons. And in 1969, the Court required Tennessee to allow one prisoner to help another with a legal petition "if there were no reasonable alternative." Perhaps most important in the long run, the Court ruled that a prisoner need not go through the state administrative process before filing a federal civil rights suit.[7]

In the fall of 1969, when Warren Burger became chief justice, there was no reason to think that any major change in the judicial attitude toward prisons was impending, certainly not at the Supreme Court level. We were pleasantly surprised. During the next few years, it seemed as if prisoners couldn't lose in the Supreme Court.

Several seemingly technical cases dealing with access to the courts were perhaps most important. In a case unanimously decided without even a signed opinion, *Haines v. Kerner* (1972), the Court made it possible for prisoners to file their own suits, a necessity given the scarcity of lawyers available for such litigation, by insisting that the suits not be dismissed unless it appeared "beyond a reasonable doubt that plaintiff can prove no set of facts in support of his claim which would entitle him to relief." And in three other cases, the Court allowed prisoners to go directly into federal court under the federal civil rights laws without having to exhaust all the judicial or administrative remedies available in the state system. State officials, like some federal judges already tired of the prisoner complaints, had hoped that the Supreme Court would insist that all prison cases first go through the state administrative agencies, the state court system, or both, which would have effectively ousted the federal courts from the prison-rights business and relegated prisoners to state judges who were then largely unsympathetic.[8]

During this period, the Supreme Court protected religious rights in prison, mail privileges, and prisoners' rights to prepare their legal matters.[9] Prisoner suits seemed to be a Court favorite. Despite Chief Justice Burger's warning in 1971 that the courts should not be looked to for social change, they did seem like a good place to achieve prison reform.

The prisoner-rights movement was at the same time fed by what has always been, unhappily, one of the more reliable stimuli to social reform—tragedy—specifically, the 1971 Attica, New York, prison riot in which forty-three people died. Because prison officials let television cameras into the prison yard while the prisoners held fifty people hostage, Americans were able to see the hatred and despair that our prison system had created. Although those of us who tried to negotiate a peaceful settlement at Attica utterly failed, we came away with some hope that the very awfulness of the tragedy would shock Americans into realizing the need for meaningful change in our system of crime and punishment, into realizing that prison was a solution that was itself a problem.

We counted on several other factors to push the cause: the sheer expense of the prison system, and the growing awareness that prison doesn't rehabilitate and does little to enhance public safety. We also thought that the obvious connection between the prison-rights movement and the black revolution would help: many prisoners were black or Hispanic, and the relation between the depredations of the prison system and the racism in the society as a whole seemed obvious, and a reason to change both.

After almost a century and a half of repeated failures, much bloodshed, and seemingly impregnable community indifference, it looked as if prison reform might be possible.

We were dreamers.

The initial successes seemed substantial. Federal judges, baptized by their activism in race cases, and with a revived Civil Rights Act to work with, after *Monroe v. Pape* (1961)[10] began to overcome their reluctance to look at prison horrors. Litigation began to expand as prisoners' rights became a part of the civil rights struggle. Foundations became interested and started to provide funding. The NAACP Legal Defense and Education Fund, Inc., entered the field in 1969; that same year I started the New York Civil Liberties Union Prisoners' Rights Project, which together with Philip Hirschkop's effort in Virginia evolved into the ACLU's National Prison Project in 1972; the New York Legal Aid Society and other lawyers also began to bring suits; many prisoners filed their own; and soon the federal courts began to complain loudly about a flood of prisoner litigation. (The complaints still continue.) In short order, mail censorship was limited, arbitrary disciplinary procedures were changed, physical abuse and corporal punishment were condemned, prisoner expression within the institution received some protection, the press was allowed into prisons, unnecessary visiting restrictions were voided, improvements in medical care were ordered, strip searches were limited, parole procedures were improved.[11] In many cases, the entire state system was condemned.

Prison administrators reacted angrily. Few had ever had their actions questioned, and especially not in a courtroom. The brutal ones obviously felt threatened, but even those honestly dedicated to running a decent system felt wronged. Many of them had spent their lives trying to improve a rotten institution, scratching for a few dollars to provide some facilities for prisoners whom the rest of the community feared and despised, and certainly didn't want to spend money on. They saw themselves as good guys, not as villains. Although a few prison administrators saw that the suits offered valuable leverage against resistant state legislatures for more resources, most of them considered prisoner-rights lawyers troublemakers who knew little about the administrators' problems and cared less. Foot dragging and other forms of resistance were common.

And soon the prison authorities began to prevail in the Supreme Court. The shift began in June 1974, with a 5–4 decision that prisoners and the press did not have a constitutional right under the First or any other amendment to have private interviews, because this might somehow inflate a prisoner's reputation in the prison community and create security problems.[12] Almost every lower court that had looked into the issue had rejected this argument for lack of substantial supporting evidence, with an occasional comment that it was not an unreasonable possibility; but that made no difference to the Burger Court, which upheld a total ban on all interviews. On the same day, a 6–3 majority told the Supreme Court of California that it was wrong in thinking that the Constitution did not allow states to continue to disenfranchise people who had been convicted and had completed their sentences. Justice William Rehnquist, writing for the Court, relied on an exhaustive analysis of the Fourteenth Amendment which, as Justice Thurgood Marshall pointed out in dissent, came down to "one explanatory reference . . . which is unilluminating at best."[13] Had the Court followed the same approach to the racial discrimination cases, we would probably still have segregated schools, antimiscegenation laws, and the poll tax.

Two days later, the Court's now solidly conservative majority struck again, this time in the matter of prison discipline. Rejecting the views of many lower courts and some twenty-eight states, the Court ruled that security considerations justified denying prisoners in disciplinary proceedings any right to cross-examine or confront adverse witnesses, or any kind of counsel, even from another prisoner; the right to call witnesses was limited by the administrators' discretion. Perhaps even more important was the fact that the Court accepted as constitutionally adequate a prison disciplinary court made up solely of prison administrators.[14]

Though the subject matter of the discipline and press-access cases seem disparate, both struck at a central strategy of the prison-reform movement: to bring outsiders, and the attendant possibility of public exposure, into the prison. One major obstacle to change and improvement was community indifference fed by ignorance, and allowing one-to-one prisoner-press interviews would make visible the problems in the normally invisible prison system. The effect of the Court's rulings was to allow prison officials to prevent contact between the press and the prisoners who had the most to say, and to relegate press contacts to what a journalist could pick up on guided tours and other casual contacts.

The discipline case also impaired this strategy of exposure. There is usually no attempt to provide procedural fairness in prison discipline proceedings. In most institutions, the only real issue is what sentence to hand out, not the guilt or innocence of the accused. And the sentences can be severe, especially those involving the loss of "good time" or other credits toward early release. Here, too, the goal of reform was to introduce outsiders into the process. Anything else is window dressing, since any bureaucracy working out of sight can manipulate merely procedural protections—it may take more paperwork and time, but a combination of witnesses lying for the administration and the tribunal readily accepting those lies, can get around procedural protections; unhappily, this combination is none too rare. Introducing an outsider into the setting would discourage this. The Supreme Court's ruling that all the judges could be prison officials, and that the prisoner was not entitled either to counsel or to cross-examine or confront the accuser, means that there is virtually no check to arbitrariness in the discipline process.

Subsequent decisions reinforced the Court's insistence that the courts stay out of prison discipline. For example, when a prisoner is charged with a disciplinary offense that could also be a crime—which is not unusual—what the prisoner says at the disciplinary hearing obviously can get him into trouble at the criminal prosecution if it can be used against him there. On the other hand, under the Court's disciplinary rulings, the prisoner has to say something to defend himself at the administrative hearing, for without the right to cross-examine or confront the adverse witnesses, he cannot even challenge the case against him, and if the administration chooses, it can deny him the right to present other defense witnesses. The prisoner is thus whipsawed: if he presents his side of the events in the disciplinary proceeding, he may incriminate himself in connection with any future criminal proceedings (a very real problem in the aftermath of the Attica uprising, when the state indicted some sixty prisoners); but if he doesn't say anything, his silence may be used against him in the disciplinary proceeding and he faces heavy prison penalties.

To alleviate these problems at least somewhat, lower courts relying on *Miranda v. Arizona* (1966),[15] had begun to allow prisoners the right to counsel in the disciplinary proceedings in order to help protect the prisoner's privilege against self-incrimination. The Burger Court promptly overturned these decisions.[16] Not even bothering to mention the serious dilemma facing the prisoner caught between disciplinary and criminal charges, it wiped out whatever additional protections the lower courts had ordered in the special civil-criminal situation. It never confronted the dilemma but simply analogized prison proceedings to ordinary civil matters, though liberty is rarely, if ever, at stake in the latter.

More recently, the Court moved again to make sure that the lower courts were not too generous to prisoners in connection with discipline. Prison officials often resort to something called "administrative segregation" when they want to isolate a troublesome prisoner but don't want to go through the paperwork required for a formal disciplinary hearing. This "segregation" is usually solitary confinement. In a case growing out of a Pennsylvania prison riot, the authorities put a prisoner against whom criminal charges were pending into this "administrative segregation" without a hearing or any other formal proceeding. The lower court thought this a serious infraction of the notion that no one should be deprived of his liberty, even in a prison setting, without some procedural formality to ensure that he is given due process of law. The Burger Court disagreed, holding that a prisoner had no constitutionally protected interest not to be put unfairly into "administrative segregation," and that even if he did have such an interest, an "informal nonadversary review of the information supporting [his] administrative confinement" was enough due process of law. And in a 1985 case, which it should probably not have bothered to hear at all, the Court went out of its way to overturn a state court's ruling that the evidence at a specific Massachusetts prison disciplinary hearing was too meager to support the finding against the prisoners.[17]

The Burger Court extended its liberality toward prison officials to a related matter of vital importance to every prison inmate—*where* he does his time. When prison officials suspect a prisoner of misconduct or consider him a bad apple, they will often transfer him to another prison. Few things can cause a prisoner greater grief. Such a transfer may send him far from home, family, and lawyers. Equally important, it may move him out of a prison where he has learned how to survive, what can get him into trouble, which guards and inmates to avoid, which are friends and allies; he may be in a useful educational or other program that is not available to him elsewhere or may have worked himself into a good job. A transfer can be so profoundly unsettling that even the Supreme Court recognized it as a "grievous loss," and lower courts insisted on a pretransfer hearing to try to minimize potential arbitrariness. Nevertheless, the Burger Court ruled that a prisoner is entitled to no protection whatsoever against an undesirable transfer.[18]

Judicial nervousness about disciplinary matters is perhaps understandable, for they often involve prisoners who are believed to threaten security in a very volatile setting. No such justification exists for many of the Burger Court's other rulings. For example, in *Houchins v. KQED* (1978), it extended its ruling in the 1974 *Pell* case on press access to prisoners, by holding that the media and the public may be *totally* denied access to prisons. "We . . . reject the . . . assertion," said Chief Justice Burger for the Court, "that the public and the media have a First Amendment right to government information regarding the condition of jails and their inmates and presumably all other public facilities . . . ."[19] Why? One of the primary purposes of the First Amendment is to hold the government accountable, to make democracy possible by ensuring that the citizenry will be able not only to speak out on public issues, to debate and vote on them, but to know enough about the government to do so knowledgeably. The Burger Supreme Court itself had said, and repeated, that the right to know is a part of the First Amendment,[20] and this would seem to be especially applicable where "public facilities" are concerned. Only the naïve or the cynical can say, as Chief Justice Burger did in *KQED*, that the citizenry should look to what official boards and other government agencies choose to disclose.

There is even less warrant for the Burger Court's refusal to insist that prison officials meet certain minimum standards with respect to physical conditions. For example, it permitted prison officials to force people held prior to trial to undergo humiliating strip searches that include an intrusion into every bodily cavity. The lower court had forbidden these "gross violations of personal privacy" unless there was some reason to believe that contraband drugs or other materials had been passed, reasoning that pretrial detainees were still considered innocent—they had not even been tried, much less convicted—and were being held to ensure their appearance at trial only because they were too poor to raise the money for bail. While proclaiming that "we do not underestimate the degree to which these searches may invade the personal privacy of the inmate . . . nor . . . doubt that on occasion a security guard may conduct the search in an abusive fashion," the Supreme Court, in an opinion written by Justice Rehnquist, nevertheless allowed such invasions without any preconditions. It brushed aside any special considerations arising from the fact that the pretrial detainees could not be considered criminals, by simply characterizing what was being done to them as not "punishment."[21]

Five years later, in 1984, the Burger Court announced flatly that prisoners have no right to privacy at all. "[T]he Fourth Amendment proscription against unreasonable searches does not apply within the confines of the prison cell,"[22] declared the Chief Justice, even when prison guards seize photos and legal materials solely for harassment. (Chief Justice Burger used to devote many of his after-dinner speeches to prison reform, but this somehow failed to carry over to his judicial decision-making.) Again, the problem is not that the Court was depriving the prisoner of what people in the free world have—prison obviously carries with it, as courts have always noted, the deprivation of many freedoms we take for granted—but, rather, that it seemed to be trying to make it clear that prisoners have virtually no rights at all that the courts should protect.

Perhaps the clearest example of this attitude appears in a case decided in 1986, during the last year of the Burger Court. New Jersey state prisoner Robert Davidson broke up a fight between two other inmates and was later threatened by one of them. Davidson reported the threat to the prison authorities in the hope that they would be able to prevent any further incidents. The authorities ignored the note. Two days later, Davidson was attacked. His nose was broken, and he was stabbed in his face and body. He had no remedy under the applicable state law and sued under the federal Civil Rights Act. The Supreme Court threw out his suit, commenting that he had no constitutional right to due care from the state even though, as dissenting Justice Harry Blackmun put it, "When the State of New Jersey put Robert Davidson in its prison, it stripped him of all means of self-protection . . . [such as] a weapon, . . . fighting back, . . . [or] avenues of escape."[23]

The Burger Court didn't really return to the bad old days when prisoner cases were thrown out without even a glance at the claims, no matter how dreadful the conditions being challenged. But the strong language in the opinions since the 1979 *Wolfish* case, and the near-uniformity with which the Court rejected claims often found meritorious by the lower courts, points to a movement back toward the old "hands-off" policy except in the most egregious cases.

That seemingly narrow exception for the "egregious" case, however, has allowed a great deal of litigation to continue. For the fact is we seem to have learned nothing from the Attica tragedy and others like it since, such as in New Mexico in 1980, where thirty-three died. The lower courts have therefore continued to order the prisons to ameliorate the more ghastly conditions, and despite its obvious distaste for judicial intrusion into prison matters, the Burger Court did not get in the way. Indeed, its 1978 affirmance of the trial court's order in the Arkansas prison case[24] can be seen as a green light to the lower courts to continue dealing with the more terrible prison conditions.

One example of such conditions is in the matter of overcrowding. The most serious problem in our prisons today is that the combination of the public's understandable fright about high crime rates, and the Draconian penalties pushed through by unscrupulous politicians quick to make political capital, has produced massive prison overcrowding. This strains the already inadequate educational, work, and recreational programs and the typically inadequate medical and other services; it increases the nervous tension in the guard force; it aggravates the frictions among men crowded together in small cages, compounding the dangers already inevitable to prison life. The Burger Court twice refused to do something about the overcrowding problem in cases raising the constitutionality of putting more than one person in a small prison cell.[25] Nevertheless, the lower courts have issued a steady stream of orders all over the country against the overcrowding, insisting that prisoners be released if necessary, and so far, the Supreme Court has not interfered.

In other cases, courts continue to order prison systems to improve sanitation and physical- and mental-health care, to provide for personal safety, to upgrade disciplinary and classification procedures, and to eliminate brutality and abusive behavior-modification programs. Revealing its continuing permissive attitude toward such judicial action, the Supreme Court refused to review a sweeping order against the Colorado prisons just two months before it decided *Rhodes v. Chapman*.[26] And after the *Chapman* case it continued to allow orders against overcrowding to stand without reviewing them.[27] As of June

1986, thirty-four states, the District of Columbia, Puerto Rico, and the Virgin Islands are operating prisons under court orders, most of which involve provisions against overcrowding; most of the major metropolitan jails are also under such court decrees.[28]

Nevertheless, most prisons remain hellholes and inevitably so. As the conditions detailed in recent court decisions make clear, a prison is inherently a terrible place that can never be made into a humane institution. But until we recognize that prison is at best only a partial and trouble-ridden solution to the problem of crime, we will be saddled with these abominable places.

The prisoner-rights movement can ameliorate things only a little. It is not an unimportant "little," but some have argued that, on balance, the benefits are not worth the effort—the overcrowding wipes out many of the gains, and the system is so innately immoral, the cruelties it imposes are so inevitable, that amelioration is worse than nothing. Those with different temperaments and styles obviously will react differently to such arguments. My own belief is that since there are no signs that prisons are withering away—prison building programs are on the increase—it makes sense to try to reduce the endemic inhumanity to be found there. For life *has* been made a little better for prisoners. There is, for example, less open physical brutality, medical care is a bit better, sanitation and other living conditions are somewhat improved. Of great importance is the fact that the courts of the United States remain available to those at society's lowest levels, who, despite their dismal status, can force government officers to obey the fundamental principles of law, justice, and decency reflected in the Bill of Rights.

·V·

FEDERAL REGULATION OF THE ECONOMY

·12·

Close Reins on the Bureaucracy: Overseeing the Administrative Agencies

ALAN B. MORRISON

Regulation, which Ronald Reagan attacked at every opportunity on his way to the White House, remains very much a fact of American life. Whatever the Burger Court may have done in other areas, it had only a modest effect on the course of regulation.

In this essay, I will use "regulation" to describe actions taken by the federal government, through decisions of administrative agencies, that prevent a person or business from doing something that it may want to do, permit it to do something someone else opposes, establish the right to do something someone else opposes, or specify the conditions under which something may be done. What I call "regulation cases" do not include challenges to the constitutionality of statutes.

The paradigm regulation case involves the industrial polluter. The Environmental Protection Agency regulates when it (1) controls the amount of some kind of emission; (2) permits a plant to continue operating on condition that it install equipment to control the emission; or (3) permits a plant to continue operation without any change. A court challenge to the first regulation would come from the company; to the third, from concerned citizens; and to the second, from either or both, claiming that the conditions were too strict or too lenient. The Supreme Court's influence in this area is measured by the degree of deference it shows to the decision-making agency as compared with its willingness to impose—or, more precisely, to construe the governing statutes as imposing—various restraints on the agency. To the extent that it overrules a federal agency, the Supreme Court, instead of the agency, can be said to be regulating.

In one important respect the Supreme Court's effect in regulation differs markedly from its effect in other areas: because its rulings are generally procedural and because different interest groups shift sides in different cases depending on what best serves their substantive interests, the long-term benefits of many of the Court's decisions in this area are hard to predict. For example, an industry trade association might decry an agency's denial of a hearing in one case while applauding it for denial in another case, simply because in the first case the industry did not get what it wanted and in the second it did.

In contrast with the lower courts, and in contrast with other areas covered in this symposium, during Chief Justice Warren Burger's tenure the Supreme Court decided relatively few regulation cases that had any effect beyond that on the specific agency and, often, the specific statute at issue. Only those decisions with broad impact will be discussed here.

OPENING THE COURTHOUSE DOORS

One of the surest ways to allow unlimited administrative discretion is to close the courthouse door to plaintiffs who challenge government agency decisions. The labels under which cases are thrown out include such picturesque examples of legalese as "standing," "committed to agency discretion," and "preclusion." They all have one clear message: no matter how wrong the agency was or what law was violated, it is not up to the courts to fix the problem. The Burger Court generally rejected such unacceptable lawlessness. The law of standing—the question of who, if anyone, has the right to go to court to test the legality of an agency decision—has been the principal focus in this area, and the Burger Court established that most agency decisions are subject to some kind of judicial review. That could not have been said with confidence in 1969.

The case that paved the way for consumer and environmental groups to sue federal agencies, *Association of Data Processing Service Organizations, Inc. v. Camp* (1970),[1] was brought by an industry group that argued that the Comptroller of the Currency was not adequately regulating banks in their nonbanking activities. The Court announced a test for standing, which requires a showing of injury to the plaintiff, a causal connection between the injury and what the agency did or did not do, a likelihood that the Court could redress the injury, and a showing that the interest the plaintiff seeks to vindicate is "arguably within the zone of interest" protected by the statute in question. Like most standards, its application is not easy, but in most cases the doubts have been resolved in favor of the plaintiff.

One particularly helpful application of the *Data Processing* test for environmental and consumer groups came four years later in *United States v. SCRAP*.[2] There the Supreme Court found that while the harm to individual plaintiffs was small, it was sufficient to enable them to attempt to prove their case (which they were eventually unable to do). As a result, the amount of harm an individual has suffered or may suffer is no longer a barrier to suing federal agencies.

Standing has been a barrier, however, in challenges to the Internal Revenue Service's enforcement of the tax laws. In *Simon v. Eastern Kentucky Welfare Rights Organization* (1976) and in *Allen v. Wright* (1984),[3] the Supreme Court refused to hear suits by poor people challenging a relaxation of IRS rules requiring hospitals to give free care to the indigent in order to be eligible to receive charitable contributions, and by black parents objecting to the IRS's nonenforcement of rules against tax-favored private academies that practice segregation. One can read these decisions as simply rejecting the broad challenges and insisting on narrow, specific allegations of harm to named individuals. Indeed, *Simon* has been a real problem only in the tax field, where the courts have always been solicitous of the IRS's policy determinations, partly because the tax status of third parties is ultimately at issue; this inevitably makes the cases more complex and raises serious issues of privacy that can be avoided by peremptory dismissals on a ground like standing. Since the Court in both cases eschewed potentially broader grounds for dismissal, more carefully prepared complaints may solve some of these problems.

While there is still a possibility of retrenchment, a decision from the 1985–86 term suggests that is not likely to occur. In *International Union, United Automobile Workers v. Brock*, the D.C. Circuit had found that a union did not have standing to represent its members in a dispute with the Department of Labor over the meaning of a trade readjustment statute, but the Supreme Court reversed. Not only did the Supreme Court decline to take a narrow view of standing, it rejected an even more threatening effort by the Justice Department to prevent associations from suing on behalf of their members except in the most unusual circumstances.[4]

Administrative agencies often claim that Congress intended their decisions to be discretionary and unreviewable. This claim had little success when challenged in cases before the Warren Court, which accepted it only when it found evidence that Congress intended to cut off access to the courts—a circumstance that rarely, if ever, obtains. And at first, the Burger Court responded similarly. In 1975, when union members sued the Secretary of Labor for not seeking to overturn a union election, which, under the Labor-Management Relations Act, only the Secretary may do, the Court in *Dunlop v. Bachowski*,[5] found that the Secretary's decision was reviewable in court, albeit under a very deferential standard. Many lower courts followed suit and held that it was proper for them to review various agency decisions not to act.

Ten years later, however, the Burger Court sounded a potentially ominous note for litigants in such cases. In *Heckler v. Chaney* (1985)[6] attorneys for death-row inmates in states using lethal injections for executions attempted to have the Food and Drug Administration prohibit the use of such drugs because they had not been proven "safe and effective" for that purpose, as the Food, Drug and Cosmetic Act requires; the FDA had refused to issue such a ban. Without reaching the merits of the case, the Court, in an opinion joined by all the justices except Thurgood Marshall, ruled that the plaintiffs were seeking to control the law-enforcement priorities of the FDA and that how that agency used its resources was not judicially reviewable, in large part because of the lack of any manageable standards by which the Court could substitute its judgment for that of the FDA. The Court went beyond the FDA, however, and established a presumption *against* judicial review of agency decisions not to enforce the law.

In theory, the Court's presumption and its underlying analysis could be applied to almost any case in which an agency refused to act. But the Court, in the text of the opinion and in a number of footnotes, was careful to make clear that it was not dealing with the refusal to issue or amend a rule, with cases in which the agency claimed it was not acting because it lacked the authority or was otherwise precluded from doing so, with constitutional challenges, or with instances where Congress had set standards for the exercise of the agency's enforcement powers.

The government has already begun to cite *Chaney* in every situation where it is being asked to do more than it wishes, but it has not generally prevailed. The question remains as to whether *Chaney* will be a limited exception, or whether it is the first in a new series of means to keep litigants out of the federal courts.

The third door-closing defense that the government trots out in almost mechanical fashion is preclusion. This argument is that Congress has decided that certain agency decisions are not subject to judicial review or that certain categories of people may not bring cases against the government. This generally met with little success in the Burger Court, although it unanimously ruled, in *Block v. Community Nutrition Institute* (1984)[7] that consumers were precluded from challenging a decision of the Department of Agriculture that made it economically impossible to produce reconstituted milk in certain areas of the country. It seems unlikely, however, that this decision will have much effect outside agricultural policy.

To a considerable extent, the Burger Court opened up the courthouse doors to challenges to decisions by administrative agencies. Despite some setbacks, only the most pessimistic observer could find reason to fear that the trend might be reversed.

DEFERENCE TO AGENCY DECISION-MAKING ON THE MERITS

Because Congress has told the courts generally to defer to agency decisions, and because the courts recognize both that they cannot hope to master the technical issues and that federal judges are not supposed to make policy, judges give agencies considerable leeway when reviewing their decisions on the merits. Quite obviously, such deference must have limits or else judicial review would be meaningless, which Congress did not intend. The question has been how to strike the balance between deference and abdication.

Congress has provided that agency decisions turning on questions of fact or on policy choices are to be upheld unless they are "arbitrary and capricious," a criterion whose meaning is not entirely self-evident. Beginning in 1971, in *Citizens to Preserve Overtone Park v. Volpe*,[8] involving a challenge to a decision to permit a highway to go through a park in Memphis, Tennessee, the Burger Court made it clear that the lower courts should make a searching review of the evidence, should be certain the legally relevant factors (and only those factors) were considered, and must insist that agencies rationally explain their decisions consistent with the statutory requirements. At the same time, it left no doubt that it did not intend lower-court judges to second-guess agencies just because the judges might have reached a different decision.

In two rulings, one favoring the position of industry and the other rejecting industry's claims, the Burger Court emphasized that federal judges should not rubber-stamp agency decisions. In *Industrial Union Department v. American Petroleum Industries* (1980)[9] it concluded that the Occupational Safety and Health Administration had not properly established that there was a "significant risk" of exposure to benzene, which the law required in order to issue a standard to protect workers. While the ruling turned in part on the meaning of the Occupational Safety and Health Act, the decision made clear that evidence, not merely conclusions, is necessary before regulations will be sustained.

The true test of whether the Burger Court would insist on rational justifications for agency decisions came three years later in *Motor Vehicle Manufacturers Association v. State Farm Mutual Automobile Insurance Co.*[10] There, the United States Court of Appeals in Washington, D.C., had overturned a Reagan administration decision jettisoning a 1977 rule mandating air bags or passive seatbelts in automobiles. In a decision that surprised many observers, the Court unanimously ruled that the agency had acted arbitrarily in failing to consider one option to total revocation and, in a 5–4 vote, agreed that another alternative had also been improperly dismissed out of hand. The ruling was particularly significant because, when considering deregulation, the Court applied the same test that it had used in determining the validity of the regulation in the first place: both require evidence and reasoned explanations. Thus, it established that a lower court would not be automatically reversed if, after a careful review of the record, it had found an agency's decision to be irrational. While the standard is still highly deferential, the rulings in the benzene and air-bag cases establish that there are limits beyond which an agency cannot go without its decisions being overturned on their merits.

Another area in which agencies ask for deference is in their interpretation of the statutes under which they operate. While generalizations in this area are not easy to make, Burger Court rulings prior to 1984 left the impression that it believed the courts' interpretation of the statute should prevail, whether that conformed to or challenged the agency's view. Most of the Court's pre-1984 opinions on this question, such as *Federal Election Commission v. Democratic Senatorial Campaign Committee* (1981),[11] had something for everyone to cite.

The high point of these mutually exclusive lines of authority occurred in June 1984 in two cases, both named *Securities Industries Association v. Board of Governors of the Federal Reserve System*,[12] brought by the securities industry against the Federal Reserve Board, challenging the Fed's decisions allowing banks to enter into non-banking activities. The Supreme Court ruled for the agency in the first case, deferring to the agency's interpretation of its statute when upholding its actions, and against it in the other, declining to defer when disagreeing with the Fed's interpretation of its congressional mandate.

However, about the same time, in *Chevron U.S.A. Inc. v. Natural Resources Defense Council* (1984),[13] the Court began taking a new approach under which an agency's interpretation of its substantive statute will be upheld if it is a "reasonable" one, unless Congress has explicitly spoken to the issue. Indeed, in *Young v. Community Nutrition Institute* (1986),[14] the Court upheld the agency's construction of the procedural requirements imposed on it by Congress, which relieved it of the obligation to hold a hearing before approving the addition of certain carcinogens to foods, on the ground that the agency's interpretation was "sufficiently rational to preclude a court from substituting its judgment for that of the [agency]." This led the sole dissenter, Justice John Paul Stevens, to remark that the majority's conclusion "reflects an absence of judgment and of judging."

To be sure, earlier in the term the Court had refused to go along with the interpretation by the Federal Reserve Board that it had the authority under its own statute to prevent "non-banks" from competing with banks in providing certain services (*Board of Governors of the Federal Reserve System v. Dimension Financial Corp.* [1986]).[15] But there now appears to be a decisive trend, with its share of exceptions, toward agencies being given substantial leeway in construing the laws that Congress has written. Whatever merits that approach may have for issues relating to the agency's general responsibilities, it threatens to undermine agency accountability in those areas where the law was intended to limit an agency's jurisdiction, to confine the sphere of its discretion, or to impose procedural requirements on it before it takes certain actions. Whether the Rehnquist Court will continue this unwarranted deference to an agency's construction of its own statute is something to be watched.

IMPOSING PROCEDURAL REQUIREMENTS

In the late 1960s and early 1970s, when federal courts began to review government agency decisions with increasing frequency and skepticism, they were often reluctant to overturn decisions on their merits. Instead, they looked for, and often found, flagrant violations of statutory requirements to give notice, to have a hearing, or to consult with persons outside the affected industry. Eventually, agencies began to follow the procedures set forth in their own statutes and regulations, although even today they do not always do so. The courts nonetheless expressed concern that the procedures followed did not always produce the kind of record or reasoned decision necessary to decide difficult questions. At the behest of both industry and its opponents (in different cases, of course), the courts began imposing on agencies procedural requirements beyond those contained in the statutes.

In 1978, however, the Supreme Court slowed this trend considerably, in *Vermont Yankee Nuclear Power Corp. v. Natural Resources Defense Council*.[16] The United States Court of Appeals had accepted an argument made by environmental groups that the Nuclear Regulatory Commission should conduct further hearings on a highly technical and controversial policy issue. A unanimous Supreme Court firmly told litigants and lower-court judges that it is up to Congress, not the courts, to decide what procedures are necessary and proper.

The philosophy enunciated in the *Vermont Yankee* case was underscored in two other Burger Court rulings—one predating *Vermont Yankee*, the other following it—both of which narrowly construed the relevant statutes in deciding whether certain procedural requirements must be followed. In the earlier case, *United States v. Florida East Coast Railway Co.* (1973),[17] the Court concluded that informal rather than formal proceedings were all that Congress had dictated, adopting a plausible but by no means compelling reading of the law. In the other, *American Textile Manufacturers Institute, Inc. v. Donovan* (1981),[18] in a significant blow to industry, the Court refused to read into the Occupational Safety and Health Act (which it had construed in favor of industry the year before in the benzene case) a requirement that the agency do a cost-benefit analysis before issuing health and safety standards. These cases expressed the Court's message clearly: We will not assume that Congress intended us to tie an agency's hands procedurally unless it makes very clear that it wanted us to do so.

THREE PRECEPTS OF JUDICIAL REVIEW OF REGULATORY ACTIONS

From this survey of the rather few Burger Court decisions affecting the manner in which courts review decisions of administrative agencies, three precepts emerge:

- You can almost always get into court and have it review your claim that an agency acted improperly.
- The court will carefully review your claim and the agency's decision, but you have an uphill road to convince a court that the agency was wrong on the facts or in resolving policy choices. However, in exceptional cases, the courts will set aside an agency's decisions on the merits.
- The courts will insist that agencies dot their procedural *i*'s and cross their procedural *t*'s, but only those *i*'s and *t*'s that are required by law and not those that the court merely thinks would be a good idea.

A NOTE ON THE LEGISLATIVE VETO DECISION

The most important Burger Court case affecting government regulation was not an administrative law decision but a constitutional law ruling, *Immigration and Naturalization Service v. Chadha, U.S.* (1983),[19] in which the Supreme Court struck down the legislative veto. The veto is a device conceived by Congress, under which powers were delegated to either an administrative agency or to the President, but over which Congress maintained a hold by allowing a particular decision to be overruled by either one House, both Houses, or sometimes even a single committee of Congress, within a fixed period provided in the statute. The theory of the veto was that it improved accountability by ensuring that the elected representatives had a say in important regulatory decisions. In practice, it was quite different: in many cases Congress used the veto to prevent a rule from going into effect that was necessary to implement broad remedial statutes requiring specific agency action before they actually benefit the public.

The issue of the constitutionality of the veto had been discussed for nearly fifty years. The case that finally went to the Supreme Court involved a decision by the Immigration and Naturalization Service to allow an alien to remain in this country, because sending him back to his native land would have resulted in "extreme hardship." The statute also had a provision that allowed either House of Congress to veto decisions regarding individual aliens. In this instance, Congress rejected the hardship determination in 6 out of 340 cases.

On the surface, this landmark case could easily have been decided on a narrow ground, since the whole notion of executive accountability to Congress in matters of broad national policy seemed inapplicable, and congressional interference in individual adjudications seemed less justified than it would have in a rulemaking context. In fact, the Ninth Circuit Court of Appeals had decided the case on a narrow ground, and declined to issue a ruling that would have applied to other vetoes in other statutes. The concurring opinion of Justice Lewis Powell in *Chadha* was similarly limited. The Supreme Court might even have ducked the issue entirely, as there were procedural grounds raised by the House and Senate that it could have accepted and thereby avoided the constitutional question. Instead, the Court issued a ruling that had the effect, as Justice Byron White's dissent pointed out, of striking down every legislative veto in every federal statute, and thereby holding unconstitutional more federal laws in one opinion than had been invalidated in the entire history of the Supreme Court.

There are several possible reasons why the Court issued such a broad ruling. First, the Solicitor General, who had agreed that the veto was unconstitutional, asked for a broad ruling, and indeed had rejected the position taken by the Attorney General in a prior administration that at least one type of veto (that contained in the Reorganization Act) was constitutional. Second, the legal arguments made by Mr. Chadha and by the Solicitor General, were, if accepted, applicable to all vetoes, and neither of them had urged a narrowing application of the constitutional ruling. Third, the *amicus* brief submitted by the American Bar Association—which was drafted by attorneys from Davis, Polk & Wardwell in New York, and future justice Antonin Scalia, a law professor at the time—pointed out the many areas in which the veto was being used and strongly recommended a broad ruling as proper, given the manner in which the veto was being employed and might be in the future. Fourth, the Court had before it, but had delayed action on, two other cases involving rule-making by federal agencies (the Federal Energy Regulatory Commission and the Federal Trade Commission), which presented problems at the other end of the spectrum from those in *Chadha*: because the lower courts in these two cases had held the veto unconstitutional, the Court could not avoid deciding the other aspects of the veto issue simply by ruling narrowly in *Chadha*.

In my view, these four factors combined to make the Court decide that Congress had begun and would continue to use the veto virtually to run federal regulatory agencies. Indeed, the House of Representatives had passed an amendment to the Administrative Procedure Act in 1976 that would have authorized a one-house veto over every rule of every regulatory agency, and similar measures had reached the floor of both Houses (they did not become law largely because of the unresolved debate over the veto's constitutionality). Thus, the Court knew the veto was not just an isolated tool for increased accountability to be used in unusual situations; both directly and indirectly, through congressional pressure, it could profoundly change the nature of our administrative state, and it was fundamentally at odds with the structure of the Administrative Procedure Act and with notions of basic due process.

Chadha provided a graphic example of how the veto was being used. Congress gave no reason when it exercised the veto; indeed, Congress was free to exercise the veto for any reason, for no reason, or for reasons that would clearly be legally impermissible were an agency to act on the same basis. Moreover, persons adversely affected by a veto, such as Mr. Chadha, were given no notice that a veto was being considered, did not know what the basis for the veto might be, and had no opportunity to argue against it.

The potential breadth of the veto's challenge to administrative law as a cause for the Court's broad opinion in *Chadha* has a correlative proposition: had Congress limited the use of the veto to cases involving agency reorganization, war powers, arms sales, or impoundment, the Court might never have issued a broad opinion or indeed might never have reached the issue at all. In those categories, it might well have been that no person would have had standing to challenge the veto, or if the Court had reached the merits in a case, it might well have upheld the use of the veto in a limited set of circumstances. But that is not what Congress did. It adopted the veto device wholesale and, as a result, lost the veto not simply in the regulatory context, but in every instance in which it might be employed.

Some of the effects of *Chadha* are already apparent. The first and most obvious is that the tide of legislative vetoes has been turned back and will never again surge forward. To me, that is far more important than the elimination of vetoes already on the books. Second, although technically invalid, the statutes still allow for vetoes in a number of instances, and the executive branch has been honoring them to the extent of delaying the effectiveness of vetoable actions until Congress has had a chance to consider these actions and pass a statute overruling them. This has resulted in substantial delays of the kind that were found before *Chadha*, but Congress has done very little to eliminate them. In addition, back-door maneuvering by congressional staffs may still affect the outcome of rules because of the theoretical possibility of a statutory override, although this is less likely than before.

As a matter of balance of power, Congress has not had its wings clipped. Similarly, administrative agencies do not seem to be much bolder now than they were, and as a result Congress has not needed to find new means of holding them accountable. Of course, administrative excess, which was the complaint of the veto's proponents, surely cannot be attributed to the Reagan administration, which is doing almost nothing to carry out its regulatory responsibilities.

Some critics of *Chadha* argue that the veto had a real use in foreign affairs, particularly concerning the war-powers resolution. I suppose I might have second thoughts about eliminating the veto if I believed that Congress would ever do anything meaningful about presidential war making. But if there was any doubt about that, Lebanon ended the issue. In the face of the massacre resulting in the death of 241 marines, Congress purported to invoke the War Powers Act and then gave the administration eighteen months to get out of Lebanon. If that is congressional power, its demise is hardly worth a passing thought.

There is one other change that is clear, unmistakable, and beneficial. Those of us who reside in the District of Columbia used to chafe under the legislative veto applicable to all statutes passed by the D.C. city council and approved by the mayor. Congress has now changed the law, not because it wished to relinquish the veto, but because bond counsel for the district said that no one would lend it money so long as the authority to issue bonds was legally questioned as a result of a potential veto affecting them. And when Congress made that change, it gave complete substantive home rule to the District of Columbia in all but criminal law, although it still has retained a major role in the district's budget. None of that would have occurred but for *Chadha*. Thus, at least one small colony is clearly better off as a result of a decision whose basic principles had nothing to do with it.

THE FREEDOM OF INFORMATION ACT

In 1966 Congress passed the Freedom of Information Act, the first significant federal open-government statute. Its purpose is to give the public access to all records of the executive branch except those that fall into nine narrow categories exempted by Congress.

The Burger Court first issued an FOIA decision in 1973, and by July 1986 had ruled on nineteen such cases. One word describes its attitude toward the public's efforts to obtain government documents: hostility.

The numbers tell the story better than anything else. From them can be gleaned three useful observations:

- The opponents of disclosure almost always win. Of the nineteen decisions, the government's position opposing disclosure prevailed in fifteen.[20] In another case, the Court ruled for the government on the principal issue and for the requesting party on a far less significant aspect.[21] In two other cases, industry intervened to prevent the government from disclosing documents requested by private parties, completely in one case and substantially in the other.[22] In only one case, involving the records of disciplinary violations at the Air Force Academy, with the names and identifying details of the individual cadets deleted, did the government's attempt to block disclosure fail.[23]

A typical example of a case denying disclosure was *Central Intelligence Agency v. Sims* (1985).[24] The case involved unclassified material containing the names of the investigators who conducted various experiments for the CIA in the 1950s, using, among other things, mind-altering drugs. Those names were withheld on the ground that their release would disclose intelligence sources. Although the agency admitted that there were essentially no limits to its definition of intelligence sources and that the term would include *The New York Times* and *Pravda*, the Burger Court, bowing to the god of "national security" and again showing its basic dislike for the FOIA, upheld its claims. As a result, virtually everything in the CIA's files can now be withheld if the CIA chooses to do so.

By contrast, when Congress has reviewed the results of FOIA decisions, it has always acted to promote greater disclosure. Thus in 1974, the year after the Supreme Court ruled, in *Environmental Protection Agency v. Mink*,[25] that the courts may not question the denial of FOIA requests for national security reasons, Congress reversed that ruling, as well as several other appellate-court decisions that gave agencies blanket authority to withhold law-enforcement records.[26] And when the Burger Court decided in *Administrator, Federal Aviation Administration v. Robertson* to give an expansive reading to the FOIA exemption incorporating other nondisclosure statutes, Congress promptly overturned that also.[27]

- The Supreme Court is likely to hear an FOIA case only if the government brings the appeal. Since the act was passed, the government has sought review in nineteen cases, and it has been granted in seventeen, or 89 percent of the time. This is extraordinary compared with the rate of 5–7 percent in all cases. It is even substantially better than the rate for all government cases, where the Solicitor General is granted 70–75 percent of his requests for review.
- The only way a person denied documents under the FOIA and not obtaining them can get the Court to take his case is if the

government also wants it reviewed. In three cases in which requests for review were granted to nongovernmental parties, the appellants were all opposing disclosure;[28] in two of them the government supported the position opposing disclosure, although it did not file its own petitions.[29]

In only three cases was an appeal granted to persons seeking disclosure, and all involved special circumstances. In each instance the government either had filed its own petition in the case or was petitioning the Court on an identical or closely related issue.[30] In no case without special circumstances has an FOIA requester been able to persuade the Supreme Court that an appellate-court ruling opposing disclosure should be reviewed. Although the number of cases in which review has been sought by a requester is not readily available, it probably runs well over one hundred.

·13·

The Burger Court and Business

JERRY S. COHEN and
HERBERT E. MILSTEIN

THE ANTITRUST LAWS

All judges, the late federal judge Braxton Craven maintained, are result-oriented—the only difference between them being that some know it and some do not.[1] In antitrust and securities law, his observation is particularly pertinent. On the Warren Court, the leaders in antitrust law were Justices Hugo Black and William O. Douglas. Both were realists and populists, and they interpreted the antitrust laws not only in economic terms but with insight into the social and political factors responsible for the laws' enactment at the end of the nineteenth century: the pressures generated by the populist and progressive movements, with their profound concern about the political and social implications of the giant corporate combinations.

Since 1890, the Sherman Act—the basic antitrust statute—has been the law of the land. And the basic premise of antitrust legislation, as described by Justice Douglas, is this:

> Industrialized power should be decentralized. It should be scattered into many hands so that the fortune of the people will not be dependent on the whim or caprice, the political prejudice, the emotional stability of a few self-appointed men. The fact that they are not vicious men, but respectable and social-minded is irrelevant. That is the philosophy and

command of the Sherman Act. It was founded on a theory of hostility to the concentration in private hands of power so great that only a government of the people should have it.[2]

Professor Eleanor Fox has defined the goals of antitrust policy, consistent with the basic thrust of the antitrust laws, as a "qualitative" rather than a quantitative measure of the impact of a particular restraint upon competition generally: "There are four major historical goals of antitrust and all should continue to be respected. These are: (1) dispersion of economic power, (2) freedom and opportunity to compete on the merits, (3) satisfaction of consumers, and (4) protection of the competitor process as market governor."[3]

The antitrust laws deal with two aspects of the marketplace, one structural and the other behavioral. Structure generally concerns the degree to which the means of production are concentrated in the hands of corporate entities. This part of the antitrust laws concerns acquisitions and mergers. Behavior concerns how firms act in the marketplace in competition with each other over such matters as pricing.

The two, of course, are related. As stated by President Johnson's Cabinet Committee on Price Stability: "Merger-achieved centralization of economic power and decision-making may seriously impair the proper functioning of our competitive, free enterprise economy, as well as threaten the social and political values associated with a decentralized economic system."[4]

Republican administrations are usually sympathetic to business. Paradoxically, the relationship between structure and behavior and the basic purpose of the antitrust laws have been best expressed by a Republican Attorney General, John N. Mitchell, who in a speech on June 6, 1969, said:

> The danger that ... super-concentration poses to our economic, political and social structure cannot be overestimated. Concentration of this magnitude is likely to eliminate existing and future competition. It increases the possibility for reciprocity and other forms of unfair buyer-seller leverage. It creates nation-wide marketing, managerial and financing structures whose enormous physical and psychological resources pose substantial barriers to smaller firms wishing to participate in a competitive market.

And, finally, super-concentration creates a "community of interest" which discourages competition among large firms and establishes a tone in the marketplace for more and more mergers.

This leaves us with the unacceptable probability that the nation's manufacturing and financial assets will continue to be concentrated in the hands of fewer and fewer people—the very evil that the Sherman Act, the Clayton Act, the Robinson-Patman Act, and the Celler-Kefauver Amendment were designed to combat.[5]

Viewed against this background, the difference between the Warren and Burger Courts is that the Warren Court was deeply concerned with the "qualitative" aspects of antitrust policies while the Burger Court was more concerned with the "quantitative" aspects.

"Competitive equality" was the hallmark of the Warren Court. Justices Black and Douglas believed deeply that one of the purposes and desirable results of the antitrust laws was to protect small business; that to have effective competition, it was necessary to have significant competitors. The Warren Court, therefore, embraced an expansive view of antitrust policy. The Burger Court showed disdain for "competitive equality" and all it implies. This disdain was rationalized under the euphemism "economic efficiency." Antitrust policy in the Burger Court was a triumph for the University of Chicago school of economics, with its emphasis on defining the rules of the game according to an abstract, artificial model of a world of perfect competition—which does not exist. To the Chicago school, all business conduct should and can be evaluated in terms of its contribution to economic allocative efficiency as predicted by a simple, static microeconomic model. The result is almost invariably resolution in favor of business, since the theory assumes that rational decision-makers are always motivated to seek greater allocative efficiency.

To a theorist like the former assistant attorney general William Baxter, a big-business practice like predatory pricing—charging below cost in order to drive out competitors—simply does not exist because, from a strictly theoretical economic point of view, such prices do not produce maximum profits. The inconvenient reality that such practices do occur is irrelevant.

The Burger Court therefore became largely a defendants' court in antitrust law. In contrast, the Warren Court found many business practices "per se" illegal—it considered them prohibited by law without regard to their particular effects or any justification given for them. This approach rested on the belief that certain business conduct was inherently and perniciously anticompetitive. As a result, the issues to be litigated before the Court were narrowly defined and antitrust cases were kept within manageable limits. The per se rule extended from price-fixing to territorial and customer restraints (allowing a purchaser to sell only within a specific geographic area or to specific customers), group boycotts, concerted refusals to deal (several sellers, for instance, agreeing not to deal with particular purchasers), and certain types of illegal tie-ins (as a condition of being sold one product, the purchaser is required to take another).[6]

The Burger Court, on the other hand, embraced the rule-of-reason test and then expanded it. Antitrust is being transferred from the practice of law to the practice of abstract economics. It opened the corral and a thundering herd of economists galloped out, arguing endlessly over abstract measures of a given market and the power within it; it is harder and harder for plaintiffs to bear their evidentiary burdens or even to consider pursuing their rights in court; economic consulting is now truly a growth industry. In the process the qualitative purposes of the antitrust laws have been abandoned and the quantitative aspect magnified until even the simplest lawsuit is becoming a nightmare of econometric models and complex algebraic formulations.

The Burger Court systematically diminished the per se rule in practically every area of antitrust except those relating to price-fixing among competitors. It held that the expulsion of a member from a cooperative buying agency did not violate the antitrust laws, and in so doing substantially weakened the per se application of the antitrust laws to group boycotts.[7]

It held that a hospital's exclusive-services contract with a firm of anesthesiologists, requiring every patient undergoing surgery at the hospital to use that firm, did not violate the antitrust laws and was not entitled to be considered under the per se rule.[8] The opinion severely weakened the possibility of per se application to any tie-ins, although the decision was significant for its lack of rational analysis as well as for its rule-of-reason results.

The Warren Court had established a per se rule for territorial and customer restraints in the *Schwinn* case (1967). In a 1977 case involving a franchise agreement between a television manufacturer and its dealers, in which the dealers were restricted to sales only at the franchised location, the Burger Court specifically overruled *Schwinn* and held that the restraint could only be judged under the rule-of-reason.[9]

The remaining area of per se illegality has been price-fixing, whether horizontal (between competing sellers) or vertical (between a seller and those of its purchasers who resell the product). The Burger Court was given the opportunity in 1984 to rule on whether or not vertical price-fixing should be measured on a rule-of-reason or per se basis in *Monsanto Co. v. Spray-Rite Service Corporation.*[10] In the Solicitor General's brief, the Reagan administration strongly urged that the Court declare that vertical price-fixing should no longer be a per se violation of the antitrust laws. The Court, however, effectively dodged the issue by basing its decision only on the horizontal aspects of the case. However, the issue of the per se status of vertical price-fixing remains murky, because the Court's rejection of the Solicitor General's attempt to force the issue was based on the defendant's failure to urge the rule of reason in the district court, and not because of the merits of the argument. Justice William Brennan suggested that the Court's refusal to reconsider the per se rule in vertical price-fixing cases was not necessarily a ringing endorsement of it either. Antitrust litigants can now be certain only that the per se rule still applies to horizontal price cases.

Implicit in all of these decisions are the incantations of the theologians of economic efficiency. Indeed, when the Burger Court reviewed a monopolization case, it went out of its way to emphasize the importance of "efficiency" even in a situation where it had been seldom applied. The case involved the issue of ski tickets and ski facilities in Aspen, Colorado.[11] Why the Court chose to accept this case is inexplicable in view of the many significant antitrust cases the Court refused to review. In any event, the Court held that an operator of three ski facilities who refused to continue a long-standing marketing arrangement whereby skiers could purchase tickets usable at a competitor's ski facility (the revenues from which were divided by the competitors), was guilty of Sherman Act monopolization. The Court said that its decision was strongly supported by the operator's failure to offer any efficiency justification whatsoever for his pattern of conduct. Again the thundering hoofbeats of the Chicago economists can be heard riding across the pages of the Supreme Court decision.

The Burger Court did not restrict its diminution of the antitrust laws to cases where it expanded the rule of reason at the expense of the per se rule. In *Copperweld Corp. v. Independence Tube Corp.* (1984),[12] the Court held that a parent and its wholly owned subsidiary "were not separate persons for the purposes of the Sherman Act's prohibition of contracts, combinations or conspiracies in restraint of trade." Again, this reversed the more realistic position recognized by the Warren Court.[13] Nor did the result conform to the formalisms of corporate personhood recognized elsewhere in the law. The Court reached this result in order to minimize the antitrust risk in operating a corporation through a parent and subsidiary structure that might be dictated by tax, business, or other consideration. Yet conglomerate subsidiaries may, in fact, be operating as specific entities. This decision shields such massive multistructured organizations from the realities of the marketplace and exposes competitors to any number of tactics aimed at reducing competition.

In keeping with its general philosophy of reducing the reach of antitrust laws, the Burger Court also undermined the utility of another antitrust law, the Robinson-Patman Act, whose purpose is to prevent unjustified price discrimination. Until *J. Truitt Payne Co. v. Chrysler Motors Corp.*,[14] circuit courts had been split on the issue of whether a jury should be permitted to infer injury or damage by a simple showing of a price discrimination. The better law had been that the injury could be measured by the amount of the discrimination between two competing purchasers. This was in line with an old Supreme Court case, *FTC v. Morton Salt Co.* (1948),[15] which allowed such injury to be inferred from the differential itself. The effect of the Burger Court decision in *J. Truitt Payne* was to apply a rule-of-reason test to Robinson-Patman violations. From the practical point of view it has made it more difficult for private plaintiffs to bring actions under that statute.

Another vital decision by the Burger Court merits mention because it was a precursor of further restraints on the reach of the antitrust laws. *Mitsubishi Motors Corp. v. Solar Chrysler Plymouth, Inc.* (1985),[16] deals with the relationship of the Federal Arbitration Act and the antitrust laws. It has generally been the law that a party to a contract cannot be required to give up its antitrust rights in agreeing to arbitration. The problem has arisen primarily in franchise agreements,

212 · Federal Regulation of the Economy

where the franchisor usually has the economic power to set whatever terms it desires. Such agreements are called "contracts of adhesion" because the franchisee must take it or leave it. In the *Mitsubishi* case, the franchisee agreement contained an arbitration clause that required all disputes to be arbitrated in Japan, to the exclusion of American antitrust rights. The law generally has been that public policy considerations do not permit a party to an agreement to waive its antitrust rights. Nevertheless, the Burger Court held that claims arising under the Sherman Act, and encompassed within valid arbitration clauses in an international commercial agreement, were subject only to arbitration. It did not say that the same rule would apply to domestic arbitration or contracts, but it certainly opened the door to this possibility. Indeed, why should an arbitration clause in an agreement under which a franchisee is selling Chevrolets in Hoboken, New Jersey, be treated differently from the arbitration clause of the franchise dealership next door who is selling Toyotas? Nor is it easy to explain to the Toyota dealer why, in his next dispute with the factory, he must travel to Japan to submit his dispute to a Japanese arbitrator, who must then determine what happened in New Jersey.

Cases involving corporate mergers show clearly how the new approach of the Burger Court has resulted in condoning market behavior totally inconsistent with the purposes of the antitrust laws. In the 1960s the Warren Court had adopted a tough standard for mergers in order "to arrest this rising tide toward concentration into too few hands and to halt the general demise of the small businessman."[17] While the Burger Court's position on mergers was never clearly defined, it indicated that it would employ a much broader range of economic data in determining the effect of a merger.

Of more significance was its signal that it was prepared to look only to purported economic efficiencies—claimed cost savings and the like—in deciding whether mergers or other potentially anticompetitive business tactics were legal. The results are what one would expect. The most massive mergers in American history are proceeding unchecked. The largest corporations in the world—Texaco, Du Pont, and others—are proceeding with mergers of a size that makes those prohibited by the Warren Court appear minuscule, apparently without fear of either the Justice Department or the Supreme Court.

The real tragedy is that Burger Court decisions weakened the ability of injured parties to act as enforcers of the antitrust law by being "private attorneys general." The Supreme Court had specifically held that one of the purposes of awarding treble damages under the antitrust law is to encourage private litigants to act as enforcers of its provisions; the possibility of violations is so great that mere government agencies should not be entrusted with its enforcement. The wisdom of that policy has never been clearer than at the present time, when the Reagan administration, the Antitrust Division of the Justice Department, and the Federal Trade Commission have taken the position that antitrust laws in fact hinder and inhibit American business in competing both at home and abroad. From a very realistic point of view, antitrust enforcement at the federal level has come to a halt. It is now clear that if the antitrust laws are to regulate a free market economy, they must be enforced by private litigants and private lawsuits. In the words of the Burger Court itself:

> Every violation of the antitrust laws is a blow to the free enterprise system envisaged by Congress . . . This system depends on strong competition for its health and vigor, and strong competition depends, in turn, on compliance with antitrust legislation. In enacting these laws, Congress had many means at its disposal to penalize violators. It could have, for example, required violators to compensate federal, state, and local governments for the estimated damage to their respective economies caused by the violations. But, this remedy was not selected. Instead, Congress chose to permit all persons to sue to recover three times their actual damages every time they were injured in their business or property by an antitrust violation. By offering potential litigants the prospect of a recovery in three times the amount of their damages, Congress encouraged these persons to serve as "private attorneys general."[18]

The irony is that when private enforcement was needed most, the decisions of the Court eroded the power of private litigants to act as "private attorneys general."

This result occurred because the Burger Court failed to consider the "qualitative" purposes of the antitrust laws. Justice Lewis Powell has stated that "competitive economies have social and political as well as economic advantages . . . but an antitrust policy divorced from market considerations would lack any objective benchmarks."[19] This, of course, is less than a thoroughgoing rejection of social and political values and broad economic goals in the interpretation of antitrust, and it does not strongly limit antitrust analysis to the sole and abstract goal of attaining economic efficiency in the unreal world of perfect competition. Yet, when joined to the other pronouncements of the Burger Court, it is a sufficient endorsement of this latter approach to suggest to the other federal courts that "efficiency" alone needs to be the primary consideration in the antitrust cases.

The ultimate question is whether a corporation should be free to compete on the merits of its products and the efficiency of its organization, rather than because of its size and economic power. If a proper goal of the antitrust laws is to guarantee entrepreneurial freedom for the victims of restraints without regard to whether the restraint injures competition generally, then economic freedom has been severely restricted.

In praising the Burger Court, Richard Posner, a major Chicago-school economic theorist and now an appellate judge, as well as one of the strongest critics of the Warren Court, has stated, "The underlying notion that the antitrust laws express the political values of Jeffersonian democracy rather than economic values rooted in efficiency, also is gone . . ."[20] So it is.

The Burger Court ignored the basic fact that the antitrust laws are not regulations in the ordinary meaning of the term but, rather, ground rules designed to keep the free-enterprise system free. A system that is not concerned with the survival of individual competitors becomes increasingly concentrated in the hands of a few large corporations. Justices Black and Douglas wished to keep the enterprise system free from the private restraints that inevitably occur when the economy is dominated by a few companies. The law of supply and demand does not work effectively when it can be manipulated by those with the economic power to do so.

THE SECURITIES LAWS

Turning from antitrust to corporate securities, the result orientation of the Burger Court is equally clear. The five securities acts passed during the Depression and New Deal, 1933–1940, were enacted mainly in response to the market excesses—including fraud, market manipulation, and illegal self-dealings—that had helped to produce the Great Depression. These laws were intended to prevent such practices and were believed to protect the investing public from such frauds as insider trading, the false prospectus, and fraud in the purchase and sale of securities.

The Warren Court took an expansive view of these federal securities laws and their basic purposes. In the mid-1960s, the Court repeatedly endorsed the idea that private enforcement of federal securities law through suits brought by victims of illegal practices is a necessary supplement to the regulatory and enforcement efforts of the Securities and Exchange Commission. As Justice Douglas wrote:

> We have said repeatedly that "the 1934 Act and its companion legislative enactments embrace a 'fundamental purpose . . . to substitute a philosophy of full disclosure for the philosophy of caveat emptor and thus to achieve a high standard of business ethics in the securities industry.' " . . .
> [It is essential] that the highest ethical standards prevail in every facet of the securities industry.[21]

The Burger Court ignored or redefined these concepts in order to achieve the results its conservative majority wanted. It also disregarded the overriding principle that the primary purpose of federal securities law is to promote the "highest ethical standards in every facet of the securities industry." Its securities-laws opinions have often been highly restrictive—indeed, in some cases vindictive—and its rhetoric has shown a marked antipathy to an expansive reading of the federal securities laws. For example, in 1975, Justice William Rehnquist wrote:

> There has been widespread recognition that litigation under Rule 10b-5 [which prohibits fraud in corporate publications] presents a danger of vexatiousness different in degree and in kind from that which accompanies litigation in general. . . .
> The potential for possible abuse of the liberal discovery provisions of the Federal Rules of Civil Procedure may likewise exist in this type of case to a greater extent than they do in other litigation. The prospect of extensive deposition of the defendant's officers and associates and the

concomitant opportunity for extensive discovery of business documents, is a common occurrence in this and similar types of litigation. . . . But to the extent that it permits a plaintiff with a largely groundless claim to simply take up the time of a number of other people, with the right to do so representing an in terrorem increment of the settlement value, rather than a reasonably founded hope that the process will reveal relevant evidence, it is a social cost rather than a benefit. . . .[22]

In its drive to weaken those laws, the Burger Court restricted many of the very areas in which the Warren Court had expanded the ability of injured parties to seek redress in federal courts. Building, in part, on claims that federal courts were overcrowded, that access to them should be limited, and that state courts should be used as much as possible, the Burger Court narrowed the definition of securities and limited the class of persons who could gain entry into those courts.

In *Blue Chip Stamps v. Manor Drug Stores* (1975), the Court dramatically restricted access to the federal courts to victims of securities fraud. As Justice Harry Blackmun noted in a dissent: "In doing so, the Court exhibits a preternatural solicitousness for corporate well-being and a seeming callousness toward the investing public quite out of keeping, it seems to me, with our own traditions and the intent of the securities laws. . . ."[23]

The next year, in *Ernst & Ernst v. Hochfelder et al.*, the Court generally limited the protections of the securities laws to those who could present an unusually high degree of proof. As Justice Blackmun again argued in dissent:

> Once again—see *Blue Chips Stamps v. Manor Drug Stores*—the Court interprets §10(b) of the Securities Exchange Act of 1934, 15 U.S.C. §78j(b) [15 U.S.C.S. §78j(b)], and the Securities and Exchange Commission's Rule 10b-5, 17 CFR-240.10b-5 (1975), restrictively and narrowly and thereby stultifies recovery for the victim. This time the Court does so by confining the statute and the Rule to situations where the defendant has "scienter," that is, the "intent to deceive, manipulate, or defraud." Sheer negligence, the Court says, is not within the reach of the statute and the Rule, and was not contemplated when the great

reforms of 1933, 1934 and 1942 were effectuated by Congress and the Commission.

Perhaps the Court is right, but I doubt it. The Government and the Commission doubt it too, as is evidenced by the thrust of the brief filed by the Solicitor General on behalf of the Commission, as amicus curiae. The Court's opinion, to be sure, has a certain technical consistency about it. It seems to me, however, that an investor can be victimized just as much by negligent conduct as by positive deception, and that it is not logical to drive a wedge between the two, saying that Congress clearly intended the one but certainly not the other.[24]

In *TransAmerica Mortgage Advisors, Inc. v. Lewis* (1979), the Court largely destroyed the possibility of any meaningful recovery by customers victimized by fraudulent practices of investment advisers. In dissent, Justice Byron White noted: "I find no such intent to foreclose private actions." The Court's opinions callously overlooked the basic purpose of the Investment Advisers Act of 1940 "to prevent fraudulent practices by investment advisers." The dissents also remark that as of December 31, 1978, a total of 5,385 investment advisers were registered with the Securities and Exchange Commission and by October 1980, more than $200 billion in assets would be under advisement by registered investment advisers.[25]

The number of investment advisers and the size of the assets under their tutelage has grown dramatically since then. Yet the protection afforded such customers by the securities laws has been dramatically limited, if not eliminated.

In *Chiarella v. United States* (1980) the Court limited the legal dangers of trading on insider information. This time the Court's narrow, restrictive opinion drew a dissent from Chief Justice Burger:

> Even at common law, however, there has been a trend away from strict adherence to the harsh maxim caveat emptor and toward a more flexible, less formalistic understanding of the duty to disclose. . . .
>
> By its narrow construction of §10(b) and Rule 10b-5, the Court places the federal securities laws in the rearguard of this movement, a position opposite to the expectations of Congress at the time the securities laws were enacted. I

cannot agree that the statute and Rule are so limited. The Court has observed that the securities laws were not intended to replicate the law of fiduciary relations. . . . Rather, their purpose is to ensure the fair and honest functioning of impersonal national securities markets where common-law protections have proved inadequate.[26]

In *Dirks v. Securities and Exchange Commission* (1983), the Court continued on its path of narrowing the possibility of recovery by those victimized by insider trading. In dissent, Justice Blackmun again wrote:

The Court today takes still another step to limit the protections provided investors by §10(b) of the Securities Exchange Act of 1934. . . . The device employed in this case engrafts a special motivational requirement on the fiduciary duty doctrine. This innovation excuses a knowing and intentional violation of an insider's duty to shareholders if the insider does not act from a motive of personal gain.

Justice Blackmun suggested that the Court appeared to be embracing a curious and radical theory:

This position seems little different from the theory that insider trading should be permitted because it brings relevant information to the market. . . . The Court also seems to embrace a variant of that extreme theory, which postulates that insider trading causes no harm at all to those who purchase from the insider. . . . Both the theory and its variant sit at the opposite end of the theoretical spectrum from the much maligned equality-of-information theory, and never have been adopted by Congress or ratified by this Court.[27]

At the same time, the Burger Court exhibited a remarkable hostility to the Securities and Exchange Commission. In *Aaron v. Securities and Exchange Commission* (1980), the Court imposed on the Commission an unnecessarily high burden of proof. Once again in dissent, Justice Blackmun noted:

In fact, the consistent pattern in both the 1933 Act and the 1934 Act is to grant the Commission broad authority to seek enforcement without regard to scienter, unless criminal punishments are contemplated. In both Acts, state of mind is treated with some precision. Congress used terms such as "knowing," "willful," and "good faith" when it wished to impose a state-of-mind requirement. . . . This pattern comports with Congress' expressed intent to give the Commission maximum flexibility to deal with new or unanticipated problems, rather than to confine its enforcement efforts within a rigid statutory framework.[28]

In *Dirks*, the Court continued to exhibit a cynical distrust of the Commission and was critical and suspicious of its investigative and enforcement efforts.

The dissenting opinion of Justices Harry Blackmun and William Brennan in *Ernst* summed up where the Burger Court was going: "Once again . . . the Court interprets §10(b) and the Securities and Exchange Commission's Rule 10b-5 restrictively and narrowly and thereby stultifies recovery for the victim." This is in sharp contrast to the Warren Court, which interpreted federal securities laws "not technically and restrictively, but flexibly to effectuate its remedial purposes," as in *Securities and Exchange Commission v. Capital Gains Research Bureau, Inc.* (1963).[29]

The fundamental function of the law, McGeorge Bundy once asserted, is "to prevent the natural unfairness of society from becoming intolerable."[30] This was certainly not a significant concern of the Burger Court.

·14·

The Burger Court and
Labor-Management Relations

DAVID M. SILBERMAN

Assessing the labor-law jurisprudence of any federal court is not easy. Under the National Labor Relations Act, a claim that an employer or a union committed an unfair labor practice must be submitted to the National Labor Relations Board; the federal courts become involved only on appeal from a decision of the Labor Board. This means that labor-law cases are, by definition, administrative law cases as well and, as Alan Morrison shows elsewhere in this volume, whenever administrative action is challenged, it is to be expected that as a general rule the agency will prevail.

This is certainly true of the labor law decisions of the Burger Court. By my count, of approximately thirty NLRB cases decided by the Court from the 1974–75 to the 1984–85 terms, the Labor Board prevailed in two-thirds. Moreover, looking only at those cases, no clear pattern emerges: the Board was upheld in ruling for employers and against employers, and in ruling for unions and against unions. The central lesson that these cases seem to teach is that the Burger Court—like its predecessors—allowed the Labor Board wide latitude to fashion the labor law. Indeed, in *Pattern Makers League of North America v. NLRB* (1985),[1] the Court, by a 5–4 vote, even permitted the (Reagan-appointed) Labor Board to read into the act a provision that Congress had considered *and rejected* in enacting the NLRA: a provision granting union members a right that is not extended to members of any other association, the right to resign at will, even at times when the union's democratically enacted constitution prohibits resignations.

In a concurring opinion in that case, Justice White—whose vote was necessary to form the majority—expressly acknowledged that he also would have voted to affirm the Board had it reached precisely the opposite conclusion.

Because decisions like *Pattern Makers* express the Supreme Court's historic practice of deferring to the Labor Board, they show us little that is unique about the labor-law jurisprudence of the Burger Court. The true measure of that jurisprudence lies elsewhere, in the decisions of the Board that it *overturned*. In overturning the agency's decisions, the Court necessarily defines the limits of NLRB discretion and makes labor law on its own, in spite of the "expert" agency. Viewed from this perspective, a much clearer picture of the Burger Court's labor-law ideology emerges.

What is most apparent is that the Burger Court was more receptive to challenges to NLRB decisions from employers than to challenges from unions. Although during the Burger Court era the Labor Board more often than not was composed of Republican appointees drawn in large part from the management bar, only once, in a case decided in 1986, did the Court overturn a decision on the ground that the Board went too far in sustaining an employer's conduct. (On one other occasion it overturned a Labor Board decision challenged solely by a union on the ground that the Board had gone too far in condemning union conduct.) But on twelve occasions from 1970–71 to 1984–85, the Burger Court overturned NLRB decisions at the behest of employers, ruling in each instance that the Board had gone too far in prohibiting the employer's conduct.

Certain values ran deep in the Burger Court's labor-law jurisprudence, values such as the sanctity of private property and of entrepreneurial freedom. These values often collided with the policies underlying the act—policies that favor collective action by employees and the equalization of bargaining power between labor and management. And when the Burger Court's values were implicated, it was quite willing to set aside the balance struck by the Board and decide for itself how much weight to give to the statutory policies and how much weight to give the employer's property interests or business needs. Indeed, the Court's concern with property interests and business needs led it to rewrite labor law as it was formulated by the Labor Board, so as to make it more difficult for employees to form unions and more difficult for those who do so to exert economic pressure against their employer; to limit the types of employees who are entitled to unionize; to restrict the subjects on which employers are required to bargain; and to minimize the legal consequences to employers of entering into collective-bargaining agreements.

Central Hardware Co. v. NLRB (1972),[2] an early Burger Court decision, illustrates the first of these points, as well as the general approach that the Court followed in labor-law cases. The case arose out of a union's effort to organize the employees of a retail hardware store; the question was whether the employer was free to exclude union organizers from the store's parking lot, which belonged to him and which he held open to the public. The significance of the issue is plain: if union organizers are to have any realistic chance of success—and it is naïve to expect an unorganized group of workers, or any other unorganized group, spontaneously to join together without the catalyst of an organizer—the organizer has to be able to talk to the workers; as a practical matter this means reaching the workers as they enter or leave work. If the employer can prevent such conversations by controlling access even to parking lots used by the general public, the opportunities for union organizing are greatly diminished.

Recognizing this, and recognizing, too, the minimal property interest that an employer has in excluding a union organizer from a parking lot that is open to every other member of the public, the Labor Board held that by excluding the organizer the employer interfered with the employees' right to form a union in violation of the act. The Board relied, in part, on a Warren Court case holding that the First Amendment requires a shopping-center owner to permit picketing on his property. And the Board distinguished a 1956 Supreme Court decision which, regarding employer property that was *not* open to the general public, had held that such property need not be open to the union except where "the location of a plant and the living quarters of the employees place the employees beyond the reach of reasonable union efforts to communicate with them."[3]

To the Burger Court, however, the *Central Hardware* case was "quite different" from the First Amendment case the Warren Court had decided and was quite similar to the older, private-property case that had arisen under the NLRA. The Court held that the NLRA permits only a "temporary and minimal" incursion on the employer's right to decide who may enter his land even where the land is a parking lot that the general public is free to use. Thus, absent proof that "no reasonable means of communication with employees were available to the nonemployee Union organizers other than solicitation in the parking lots,"[4] the Burger Court held that the employer's property rights must prevail. The Court remanded the case for a decision on that narrow question.

In *Hudgens v. NLRB* (1976),[5] the Burger Court applied *Central Hardware* in a different and equally significant context. There a union was engaged in a labor dispute with an employer who operated a store in an indoor mall; the union sought to place four pickets on property belonging to the mall's owners in order to communicate with customers of the struck employer. The Labor Board concluded that the employees' statutory right to engage in "concerted activities" encompassed a right to place pickets on property that is privately owned but open to the entire public. Again, the Burger Court reversed and remanded the case to the Board to redecide in a way that would give greater sweep to the property rights of the mall owner and correlatively lesser weight to the employees' statutory rights.

The Burger Court was equally solicitous of what it perceived to be the managerial prerogatives of employers. Three sets of cases illustrate this tendency.

The first set raised an issue as to whether particular categories of workers were entitled to the protection of the NLRA. That act, by its very language, applies to "*any* employee" except those falling under certain limited exceptions. But in two cases the Burger Court overturned NLRB decisions and held that employer interests warranted creating an exception not contained in the act, thus excluding from the act a group of workers who in fact met the statutory definition of "employee."

NLRB v. Bell Aerospace Co. (1974)[6] was the first such case. There, employees who worked as buyers for Bell Aerospace opted to form a union to negotiate their salaries and other employment conditions on a collective basis. The employer argued to the Board that the buyers were not entitled to do so because they made procurement policy for the company and in that sense were managerial employees. The Board rejected the argument, reasoning that so long as the buyers did not formulate the employer's labor relations policy, there was no reason to stop them from forming a union to negotiate the terms and conditions of their employment. But the Burger Court disagreed and read into the act an exclusion for "managerial employees" that Congress had never enacted and that is far broader than the exclusion Congress did enact for employees who supervise others.

The breadth of the *Bell Aerospace* "managerial" exclusion became apparent a few years later in *NLRB v. Yeshiva University* (1980).[7] There the Burger Court—to the undoubted surprise of higher-education faculty and administrators alike—held that the faculty of Yeshiva University, no less than the university president and the various deans, are university "managers" and hence not entitled to form a union to negotiate salaries and the like with the administration. The Court easily looked past the facts on which the NLRB had relied: that unlike virtually any other "manager," no individual faculty member makes policy for the employer; no faculty member is accountable to the administration for developing academic policy (indeed, the concept of academic freedom negates any such accountability); and the only policy making in which the individual faculty member participates is, in collective bodies (such as departments), to join in formulating professional judgments on academic affairs—judgments that the administration, which evaluates them from the vantage point of the university as an institution, is free to accept or reject. To the Burger Court, the fact that faculty necessarily participated in "the formulation and implementation of academic policy" required excluding them from the protection of the NLRA; it reasoned that a university's reliance on the faculty's "professional expertise" made unionization unacceptable, as faculty members might "divide their loyalty between employer and union." Indeed, the Court hinted that because of the (hypothesized) risk of divided loyalty the same result would obtain with respect to any professional employees except those "whose decisionmaking is limited to the routine discharge of professional duties in projects to which they have been assigned"—notwithstanding the fact that the act expressly covers *all* professional employees.

In other words, the Burger Court placed the university's supposed interest in maintaining the undivided loyalty of its faculty—an interest that only the Court, and not the Board, believed would even be jeopardized by the formation of a faculty union—over the faculty's statutory interest in bargaining collectively for salary and the like. And although in an almost obligatory final footnote it tried to limit the sweep of its decision to the particular facts before it, the result was all too predictable: except in rare cases, faculty at other institutions have been held, under *Yeshiva*, to be managers and on that basis have lost the benefits of the collective-bargaining system the NLRA seeks to foster.

The second set of cases in which the Burger Court invoked business interests of employers to overturn Labor Board rulings concerned the question of whether employees are entitled to the benefit of their collective-bargaining agreement when, as a result of a merger, sale of assets, or other corporate reorganization, a new corporate entity takes over the business for which they work. The Warren Court had answered that question in the affirmative, in a suit to compel a new owner to arbitrate grievances arising under the predecessor's labor agreement, pursuant to an arbitration clause in that agreement. Relying on that ruling, the Labor Board later held that the NLRA prohibited an employer from renouncing a predecessor's collective-bargaining agreement during the term of that agreement. But in *NLRB v. Burns International Security Service* (1972),[8] the Burger Court reversed that holding and concluded that it is not an unfair labor practice under the NLRA for the new employer to repudiate the predecessor's agreement. And in *Howard Johnson Co. v. Detroit Local Jt. Exec. Bd., Hotel Employees* (1974)[9] the Court went further. In a decision that expressly called the Warren Court's decision into question, the Burger Court held that it is not a *breach of contract* for the successor to repudiate the predecessor's agreement or to refuse to arbitrate disputes under it even where the contract, in terms, states that it is binding on "successors, assigns, purchasers, lessees, or transferees."

In both these cases the Burger Court was concerned that "holding a new employer bound by the substantive terms of the preexisting collective-bargaining agreement might inhibit the free transfer of capital, and that new employers must be free to make substantial changes in the operation of the enterprise."[10] In the face of those employer interests, the interests of the *workers* were required to give way—to the point that in *Howard Johnson* discharged workers who claimed that they had a contractual right to be retained by the new employer were denied any hearing on the merits of their claim.

The third set of cases in which the Burger Court allowed entrepreneurial values to override Labor Board decisions favoring the collective rights of employees concerned the limits on an employer's duty to bargain. The NLRA makes it unlawful for an employer to refuse to bargain in good faith with the representative of his employees with respect to wages, hours, and other terms and conditions of employment. But in two recent cases, the Burger Court placed important limits on that duty.

In *NLRB v. Bildisco & Bildisco*,[11] the Court held, reversing the

NLRB, that after filing a petition in bankruptcy, the employer is free to repudiate his labor contract without bargaining with the union and without even waiting for a ruling from the bankruptcy court permitting contract repudiation. Again, in the Court's view, the interests of the employer were paramount: to require prior bargaining and/or the approval of the bankruptcy court before the employer could repudiate "would largely, if not completely, undermine whatever benefits the debtor-in-possession [i.e., the bankrupt employer] otherwise obtains by its authority to request rejection of the agreement."[12] The consequence of that holding—until it was reversed by Congress—was to benefit not only employers who are bankrupt but also nonbankrupt employers seeking wage reductions from their employees.

All the Burger Court's tendencies in the labor-law area reached what may fairly be called their apex in *First National Maintenance Corp. v. NLRB* (1981),[13] the second case involving the duty to bargain. The question was whether the employer was obligated to bargain with the representative of his employees before deciding to close part of his business. The NLRB had ruled that bargaining over "partial closing" decisions is required, at least where the employer's decision does not involve a "significant investment or withdrawal of capital"; the Board based its ruling on the effect a partial closing has on the tenure of employees, which it reasonably viewed as one of the "terms of employment" as to which the Act requires bargaining. Indeed in *First National Maintenance* the Board viewed the matter as so clearly settled that it was content merely to affirm without opinion a decision by an administrative-law judge.

Notwithstanding the fact that, as the Court acknowledged, Congress adopted a general definition of the mandatory subjects of bargaining so as to "preserve future interpretation by the Board," the Burger Court overturned the NLRB's decision in *First National Maintenance*. The decisive consideration was that

> [m]anagement must be free from the constraints of the bargaining process to the extent essential for the running of a profitable business. . . . In view of an employer's need for unencumbered decisionmaking, bargaining over employment decisions that have a substantial impact on the continued availability of employment should be required only if that benefit, for labor-management relations and the col-

lective bargaining process, outweighs the burden placed on the conduct of the business.[14]

Applying this "test" was a simple matter for the Burger Court, as it could find no real "benefit" in mandating bargaining over a decision to close part of the business: in the Court's view, management would bargain voluntarily if there was anything it wanted from labor in the way of wage reductions, and thus there was no reason to *require* bargaining; the only consequence of doing so, it concluded, would be to jeopardize management's need for "speed, flexibility, and secrecy in meeting business opportunities and exigencies." So the Court decided that a partial closing decision simply is not "amenable to resolution through the bargaining process."

This is labor law, Burger Court–style, at its very worst. Despite a statute that Congress enacted for the purpose of "encouraging the practice and procedure of collective bargaining," the Court's decision as to whether bargaining is required in a particular case turned on an assessment of the costs and benefits of collective bargaining, which the Court took it upon itself to make, ignoring the judgment of the Labor Board. And it ultimately concluded that the "cost" of mandatory bargaining—measured in terms of the effect on management's ability to "run a profitable business"—outweighs the benefits, and thereby overturned the Board's decision to require bargaining in favor of a Court-created rule freeing employers from a bargaining obligation.

When the National Labor Relations Act was being considered in Congress over fifty years ago, Senator Huey Long told Senator Robert Wagner, the principal author of the bill, that "[i]f the Senator from New York can draft an act that will protect labor, he will be the only man who has ever been able to do it. Nobody else has ever been able to do it with the court interpretations." Reviewing the Burger Court's labor-law cases, one cannot escape the conclusion that Senator Long was more right than wrong. For when the proverbial chips were down, the Burger Court was more than willing to abandon its traditional deference to the Labor Board and, without any clear statutory basis for doing so, to rescue employers from the Board's attempts to allow employees to form unions and to participate in shaping the terms and conditions of their employment through the process of collective bargaining.

·15·

Showing Workers Who's Boss

ARTHUR FOX

Worker-employer relationships are governed principally by the National Labor Relations Act, and worker-union relations by the Landrum-Griffin Act. Both these laws depend heavily on the judicial process for elaboration because they were so generally, often ambiguously, drafted. As a result, the Supreme Court has played an unusually significant role in defining the scope of workers' rights.

THE CONTRACTUAL RIGHTS OF EMPLOYEES IN THE WORKPLACE

No one will seriously suggest that workers and their unions are on an equal footing with employers in the "economic state of nature." In the absence of laws prohibiting various forms of discrimination, the boss can hire and fire at will, and pay as little as he can manage while still attracting workers. The function of the law has been to confer certain rights upon employees and their unions, and concomitantly to limit the otherwise unfettered discretion of employers, in an effort to create a more socially acceptable balance between the two competing interest groups. The National Labor Relations Board and the federal courts have been given the responsibility of enforcing the law. The Supreme Court is the final arbiter of this adjudicatory process, and under Chief Justice Warren Burger its decisions created a serious tilt in favor of business interests.

Because so much money is often at stake depending upon which way the law may lean, employers have enormous incentives to litigate every nuance of labor law, just as they do with tax laws. Over the years, the body of decisional law has snowballed to the point where its breadth and complexity far exceed those of tax laws. Unlike the latter, which are largely codified and can easily be discovered, the laws governing labor relations must often be divined by studying scores of agency and judicial decisions, often seemingly in conflict. Indeed, we are fast arriving at a point where there is such a plethora of law governing labor relations that workers and their unions can barely sneeze without first consulting a lawyer to determine when, where, and how they may do so. In such circumstances, one can readily see that those who can least afford legal counsel are the ones who are increasingly disadvantaged.

Unfortunately, the Burger Court added layer upon layer to the law without showing any sensitivity to this basic inequity. While it occasionally upheld the rights of individual employees, workers have been the losers overall. Even in cases where employees were technically the winners, their victory often came at the expense of their unions, thus weakening their collective strength. All told, the employer has finished first in the Court's standings; unions, second; and employees, last.

Although the Burger Court did not radically change the fundamental principles established by the Warren Court with regard to labor contracts and their enforcement, it extended some of those principles in a manner that impairs the workers' opportunity to remedy violations. To appreciate this drift, we must first understand a few basic propositions.

Unlike ordinary contracts, leases, warranties, and the like, collectively bargained labor agreements are not ordinarily enforceable in courts of law. Under Chief Justice Earl Warren, the Supreme Court recognized that the courts might be inundated and the judicial system might grind to a standstill if every alleged violation of a labor contract was litigated in the courts. Hence, it declared that federal policy required the parties to labor agreements to develop their own processes for adjudicating disputes and remedying violations. As a result, one can find in almost every collective-bargaining agreement some sort of grievance-arbitration procedure. Unions customarily agree to utilize this mechanism for securing employer compliance with the contract, and employers agree to be bound by the results of the process as an alternative to economic pressures such as strikes and lock-outs.

Of course, unions are concerned primarily with the collective rights of all the workers in any given shop. And when an employer unjustly terminates or otherwise discriminates against an individual worker, the union, which functions like a state's attorney in deciding what grievances to prosecute, may choose not to press the grievance for reasons unrelated to the merits of the employee's case.

This "prosecutorial discretion" is a power that can be abused. Like the rest of us, union officials are only human. For example, they might be biased against a complaining worker, perhaps because he or she threatens their own prospects for reelection to office. In such cases, the official may be as eager as the employer to be rid of the worker and may refuse altogether to prosecute his or her grievance, or may sabotage the grievance procedure more subtly, such as by failing to offer crucial evidence or argument. While this would constitute malpractice if the union official were a lawyer, the law as developed by the Supreme Court imposes on union officials no affirmative duty to represent workers. If there were such a duty, workers and unions might become regular adversaries in a wholly overcrowded court system.

Given these considerations, the Supreme Court has held that employees must exhaust their contractual grievance procedures before going to court, and the courts must then defer to the outcome of the grievance process. The employee would certainly seem to be up the proverbial creek, but the Court did not leave workers at the total mercy of their unions. In a famous decision, *Vaca v. Sipes* (1967),[1] the Warren Court recognized that these procedural rules could expose workers to serious injustices. So the Court created what it called a "bulwark to prevent arbitrary union conduct against individuals stripped of traditional forms of redress by provisions of Federal labor law."[2] When the individual worker can prove that a grievance was not prosecuted because of union animus or some nearly outrageous form of malfeasance, the Court carved an exception to its hands-off rule and instructed the federal courts to accept and adjudicate employees' breach-of-contract claims.

The Burger Court subsequently extended that ruling to situations in which the union had pressed the grievance to arbitration but had not fairly represented the worker in that proceeding. In *Hines v. Anchor Motor Freight* (1976),[3] the Court held that if the worker could demonstrate that the union had sabotaged the arbitration proceeding, the award would be invalidated and the employee granted a hearing. Thus, only when the employee can first prove a union breach of the so-called "duty of fair representation" in what is the equivalent of a judicial semifinal, may he or she qualify for the final against the employer on the breach-of-contract claim.

After *Hines*, employers cried "foul." While they had formerly been protected from most employee suits by the arbitration process, they finally came out from behind the unions' skirts and mounted an attack on the "fair representation" doctrine, complaining that their liability to unlawfully terminated employees might multiply because of delays in adjudicating contract claims. They argued that they had bargained for an expedited arbitration process to resolve such claims and should not have to pay damages that accrued subsequent to the union's breach of its duty of fair representation in handling an employee grievance. And, in 1983, the Court embraced that argument in a 5–4 decision even though it had been rejected by every appeals court that had previously considered it. In *Bowen v. United States Postal Service*,[4] the Court ruled that the lion's share of a back-pay award to an employee who sued for wrongful discharge and won could be assessed against the union, even though the union had had nothing to do with the employee's illegal termination.

Of course, individual workers may not particularly care where their back pay comes from, but in the long run they will have more problems dealing with employers if they are represented by unions that have been seriously weakened by damage awards. Moreover, the Court's ruling pits workers against their unions any time they are the victims of employer contract violations that the grievance machinery did not remedy. The union has thus been judicially maneuvered into a position in which it serves as the employer's first line of defense against workers suing to vindicate their rights under collective-bargaining agreements. And to protect their own interests, unions have become as zealous as employers in stifling these suits. As if employers were not a sufficiently formidable opponent, unions are now forced into a quasi-partnership with them to enforce workplace discipline; the odds against an employee's securing workplace justice become staggeringly long.

Moreover, as a result of other Burger Court decisions, workers must fulfill strict procedural requirements before they may even attempt to bring their claims to court. In *Clayton v. International Union*,

United Automobile Workers (1981),[5] the Court held that employees must exhaust not only their contract grievance procedures but also lengthy and complex internal union appellate procedures before they may sue an employer for breach of contract. During the same term, in United Parcel Service v. Mitchell,[6] the Court reduced the time limit for filing such suits from the existing three to six years (depending on state laws) to a scant 30 to 120 days. However, even the Burger Court soon recognized that this limitation was too severe. Two terms later, it extended the period to six months in Del Costello v. Teamsters (1983).[7] The practical effect of such procedural obstacles has been to dry up breach-of-contract litigation. Today few employees can secure relief from workplace injustices except through union grievance machinery. Thus, while the Warren Court's "bulwark" against such injustices is still alive in theory, the Burger Court rendered it of little practical value.

And finally, when attorneys representing workers began finding creative methods for breaking their clients out of the breach-of-contract/duty-of-fair-representation straitjacket, with its maze of procedural booby traps, the Burger Court undermined their efforts in Allis-Chalmers Corp v. Lueck (1985).[8] Rather than permit unionized workers to use conventional remedies available under state law to redress legal injuries inflicted upon them by their employers, the Court held that they had to look to their contract grievance machinery as the exclusive remedy. Thus, when Allis-Chalmers ordered a private insurance company to terminate an employee's disability coverage for "a non-occupational back injury [suffered] while carrying a pig to a friend's house for a pig roast," the Court said that the employee's only avenue of redress against Allis-Chalmers would be a classic breach-of-contract suit, complete with its procedural minefield that is usually fatal to employee-plaintiffs. Although the employee's claim more closely resembled a tort, the Court rationalized this result on the tenuous ground that Allis-Chalmers had agreed to pay its employees' insurance premiums in its collective-bargaining agreement.

EMPLOYEES' STATUTORY RIGHTS IN THE WORKPLACE

Collective-bargaining agreements are not, of course, the only source of employees' rights in the workplace. In the 1930s, Congress conferred upon workers the right to engage in "concerted activities for mutual aid and protection." Enforcement of this law was entrusted to the exclusive jurisdiction of the National Labor Relations Board; in other words, employees are not permitted even to initiate legal actions against employers for retaliating against the employees for engaging in statutorily protected activities.

Obviously, these statutory rights cannot be exercised if employees are afraid to talk to one another about workplace problems. One increasingly popular management device for chilling employee efforts to engage in statutorily protected "concerted activities," or for nipping them in the bud, is the libel/defamation action. If employees say something critical about management, they may suddenly find themselves having to defend a multi-million-dollar lawsuit. In *Bill Johnson's Restaurants v. National Labor Relations Board* (1983),[9] the Court overruled a line of NLRB decisions that had barred such suits. Although the Court upheld the Board's authority to order companies to reimburse employees for legal fees in cases the employees won, the Court sharply tilted the balance between the rights of employers and employees against the latter. These suits are very expensive to litigate. To defend against such actions, which may have been brought for the sole purpose of intimidation, employees must usually raise tens of thousands of dollars "up front" before lawyers will agree to handle their cases. Employers, on the other hand, can usually afford to pay hefty legal fees, partly because they are generally tax-deductible. In effect, the Burger Court gave employers license to use public funds to undermine the employees' right to free speech.

An equally damaging decision for workers came in 1981 in a case involving a company that had decided to shut down one of its facilities and terminate the employees there. Although the Supreme Court traditionally has upheld the absolute right of employers to go out of business, it has also held that employers must bargain with unions over partial shutdowns. In *First National Maintenance Corp. v. National Labor Relations Board* (1981),[10] the Court removed this particular category of management decision-making from the list of mandatory subjects of bargaining. The Court speculated that bargaining over decisions to shut down facilities would be unproductive, would increase the employer's financial losses, and could even exacerbate conflict. The presumption that the collective-bargaining process itself provided a vehicle for ventilating conflict, thus alleviating tensions between labor and management, was effectively overruled.

By weighing the subjective costs and benefits of bargaining from a management perspective, the Burger Court gave the ardently pro-management Reagan appointees on the NLRB a license to overhaul long-settled labor principles. And the Board has been doing that with a vengeance. Although the Court and the NLRB continue to pay lip service to the principle that plant closings and job subcontracting motivated primarily by a desire to reduce labor costs are illegal, the burden of proof has been put on those who would challenge an employer's action. That burden is practically impossible to meet, since such policies are adopted in the security of the board room by managers who can always cloak their decisions in complex economic justifications, hiding their real, unlawful motivation to cut labor costs. Moreover, NLRB procedures do not grant the subpoena power needed to develop evidence to refute management claims.

In another case, the Court struck a blow at labor's efforts to organize new categories of workers with its ruling in 1980 that faculty members at Yeshiva University were not entitled to unionize because they were part of management, a view that anyone familiar with the way universities are run knows is unfounded.[11] In the most notorious (though short-lived) decision harmful to workers, *National Labor Relations Board v. Bildisco & Bildisco* (1984),[12] the Burger Court held that employers who had filed for protection under the Bankruptcy Act could abrogate their collective-bargaining agreements. That tipped the balance so far in favor of employers that Congress was forced to quickly pass a law requiring bankruptcy judges to approve any modifications of labor agreements before they could be implemented.

The Burger Court may have believed that congressional activism to overrule its decisions shows a healthy functioning of our constitutional system. In truth, it shows that the Court is well to the right of public opinion. When Congress speaks—as it has on many of these matters—it is the Court's job to construe the statutes so as to promote the lawmakers' objectives, not to undermine them and force Congress to enact yet another law. Congress, after all, is functionally incapable of supervising the Court. Only the most extreme decisions are likely to be overruled legislatively. The result in labor law is that employees' rights will be narrowly confined and Congress' objectives frustrated.

The picture is not totally bleak, however. In two decisions, the Burger Court strengthened the hand of individual workers involved in safety disputes with employers. In *Whirlpool Corp. v. Marshall* (1980),[13] it upheld a Labor Department regulation that prohibits employers from firing workers who refuse to perform abnormally dangerous assignments, despite the absence of any explicit statutory authorization for the regulation. And in *National Labor Relations Board v. City Disposal Systems* (1984),[14] it affirmed an NLRB decision ordering the reinstatement of a truck driver who refused to drive a vehicle with faulty brakes. (The company had attacked the Board's decision on the ground that the driver's conduct was not taken "in concert" with other employees, so that the Board lacked the authority to order his reinstatement.)

Unfortunately, at the same time the Court was affirming the NLRB doctrine protecting "individual concerted activity," the newly constituted Reagan Board was publishing its own decision rescinding that doctrine. Overturning decades of legal precedent, the NLRB decided in 1984 to withhold its remedial processes from an employee who is the victim of unlawful employer reprisals if he has available to him a union grievance procedure.[15] Not only does this place employees at the total mercy of their unions, but it also overburdens unions, which are functionally and financially incapable of shouldering the burden of enforcing an act of Congress as well as their own agreements.

The government has always absorbed the cost of NLRB proceedings, while unions have absorbed the costs of arbitral proceedings. With the entire burden of adjudicating every kind of controversy shifted to unions, recalcitrant employers who are willing to flout their lawful obligations can easily break a union's financial back and put its workers in a position where they have to decide which of their legal rights they wish to vindicate and which they will do without. It is no wonder that workers are becoming increasingly contemptuous of the legal process, an unhealthy phenomenon in a nation under law.

The Board found support for its reliance on the private grievance adjustment process in *Gateway Coal Co. v. United Mine Workers* (1974).[16] In that case, despite the UMW's deliberate removal of its "no-strike" commitment from the contract, the Court adopted an inference that whenever a collective-bargaining agreement contains a grievance procedure, the union *must* employ that procedure to adjust every kind of dispute; the effect was to insert a no-strike clause in every labor agreement, overriding union efforts to reserve the right to apply economic pressure on employers as a means of obtaining the favorable adjustment of contract disputes, even life-threatening safety disputes in the nation's mines.

THE RIGHTS OF UNION MEMBERS

Employees fare little better in their efforts to secure their "civil" rights within their unions. In 1959, Congress enacted the Landrum-Griffin Act in response to revelations of corrupt and undemocratic union practices made during the McClellan Committee hearings on labor racketeering. Congress concluded that since unions possessed such power and discretion over the lives and welfare of the employees they represented, they should at the very least be democratically accountable to their members.

The Landrum-Griffin Act bore the Kennedy stamp: Robert Kennedy was chief counsel to the McClellan Committee and was largely responsible for conducting the hearings, and John Kennedy managed the bill on the floor of the Senate. Its overall objectives were to make unions accountable to their members through the democratic process and to strengthen the hand of workers in their dealings with their union officials.

These are particularly difficult goals to attain, since unions are one-party states. The union and its administration are wrapped in the flag, and dissent is equated with disloyalty. The leadership dominates communication and controls the union newspaper, which typically presents only its views, usually with much adulation; incumbent officials hold the keys to the union treasury and can take full advantage of political patronage. They can groom their successors, reward loyal subordinates, and eliminate potential opposition through appointments. Through their control over "hiring hall" referrals for jobs and the grievance procedure—which means, of course, their members' jobs—officers can reward their friends and punish their political enemies. Under those circumstances there is little opportunity to form any kind of organized opposition.

The cornerstone of the Landrum-Griffin Act is a Union Members' Bill of Rights patterned after the Constitution's Bill of Rights. For example, the statute prohibits unions from infringing members' freedom of speech and assembly and requires unions to conduct periodic secret-ballot elections for officers. However, possessing a right is only half the battle; one must also be able to secure relief when the right is infringed. For better or worse, the Union Members' Bill of Rights was left to members to enforce by bringing suits in federal courts. To some extent, the Court has facilitated member suits to vindicate their rights. In *Hall v. Cole* (1973),[17] the Court held that unions found guilty of interfering with members' freedom of speech would normally have to pay the members' attorney fees. As a result, some attorneys are now willing to represent unionists on a contingent-fee basis. And in *Local 82, Furniture and Piano Movers v. Crowley* (1984),[18] the Court ruled that member suits arising out of an election could be heard and violations remedied during the election, so long as the remedy did not delay the election or force a rerun.

But these two victories pale beside two 1982 decisions that strengthened the hand of officials intent on repressing democracy and retaining dynastic control of unions. Incumbent union officials not only possess vast political advantages over insurgent candidates, but also have ready access to campaign funds from the union staff. Insurgent candidates have no comparable sources and often must raise funds from outside the union. While no candidate should solicit or accept contributions from employers with whom the union bargains or whose shop it might seek to organize, there is no reason why candidates should be prohibited from accepting contributions from friends who do not hold a card in their particular union. Barring contributions from any "outsider" serves only to increase the already overwhelming advantages of the incumbents.

Nevertheless, in *United Steelworkers of America v. Sadlowski* (1982),[19] the Court upheld a union ban on outsider contributions. In 1977, rank-and-file candidate Ed Sadlowski mounted a substantial challenge to the incumbent, Lloyd McBride, for the presidency of the steelworkers' union. McBride raised 85 percent of his campaign funds from the union's staff. Sadlowski had to look to family, friends, and others; none of the money he raised came from anyone with actual or potential collective-bargaining relations with the union.

Sadlowski lost, but he came closer than comfort, from the incumbent administration's perspective. Following its electoral scare, the administration crafted a rule forbidding candidates to accept contributions from nonmembers, a rule that would have barred even Sadlowski's father, a retired steelworker with thirty years' service, from contributing. Both the district court and the court of appeals concluded that the rule violated the Landrum-Griffin Act. The appellate court relied on the Supreme Court's opinion on the Federal Election Law in *Buckley v. Valeo* (1976)[20] and reasoned that by denying Sadlowski funds, the union was infringing his right of free speech, making it difficult, if not impossible, for him to communicate his views to other members. The Supreme Court reversed this decision, stating simply that while Title I may have been modeled after the Bill of Rights, union rules need not meet stringent First Amendment standards and are valid "so long as they are reasonable." But, as Professor Clyde Summers, the architect of Title I, so poignantly observed:

> This reverses reality. Free speech needs even wider scope in a one-party state . . . because there is no free press and no established opposing party to criticize those in power. . . . The purpose of the statute was to loosen the iron grip of oligarchy, not tighten its stranglehold.[21]

Following the Burger Court's decision, a number of unions quickly adopted their own outsider rules, and it is just a matter of time before most union oligarchies follow the United Steelworkers' lead. Sadly, only in those unions where democracy is already alive and well, and where the protections of Title I are less crucial, will opposition groups be able to block administration moves to amend their constitutions to prohibit outsider campaign contributions.

The other decision by the Burger Court that seriously undermined union democracy and fortified the political power of incumbent officials, is *Finnegan v. Leu* (1982).[22] There, an insurgent in a local union won an election and promptly fired all the appointed business agents who had supported the incumbent. The agents argued that they should not have been punished solely for their political beliefs, an argument that has been successfully made by public officials. Contrary to the normal practice of broadly interpreting remedial statutes, the Court read the Landrum-Griffin Act narrowly and ruled that it proscribed only retaliatory actions that affected an employee's *membership* rights. Thus, while a union cannot suspend or expel the business agent from the union, it can take away his or her livelihood as a staff employee because of political beliefs, speech, or association.

At first blush, this decision appears to be correct. Certainly the President of the United States must be able to hire and fire his cabinet secretaries, albeit with the advice and consent of the Senate. But this analogy is not entirely apt in the one-party union political state. In the first place, members who hold union jobs are among the few who have the knowledge and experience to mount credible campaigns against incumbent officials. Now they can be muzzled unless they are willing to forfeit their jobs. The dangers that patronage poses for the democratic process have been recognized in the Hatch Act and by various Supreme Court decisions that limit the circumstances under which public employees may be discharged because of their political affiliation or activities. In these labor cases, however, the Burger Court ignored the obvious analogy and found that the protections necessary to democracy in an open two-party system were not required in a one-party system.

Another problem is that the lower courts have carried *Finnegan* one tragic but predictable step further by holding that unions may remove not only appointed, but also elected officials so long as they do not deny them the privileges of membership in the process.[23] In other words, national union officials no longer need to impose trusteeships on locals with popular, independent officers who refuse to toe their line in order to take over such locals. So long as they do not deny these local officials their membership right to attend meetings and to vote, *Finnegan*, according to the unanimous holding of the lower courts, permits the national officials to remove them from office. As a result, entrenched officers in national unions can now prevent political opponents from gaining even a local foothold while simultaneously depriving members of their right to govern themselves through elected local leaders.

Finnegan has given top union officials license to impose *de facto* trusteeships on independent locals. Between *Sadlowski* and *Finnegan*, the Burger Court prevented the Landrum-Griffin Act from "loosening the iron grip" of union oligarchy, as Congress intended. All told, the legal plight of the worker and union member worsened measurably under the Burger Court.

NOTES

Introduction

1. Mapp v. Ohio, 367 U.S. 643 (1961); Miranda v. Arizona, 384 U.S. 436 (1966); Moran v. Burbine, 106 S. Ct. 1135, 1144 (1986).
2. *See, e.g.*, Wallace v. Jaffree, 105 S. Ct. 2479 (1985) (religion); Akron v. Akron Center for Reproductive Health, 462 U.S. 416 (1983) (abortion).
3. New York Times, July 4, 1971, p. 1, col. 5.
4. Younger v. Harris, 401 U.S. 37 (1971) ("our federalism"); *e.g.*, Stone v. Powell, 428 U.S. 465 (1976) (habeas corpus).
5. 444 U.S. 507 (1980).
6. 468 U.S. 222 (1984).
7. 106 S. Ct. 1310 (1986).
8. *E.g.*, Epstein, Takings: Private Property and the Power of Eminent Domain (1985).
9. 198 U.S. 45 (1905).
10. Lloyd Corp. v. Tanner, 407 U.S. 551 (1972) (leaflets); Hudgens v. NLRB, 424 U.S. 507 (1976) (labor activity).
11. Dorsen and Gora, *The Burger Court and the Freedom of Speech*, in The Burger Court: The Counter-Revolution That Wasn't 28, 31 (V. Blasi ed. 1983).
12. Harper & Row v. Nation Enterprises, 105 S. Ct. 2218 (1985).
13. Tribe, *Compensation, Contract & Capital: Preserving the Distribution of Wealth*, in Constitutional Choices 165, 186 (1985).
14. *E.g.*, Penn Central Transportation Co. v. New York, 438 U.S. 104 (1978) (taking); Energy Reserves Group, Inc. v. Kansas Power & Light Co., 459 U.S. 400 (1983) (contract clause).

15. *E.g.*, Dandridge v. Williams, 397 U.S. 471 (1970) (welfare).
16. Plyler v. Doe, 457 U.S. 202 (1981) (education); Wohlgemuth v. Williams, 416 U.S. 910 (1974) (welfare); Memorial Hospital v. Maricopa County, 415 U.S. 250 (1974) (health care); U.S. Department of Agriculture v. Moreno, 413 U.S. 528 (1973) (food stamps), *but see* Lyng v. Castillo, 106 S. Ct. (1986) (food stamps denial allowed).
17. 376 U.S. 254 (1964).
18. Bowers v. Hardwick, 106 S. Ct. (1986); Gewirtz, *The Court Was "Superficial" in the Homosexuality Case*, New York Times, July 8, 1986, p. A21, col. 1. The four critics of the abortion decision were Chief Justice Burger and Justices White, Rehnquist, and O'Connor.
19. *E.g.*, Armco, Inc. v. Hardesty, 467 U.S. 638 (1984). Its hostility to local restraints was so great that it even invoked the usually toothless equal-protection clause to strike down protectionist state legislation, when the commerce clause was inapplicable. Metro. Life Ins. Co. v. Ward, 105 S. Ct. 1676 (1984).
20. National League of Cities v. Usery, 426 U.S. 833 (1976); Garcia v. San Antonio Metro. Transit Authority, 105 S. Ct. 1005 (1985); *id.* at 1033, 1038 (dissents).
21. Allen v. Wright, 468 U.S. 737 (1984); Bob Jones University v. United States, 461 U.S. 574 (1983).
22. United States v. Leon, 468 U.S. 897 (1984); Grove City College v. Bell, 465 U.S. 555 (1984).
23. Meese, Address before the Federal Bar Association, Detroit, Mich. (Sept. 13, 1985); the *Gramm-Rudman* case is Bowsher v. Synar, 106 S. Ct. 3181 (1986), *aff'g* 626 F. Supp. 1374 (D.D.C. 1986) (3-judge); Humphrey's Executor v. United States, 295 U.S. 602 (1935). For Judge Scalia's comment on the independent agencies, see 626 F. Supp. at 1398.
24. Garcia v. Metro. Transit Authority, 105 S. Ct. at 1023 (Powell, J., dissenting).
25. 106 S. Ct. 2101 (1986).
26. Monsanto Co. v. Spray-Rite Service Corp., 465 U.S. 752, 761 (1984).
27. *Reagan Crusade Before the Court Unprecedented in Intensity*, 44 Cong. Q. 616 (Mar. 15, 1986).
28. Bowers v. Hardwick, 106 S. Ct. at 2841; Davis v. Bandemer, 106 S. Ct. 2797 (1986).
29. Address before the Federalist Society Lawyers Division, Washington, D.C. (Nov. 15, 1985), pp. 14, 8–9 (mimeo).
30. 60 U.S. 393 (1857).
31. 347 U.S. 483 (1954).
32. Bickel, *The Original Understanding and the Segregation Decision*, 69 Harv. L. Rev. 1, 58–59 (1955).
33. Cong. Globe, 39th Cong., 1st Sess. 401 (1866) (remarks of Sen. McDougall).
34. Wallace v. Jaffree, *supra* note 2 at 2503.
35. Quoted in Bickel, *supra* note 32.

36. Powell, *The Original Understanding of Original Intent*, 98 HARV. L. REV. 885, 894–902 (1985).
37. FARRAND, THE RECORD OF THE FEDERAL CONVENTION OF 1787 xiii, xv, xvii (1937).
38. Levy, *The Legacy Reexamined*, 37 STAN. L. REV. 767, 770 (1985).
39. Batson v. Kentucky, 106 S. Ct. 1712, 1742 (1986).
40. *See, e.g.*, Ollman v. Evans & Novak, 750 F.2d 970 (D.C. Civ. 1984); Tavoulareas v. Washington Post, 763 F.2d 1472 (D.C. Cir.), *reh'g en banc granted*, 773 F.2d 1325 (1985).
41. Fullilove v. Klutznick, 448 U.S. 48 (1980); Roe v. Wade, 410 U.S. 113 (1973).
42. *See, e.g.*, Rawlings v. Kentucky, 448 U.S. 98 (1980); National League of Cities v. Usery, *supra* note 20.
43. Morrison and Stenhouse, *The Chief Justice of the United States: More Than Just the Highest Ranking Judge*, 1 CONST. COMMENTARY 57 (1984).
44. Three famous examples of such disappointment are Theodore Roosevelt's unhappiness with Justice Oliver Wendell Holmes over the latter's vote in an antitrust case, Eisenhower's unhappiness with Chief Justice Warren, and Nixon's with Justice Blackmun's shift and with the overall record of the Burger Court. But on the crucial issue of the early twentieth century, the Court's interference in state efforts to regulate the economy, Holmes voted consistently as Roosevelt wanted. See, *e.g.*, Holmes's dissent in Lochner v. New York, 198 U.S. 45 (1905). Eisenhower did not deplore either Warren's segregation decision, the most important case pending when Warren was chosen, or even the choice of Warren as Chief Justice (*see* AMBROSE, EISENHOWER: THE PRESIDENT 128, 129 [1985]), until the 1960s, when the Court issued its criminal law and national security decisions, *id.* at 190; by this time Eisenhower had moved sharply to the right. Nixon's primary concern was law and order, and Justice Blackmun and the other Nixon appointees have consistently voted against defendants' rights.
45. *The Burger Court Holds The Line*, 229 NATION 495, 497 (1979).

1. Justiciability, Remedies, and the Burger Court

1. 5 U.S. (1 Cranch) 137 (1803).
2. *United States v. Carolene Products Co.*, 304 U.S. 144, 152 n. 4 (1938).
3. DWORKIN, TAKING RIGHTS SERIOUSLY (1977); Dworkin, *The Forum of Principle*, 56 N.Y.U. L. Rev. 469 (1981).
4. ELY, DEMOCRACY AND DISTRUST (1980).
5. 369 U.S. 186 (1962).
6. 392 U.S. 83 (1968).
7. 408 U.S. 1 (1972).
8. 418 U.S. 208 (1974).
9. 418 U.S. 166 (1974).

10. 422 U.S. 490 (1975).
11. 423 U.S. 362 (1976).
12. 461 U.S. 95 (1983).
13. 454 U.S. 464 (1982).
14. 410 U.S. 614 (1973).
15. 426 U.S. 26 (1976).
16. 468 U.S. 737 (1984).
17. 438 U.S. 59 (1978).
18. 106 S. Ct. 1326, 1336 (1986).
19. 419 U.S. 393 (1975).
20. *See also* Richardson v. Ramirez, 418 U.S. 24 (1974); Franks v. Bowman Trans. Co., 424 U.S. 747 (1976).
21. 416 U.S. 312 (1974).
22. 416 U.S. 115 (1974).
23. 365 U.S. 167 (1961).
24. 436 U.S. 658 (1978).
25. 445 U.S. 622 (1980).
26. *E.g.*, Harlow v. Fitzgerald, 457 U.S. 800 (1982); Wood v. Strickland, 420 U.S. 308 (1975).
27. 403 U.S. 388 (1971).

2. The Burger Court and the Press

1. 376 U.S. 254 (1964).
2. Brennan, *The Supreme Court and the Meiklejohn Interpretation of the First Amendment*, 79 HARV. L. REV. 1 (1965).
3. Professor Meiklejohn had suggested that

> the principle here at stake can be seen in our libel laws. In cases of private defamation, one individual does damage to another by tongue or pen; the person so injured in reputation or property may sue for damages. But, in that case, the First Amendment gives no protection to the person sued. His verbal attack has no relation to the business of governing. If, however, the same verbal attack is made in order to show the unfitness of a candidate for governmental office, the act is properly regarded as a citizen's participation in government. It is, therefore, protected by the First Amendment. [Meiklejohn, *The First Amendment Is an Absolute*, 1961 SUP. CT. REV. 245, 259.]

It is worth noting that Professor Meiklejohn would extend First Amendment protection to "many forms of thought and expression within the range of communications" (*id.* p. 256), and he enumerated some of those: "education, in all its phases . . . [t]he achievements of philosophy and the sciences . . . literature and the arts" (*id.* p. 257). But, again, Meiklejohn suggested constitutional protection for those modes of expression because they would tend to inform the judgment of the voter taking part in the process of self-government. Those other forms, he said, had constitutional value in contributing to "the capacity for sane and objective judgment which, so far as possible, a ballot should express" (*id.* p. 256). Again, that approach to the First Amendment reinforces the classification of expression in terms of social utility. Although Meiklejohn personally might have assumed that a voter, as Renaissance man, would be protected in the pursuit of all manner of "literature and the arts," for example, it would be easy enough for a censor or regulator with a more limited view of the average voter to conclude that some kinds of literature (explicit sexual expression, perhaps) would have no bearing upon exercise of the franchise, and thus should be denied constitutional protection.

4. For example: Jerry W. Friedheim, executive vice-president of the American Newspaper Publishers Association, remarked in an address in 1984:

> When we talk here today about a free press, we must know— and we must remind our people—that freedom of the press is a unique right of the American people; it's their freedom. . . . We must remind our people to guard and protect that right. For, if they do—and, if we of the press meet our Constitutional task with dignity and responsibility—those who meet here 100 years from now . . . will still be a part of the greatest, most free, most successful society ever devised by man. [*The American People's First Amendment*, Biloxi, Miss., (Oct. 25, 1984). Full text available from ANPA, 11600 Sunrise Valley Drive, Reston, Va. 22091.]

5. *See* Near v. Minnesota, 283 U.S. 697 (1931); New York Times v. U.S. (the "Pentagon Papers" case) 403 U.S. 713 (1971); and Nebraska Press Association v. Stuart, 427 U.S. 539 (1976). This is the doctrine going back to Blackstone's commentaries that there can be no restraint on publication by requiring a license, censorship, or prohibition—though there may be postpublication punishment or other consequences.

6. 376 U.S. 301.

7. Rosenblatt v. Baer, 383 U.S. 75 (1966) (non-public officials and subordinate officials); Curtis Publishing v. Butts, 388 U.S. 130 (1967) ("public figures"); Greenbelt Publishing v. Bresler, 398 U.S. 6 (1970) (public hearings); Monitor Patriot v. Roy, 401 U.S. 265 (1971) (candidates); Time v. Pape, 401 U.S. 279 (1971) (government documents).

8. 403 U.S. 29, 44, 46 (1971).

9. *Id.* at 79.

10. 418 U.S. 323, 346 (1974).

11. Time v. Firestone, 424 U.S. 448 (1976) (civil-court proceedings); Hutch-

inson v. Proxmire, 443 U.S. 111 (1979) (public funds); Wolston v. Reader's Digest, 443 U.S. 157 (1979) (crime).

12. Herbert v. Lando, 441 U.S. 153 (1979). The Court's decision set off further discovery in that case, prolonging the process into a marathon. Ultimately, without ever having gone to trial, the case was ordered dismissed on January 15, 1986—almost exactly twelve years after its initial filing January 25, 1974. Herbert v. Lando, 781 F.2d 298 (2d Cir. 1986), cert. denied, 106 S. Ct. 2916 (1986).

13. The decision expanded enormously the scope and cost of pretrial preparations in all public-figure libel cases. After the Supreme Court, in that same year, implied that more public-figure libel cases should go to trial rather than be dismissed early on summary judgment in favor of the press (Hutchinson v. Proxmire, 443 U.S. 111, 120 n. 9 [1979]), the Herbert decision seemed to translate into a serious new risk that more of those cases would be lost before juries. Some of that risk diminished when the Court in June 1986 apparently backed away from the implied suggestion of the Hutchinson footnote, and made it more difficult for public figures to force their libel cases to trial by overcoming summary judgment motions by the press (Anderson v. Liberty Lobby, 106 S. Ct. 2505 [1986]).

14. 465 U.S. 770, 776 (1984).

15. Dun & Bradstreet v. Greenmoss Builders, 105 S. Ct. 2939, 2945 (1985).

16. Id. at 2961, 2964. A year after Dun & Bradstreet, the Court removed all conjecture that that decision meant that the public/private distinction would be relevant only in libel cases involving publications special in nature, like a credit report, or limited in distribution, as Dun's report was. In Philadelphia Newspapers v. Hepps, 106 S. Ct. 1558 (1986), the Court said explicitly that a "media defendant" would be entitled to constitutional protection against having to prove the truth of its stories only when the stories dealt with matters "of public concern." The Hepps case, of course, involved a "regular" media defendant, a newspaper.

17. Fortunately, in Dun & Bradstreet the Court declined to create a new layer or category for libel, one that would measure constitutional protection according to whether the party sued was "media" or "nonmedia." That was the sole issue before the Court when it granted review of the case, because the Vermont Supreme Court had ruled that the Sullivan-Gertz protections simply were unavailable to nonmedia defendants. Aside from the obvious imprecision of such broad groupings as media and nonmedia, the recognition of that supposed distinction would have opened a new avenue for variable social value to dictate the scope of protected and unprotected expression.

18. See Richmond Newspapers v. Virginia, 448 U.S. 555 (1980) and related cases, discussed below.

19. New York Times v. U.S., 403 U.S. 713 (1971).

20. Id. at 749–51.

21. 408 U.S. 665 (1972).

22. Id. at 697.

23. *Id.* at 688.
24. *Id.* at 726 n. 2.
25. *Id.* at 727.
26. *Id.* at 681.
27. *Id.* at 721.
28. Pell v. Procunier, 417 U.S. 817 (1974); Saxbe v. Washington Post, 417 U.S. 843 (1974); Houchins v. KQED, 438 U.S. 1 (1978); Nixon v. Warner Communications, 435 U.S. 589 (1978); Gannett Co. v. DePasquale, 443 U.S. 368 (1979). (The *Gannett* decision appears no longer to be good law, since the Court found a First Amendment right of access to pretrial hearings in criminal cases in Press-Enterprise Co. v. Superior Court, 106 S. Ct. 2735 [1986]).
29. 448 U.S. 555 (1980); 582 (Stevens); 589 (Brennan).
30. Waller v. Georgia, 467 U.S. 39 (1984).
31. Press-Enterprise Co. v. Superior Court, 106 S. Ct. 2735 (1986).
32. Seattle Times v. Rhinehart, 467 U.S. 20, 33 (1984); *see also* Globe v. Superior Court, 457 U.S. 596 (1982) (sex crimes); Press-Enterprise Co. v. Superior Court, 464 U.S. 501 (1984) (jury selection); Waller v. Georgia, 467 U.S. 39 (1984) (suppression hearing).
33. Houchins v. KQED, 438 U.S. 1 (1978), at p. 14.
34. *See* Estes v. Texas, 381 U.S. 532 (1965).
35. *Id.* at 544, 549.
36. *Id.* at 541–42.
37. 449 U.S. 560 (1981), 569, 589 (White).
38. Red Lion Broadcasting v. Federal Communications Commission, 395 U.S. 367.
39. CBS Inc. v. Federal Communications Commission, 453 U.S. 367 (1981).
40. *See* Miami Herald Pub. Co. v. Tornillo, 418 U.S. 241 (1974).
41. 105 S. Ct. 2218, 2230 (1985).
42. *Id.* at 2230.
43. 750 F.2d 970, 1036, *on rehearing en banc* (D.C. Cir. 1984) (Scalia, J., dissenting in part).
44. 759 F.2d 90 (D.C. Cir.); *on motion for rehearing en banc*, 763 F.2d 1472 (D.C. Cir. 1985).
45. 746 F.2d 1563 (D.C. Cir. 1984), *rev'd,* 106 S. Ct. 2505 (1986), discussed at *supra* note 13.
46. In re Reporters Comm. for Freedom of the Press, 773 F.2d 1325 (D.C. Cir. 1985).

3. Freedom of the Press: A Tale of Two Libel Theories

1. Bose Corp. v. Consumers Union, 466 U.S. 485 (1984).
2. Branzburg v. Hayes, 408 U.S. 665 (1972) (no constitutional privilege re sources); Zurcher v. Stanford Daily, 436 U.S. 547 (1978) (newsroom search);

Reporters Comm. for Freedom of the Press v. A.T.&T., 593 F.2d 1030 (D.C. Cir. 1978); Herbert v. Lando, 441 U.S. 153 (1979) (discovery of journalists' notes); Gannett Co. v. DePasquale, 443 U.S. 368 (1979) (closed courtroom).
3. 424 U.S. 693 (1976).
4. 443 U.S. 157 (1979).
5. *Id.* at 168–69.
6. 443 U.S. 137 (1979).

4. The National Security State: Never Question the President

1. Korematsu v. U.S., 323 U.S. 214 (1944); Dennis v. United States, 341 U.S. 494 (1951).
2. Youngstown Sheet & Tube Co. v. Sawyer, 343 U.S. 579 (1952) (steel seizure); Kent v. Dulles, 357 U.S. 116 (1958) (travel); U.S. v. Robel, 389 U.S. 258 (1967) (hiring).
3. HALPERIN AND HOFFMAN, FREEDOM VS. NATIONAL SECURITY: SECRECY AND SURVEILLANCE (1977).
4. 403 U.S. 713 (1971).
5. *Id.* at 747.
6. 444 U.S. 507 (1980).
7. *Id.* at 509 n. 3.
8. 453 U.S. 280 (1981).
9. Title I, § 101, of Pub.L. 95–223, 91 Stat. 1625.
10. 357 U.S. 116 (1957).
11. 468 U.S. 222 (1984).
12. *Id.* at 242, 243.
13. 454 U.S. 139 (1981).
14. *Supra* note 11 at 262.
15. United States v. Robel, 389 U.S. 258 (1967).
16. In cases involving constitutional rights where the military is involved, the Court also accepted at face value the claims of harm put forward by the military and refused to undertake its own balancing of that harm against the right of the individual. Whatever the military says is necessary, is constitutional. As Chief Justice Rehnquist put it in an opinion for the Court in March 1986 holding that the military could prevent a religious Jewish officer from wearing a yarmulke while on duty:

> The desirability of dress regulations in the military is decided by the appropriate military officials, and they are under no constitutional mandate to abandon their considered professional judgment . . . [T]he First Amendment does not require the military to accommodate such [religious] practices in the face of its view that they would detract from the uniformity

sought by the dress regulations. [Goldman v. Weinberger, 106 S. Ct. 1310, 1314 (1986).]

As Justice O'Connor pointed out in dissent, the Court completely abdicated its responsibility to determine for itself whether granting the exemption would do substantial harm to the government interest. In cases not involving the military the Court would determine for itself both whether an important government interest was at stake and whether accommodating religious convictions or other basic rights would jeopardize those interests. In cases involving the military it no longer did either. *See,* Orloff v. Willoughby, 345 U.S. 83, 94 (1953); Parker v. Levy, 417 U.S. 733, 743 (1974); Schlesinger v. Councilman, 420 U.S. 738, 757 (1975); Greer v. Spock, 424 U.S. 828, 843–44 (1976); Rostker v. Goldberg, 453 U.S. 57, 70 (1981); Chappell v. Wallace, 462 U.S. 296, 300 (1983).

5. The Separation of Church and State: The Burger Court's Tortuous Journey

1. U.S. CONST. amend. I.
2. 330 U.S. 1 (1947).
3. The Remonstrance was included as an appendix to Justice Rutledge's dissent. *See* 330 U.S. at 63 (1947).
4. *See* Wallace v. Jaffree, 105 S. Ct. 2479, 2508 (1985) (Rehnquist, J., dissenting).
5. 330 U.S. at 15–16 (1947) (citation omitted).
6. *Id.* at 31.
7. *See* I. BRANT, JAMES MADISON: THE NATIONALIST 343–55 (1948); L. Levy, *No Re-establishment of Religion: The Original Understanding* in JUDGEMENTS: ESSAYS ON AMERICAN CONSTITUTIONAL HISTORY 169 (1972); Cahn, *The Establishment of Religion Puzzle,* 36 N.Y.U. L. REV. 1274 (1961); Sky, *The Establishment Clause, the Congress and the Schools: A Historical Perspective,* 52 VA. L. REV. 1395 (1966). *See also* Abington School Dist. v. Schempp, 374 U.S. 203, 238–42 (1963) (Brennan, J., concurring), in which he described as "futile and misdirected" a "too literal quest for the advice of the Founding Fathers" to help decide the specific issue of the validity of the reading of the Bible or the Lord's Prayer at the start of the school day. Justice Rehnquist's dissent in Wallace v. Jaffree, 105 S. Ct. 2479, 2508 (1985), is the product of historical research, as were the opinions of Justices Black and Rutledge in *Everson.* Justice Reed questioned the *Everson* historical analysis in his dissent in McCollum v. Board of Educ., 333 U.S. 203, 238 (1948).
8. 330 U.S. at 16–17.
9. 333 U.S. 203 (1948).
10. 343 U.S. 306 (1952).
11. *Id.* at 313–14.
12. 370 U.S. 421 (1962).

13. *Id.* at 430.
14. 374 U.S. 203 (1963).
15. *Id.* at 222.
16. *See* Note, *Religious Holiday Observances in the Public Schools*, 48 N.Y.U. L. REV. 1116 (1973). *See also* Florey v. Sioux Falls School Dist., 19 F.2d 1311 (8th Cir. 1980).
17. McGowan v. Maryland, 366 U.S. 420, 445 (1961).
18. Epperson v. Arkansas, 393 U.S. 97 (1968) was also decided at this time. The Court found that an Arkansas law banning the teaching of Darwin's theory of evolution originated in "fundamentalist sectarian conviction." This finding compelled the conclusion that the law was an establishment of religion. In other contexts, however, efforts by religious groups to influence educational policy could not be viewed as establishments. The critical issue is whether or not the state is adopting religious beliefs, as distinct from moral values. *Epperson* has been relied on by those challenging laws that require the teaching of "scientific creationism." *See* McLean v. Arkansas, 529 F. Supp. 1255 (E.D. Ark. 1982); Aguillard v. Edwards, 765 F.2d 1251 (5th Cir. 1985), *prob. juris.* noted, 106 S. Ct. 1946 (1986).
19. 392 U.S. 326 (1968).
20. 392 U.S. at 250 (Black, J., dissenting); 392 U.S. at 254 (Douglas, J., dissenting); 392 U.S. at 269 (Fortas, J., dissenting).
21. 397 U.S. 664 (1970). The author, as New York City's first assistant corporation counsel, participated in the *Walz* case.
22. *Id.* at 674.
23. 403 U.S. 602 (1971); Earley v. Di Censo and Robinson v. Di Censo, 403 U.S. 602 (1971).
24. 403 U.S. at 612–13.
25. *Id.* at 619.
26. *Id.* at 621.
27. *Id.* at 625.
28. *Id.* at 622–23 (citations omitted).
29. *Id.* at 624–25.
30. 403 U.S. 672 (1971).
31. Chief Justice Burger's opinion was joined by Justices Harlan, Stewart, and Blackmun. Justice White concurred in the judgment. The Court's judgment invalidated a portion of the federal statute that imposed a twenty-year limitation on the government's right to recover a portion of the grant if the facility was no longer being used for secular purposes. Justices Black, Douglas, and Marshall agreed with the latter conclusion, but would also have held the entire program invalid. Justice Brennan would have held the program invalid only as to sectarian institutions and would have remanded to determine the sectarian character of the colleges.
32. 413 U.S. 756 (1973).
33. *Id.* at 779–80.
34. *Id.* at 783.

35. *Id.* at 790, 790–91.
36. *Id.* at 794.
37. Justice Powell's opinion contains a long footnote adopting the *Everson-McCollum-Engel* view of the historical basis of the establishment clause. 413 U.S. at 770–71 n. 28.
38. 413 U.S. 734 (1973).
39. 426 U.S. 736 (1976).
40. 413 U.S. 472 (1973).
41. *See, e.g.,* Wollman v. Walter, 433 U.S. 229, 238–42 (1977).
42. 421 U.S. 349 (1975).
43. Justices Harry Blackmun and Powell joined Part V of Justice Stewart's opinion invalidating the "remedial" auxiliary services provision of the Pennsylvania program. Justices Brennan, Douglas, and Marshall joined Part V, in an opinion by Justice Brennan, dissenting from the majority's sustaining of textbook loan provisions that were upheld on the basis of Board of Educ. v. Allen, 392 U.S. 236 (1968).
44. 421 U.S. at 371.
45. *Id.* at 372 n. 22.
46. The lineup of the Court on this issue was the same as in Part V. *See supra* note 43.
47. 421 U.S. at 386–87.
48. The Chief Justice and Justices White and Rehnquist would have also upheld lending instructional materials.
49. 433 U.S. 229 (1977).
50. The Chief Justice's position after *Wollman* was not completely clear, since he joined in Part VI of the Court's opinion, which upheld the provision of therapeutic services off the premises of the religious schools, and which reaffirmed the *Meek* distinction between the religious-school premises and a "neutral" site. However, in light of the Chief Justice's strong dissent from that portion of the *Meek* opinion, the Chief Justice in *Wollman* undoubtedly was simply agreeing with the majority's conclusion that the provision was valid.
51. 449 U.S. 39 (1980).
52. *Id.* at 41. The Chief Justice, and Justices Blackmun and Stewart, objected to the Court's summary reversal, without indicating their views on the merits.
53. *See, generally, Proposed Constitutional Amendment to Permit Voluntary Prayer: Hearings Before the Senate Comm. on the Judiciary,* 97th Cong., 2d Sess. (1982). For the 1984 voluntary school-prayer amendment debate, see 130 CONG. REC. S2879 (daily ed. Mar. 20, 1984). A silent-prayer amendment was tabled prior to the above debate. *See* 130 CONG. REC. S2850 (daily ed. Mar. 19, 1984).
54. S. 528, 98th Cong., 1st Sess., 129 CONG. REC. S1335–38 (daily ed. Feb. 17, 1983). In November 1983, the Senate rejected the President's proposed tuition tax-credit program; *see* NEW YORK TIMES, Nov. 17, 1983, at A1, col. 1.
55. 343 U.S. at 314. *See also* Walz v. Tax Commission, 397 U.S. at 669–70.

56. 374 U.S. 398 (1963).
57. Braunfeld v. Brown, 366 U.S. 599 (1961).
58. Such an exemption was upheld in Arlan's Dep't Store of Louisville, Inc. v. Kentucky, 357 S.W.2d 708 (Ky. 1962), *appeal dismissed,* 371 U.S. 218 (1962).
59. 454 U.S. 263 (1981).
60. *Id.* at 273 n. 13.
61. *See* Bender v. Williamsport Area School Dist., 741 F.2d 538 (3d Cir. 1984), *rev'd for lack of standing,* 106 S. Ct. 1326 (1986); Nartowicz v. Clayton County School Dist., 736 F.2d 646 (11th Cir. 1984); Brandon v. Board of Educ. of Guilderland Central School Dist., 635 F.2d 971 (2d Cir. 1980); Lubbock Civil Liberties Union v. Lubbock Indep. School Dist., 669 F.2d 1038 (5th Cir. 1982); Bell v. Little Axe Indep. School Dist. No. 70, 766 F.2d 1391 (10th Cir. 1985). Congress provided for limited "equal access" to religious groups in public schools through the Equal Access Act, Pub. L. No. 98–377, 98 Stat. 1302 *et. seq.* (1984).
62. 463 U.S. 388 (1983).
63. *Id.* at 397.
64. *Id.* at 409 (Marshall, J., dissenting).
65. *Id.* at 401.
66. *Id.* at 416–17.
67. 463 U.S. at 403–4 n. 11.
68. 463 U.S. 783 (1983).
69. *Id.* at 795 (Brennan, J., dissenting).
70. *Id.* at 792.
71. *Id.* at 816–17, 819.
72. *See* Walz v. Tax Commission, 397 U.S. 664 (1970).
73. *See* Gillette v. United States, 401 U.S. 437 (1971).
74. *See* Lynch v. Donnelly, 465 U.S. 668, 718–21 (1984) (Brennan, J., dissenting).
75. *Id.* at 673.
76. *Id.* at 674.
77. *Id.* at 679.
78. *Id.* at 680.
79. *Id.* at 684; 683 (effect), 683–685 (entanglement).
80. *Id.* at 689 (O'Connor, J., concurring). No Supreme Court decision has relied on political divisiveness as an "independent ground."
81. *Id.* at 690.
82. *Id.* at 690–91.
83. *Id.* at 692.
84. *Id.* at 685.
85. *Id.* at 711–12.
86. *See* Redlich, *Nativity Ruling Insults Jews,* NEW YORK TIMES, Mar. 26, 1984, at A19, col. 2; Van Alstyne, *Trends in the Supreme Court: Mr. Jefferson's Crumbling Wall—A Commentary on* Lynch v. Donnelly, 1984 DUKE L.J. 301.

87. 459 U.S. 116 (1982). Larson v. Valente, 456 U.S. 228 (1982), might possibly be considered another example of a strong reaffirmation of establishment-clause principles. The case involved a Minnesota law that imposed registration and reporting requirements on charitable organizations, but exempted from regulation those religions that received less than half of their contributions from nonmembers. The Court accepted the argument of the Unification Church that the law established a governmental preference in favor of those religions that did not rely on nonmembers for principal financial support. Given this interpretation, the result was clear. As Justice Brennan's majority opinion stated: "The clearest command of the Establishment Clause is that one religious denomination cannot be officially preferred over another" (456 U.S. at 244). The majority applied a "compelling governmental interest" test and rejected the asserted justifications proffered by the state. In addition, the entanglement prong of the *Lemon* three-part test was applied and the distinctions drawn by the statute were held to engender a risk of politicizing religion. Justices White and Rehnquist argued that the record was not adequate to support the finding of religious preference, or to reject the state's justifications. Four justices (the Chief Justice and Justices White, Rehnquist, and O'Connor) dissented on the tangential issue of standing that was present in the case.

88. These provisions are set forth in Wallace v. Jaffree, 105 S. Ct. 2479, 2481–82 (1985).

89. Wallace v. Jaffree, 465 U.S. 920 (1984).

90. The history of the litigation under the three statutes is set forth at 105 S. Ct. at 2482–86.

91. *Id.* at 2490.

92. *Id.* at 2494–95 (Powell, J., concurring).

93. *Id.* at 2490.

94. 465 U.S. at 690–91 (O'Connor, J., concurring).

95. 105 S. Ct. at 2492.

96. *Id.* at 2507 (Burger, C.J., dissenting).

97. Lynch v. Donnelly, 465 U.S. at 686.

98. 105 S. Ct. at 2507–8.

99. *See* 105 S. Ct. at 2502 (O'Connor, J., concurring).

100. *Id.* at 2491 n. 45.

101. *Id.* at 2504.

102. *Id.* at 2505.

103. 105 S. Ct. at 2520. Justice Rehnquist relied heavily on the historical analysis in R. CORD, SEPARATION OF CHURCH AND STATE (1982). *See also* M. HOWE, THE GARDEN AND THE WILDERNESS (1965).

104. *See* Powell, *The Original Understanding of Original Intent*, 98 HARV. L. REV. 885 (1985); Richards, *Interpretation and Historiography*, 58 S. CAL. L. REV. 489 (1985).

105. 105 S. Ct. at 2488.

106. *Id.* at 2488 n. 37.

107. *Id.* at 2493 (emphasis added); *see* Justice O'Connor's comment in her concurring opinion: "It is difficult to discern a serious threat to religious liberty from a room of silent, thoughtful school children" (*id.* at 2499).
108. *Id.* at 2495 (Powell, J., concurring).
109. *Id.* at 2501 (O'Connor, J., concurring).
110. *Id.* at 2495 (Powell, J., concurring).
111. *Id.* at 2491.
112. *See* May v. Cooperman, 572 F. Supp. 1561 (D. N.J. 1983) ("one-minute period of silence" held invalid) *aff'd*, 780 F.2d 240 (3d Cir. 1985); *contra* Gaines v. Anderson, 421 F. Supp. 337 (D. Mass 1976).
113. *See* Duffy v. Las Cruces Pub. Schools, 557 F. Supp. 1013 (D. N.M. 1983) ("or prayer" statute held unconstitutional).
114. 374 U.S. 398 (1963).
115. 450 U.S. 707 (1981).
116. 432 U.S. 63 (1977).
117. 105 S. Ct. 2914 (1985).
118. Conn. Gen. Stat. 53–303e(b) (Supp. 1962–1984), reproduced at 105 S. Ct. at 2916.
119. *Id.* at 2918.
120. *Id.*
121. 105 S. Ct. 3216 (1985); 105 S. Ct. 3232 (1985).
122. Only Justices White and Rehnquist voted to uphold the Community Education Program.
123. 105 S. Ct. at 3218–19 (citations to district court opinion omitted).
124. *Id.* at 3223. Elsewhere in the opinion the schools are described as "pervasively sectarian" (*id.* at 3223).
125. *Id.* at 3225–26.
126. *Id.* at 3227.
127. *Id.* at 3226.
128. *Id.* at 3227, *quoting* Felton v. Secretary of United States Dept. of Educ., 739 F.2d. 48, 67–68 (2d. Cir. 1984).
129. 105 S. Ct. at 3229.
130. *Id.* at 3230. The importance of keeping the "genie" in the bottle was emphasized by Judge Friendly. *See* Felton v. Secretary of United States Dept. of Educ., 739 F.2d at 67; Americans United for Separation of Church and State v. School Dist. of Grand Rapids, 718 F.2d 1389 (6th Cir. 1983).
131. Title I of the Elementary and Secondary Education Act of 1965, 20 U.S.C., 92 Stat. 2153, 2701 *et. seq.* (1982).
132. Felton v. Secretary of United States Dept. of Educ., 739 F.2d at 71–72.
133. 105 S. Ct. at 3239.
134. In Bender v. Williamsport Area School Dist. (*see supra* note 61), the Court failed to resolve the issue of the applicability of the *Widmar* principle to public secondary schools. Four justices (the Chief Justice and Justices White, Rehnquist, and Powell) would have followed *Widmar* and recognized a free-speech right for student religious groups, but

the majority concluded that a single school-board member did not have standing to appeal a lower-court decision.

135. *See supra* note 112.

136. *See* McCreary v. Village of Scarsdale, 739 F.2d 716 (2d Cir. 1984) (city could not exclude crèche from a public park when other free-standing displays were permitted), *aff'd by equally divided Court*, Scarsdale v. McCreary, 105 S. Ct. 1859 (1985).

137. In Witters v. Washington, 106 S. Ct. 748 (1986) a unanimous Court upheld the expenditure of public funds to enable a person to attend a divinity school under a state vocational rehabilitation program for the visually impaired. The majority did not refer to Mueller v. Allen, prompting Justice Powell to reaffirm his position in *Mueller* that "state programs that are wholly neutral in offering educational assistance to a class defined without reference to religion do not violate the second part of the *Lemon v. Kurtzman* test, because any aid to religion results from the private choices of individual beneficiaries" (*id.* at 754). The Chief Justice and Justices White, Rehnquist, and O'Connor indicated their agreement with this position.

6. The Activism Is Not Affirmative

1. *See, e.g.*, Warth v. Seldin, 422 U.S. 490 (1975); Allen v. Wright, 468 U.S. 737 (1984).

2. Edelman v. Jordan, 415 U.S. 651 (1974) (state immunity); Stump v. Sparkman, 435 U.S. 349 (1978) (judicial immunity); Imbler v. Pachtman, 424 U.S. 409 (1976) (prosecutors).

3. *See, e.g.*, Washington v. Davis, 426 U.S. 229 (1976).

4. For an excellent treatment of this subject, arriving at similar conclusions, see Brest, *Race Discrimination*, in THE BURGER COURT: THE COUNTER-REVOLUTION THAT WASN'T 113–131 (V. Blasi ed. 1983).

5. 347 U.S. 483 (1954).

6. 402 U.S. 1 (1971).

7. 413 U.S. 189 (1973).

8. 418 U.S. 717 (1974).

9. Columbus Board of Education v. Penick, 443 U.S. 449 (1979); Dayton Board of Education v. Brinkman, 443 U.S. 526 (1979).

10. 163 U.S. 537 (1896).

11. 403 U.S. 217 (1971).

12. 401 U.S. 424 (1971).

13. 426 U.S. 229 (1976).

14. 446 U.S. 156 (1980).

15. 446 U.S. 55 (1980).

16. 458 U.S. 613 (1982).

17. P.L. No. 97–205, 96 Stat. 131. An effort by the Justice Department to have the Court interpret the statute as requiring proof of intent was

unanimously rebuffed. Thornburg v. Gingles, 106 S. Ct. 2752 (1986).

18. 60 U.S. 393 (1857).
19. 438 U.S. 265 (1978).
20. 443 U.S. 193 (1979).
21. 448 U.S. 448 (1980).
22. 467 U.S. 561 (1984).
23. 106 S. Ct. 1842 (1986).
24. 106 S. Ct. 3063 (1986).
25. 106 S. Ct. 3019 (1986).
26. 465 U.S. 555 (1984).
27. 461 U.S. 574 (1983).
28. 468 U.S. 737 (1984).

7. Sex Discrimination: Closing the Law's Gender Gap

1. 404 U.S. 71 (1971).
2. 411 U.S. 677 (1973).
3. 429 U.S. 190 (1976).
4. *See, e.g.*, Frontiero v. Richardson, 411 U.S. 677 (1973); Califano v. Gold-farb, 430 U.S. 199 (1977); Califano v. Westcott, 443 U.S. 76 (1979); Wengler v. Druggist Mutual Insurance Co., 446 U.S. 142 (1980); Weinberger v. Wiesenfeld, 420 U.S. 636 (1975); Stanton v. Stanton, 421 U.S. 7 (1975); Orr v. Orr, 440 U.S. 268 (1979); Kirchberg v. Feenstra, 450 U.S. 455 (1981); Reed v. Reed, 404 U.S. 71 (1971).
5. 458 U.S. 718 (1982).
6. 433 U.S. 321, 336 (1977). *Dothard* was decided under Title VII of the Civil Rights Act of 1964 rather than under the Fourteenth Amendment; the Court concluded that because a woman's "very womanhood" rendered her unable to perform the job, sex was, in the language of the statute, a "bona fide occupational qualification" and the employer was therefore authorized to treat men and women differently.

The Court chose not even to seriously entertain another and controversial gender and sexuality issue—pornography. The Court summarily affirmed, without briefing or oral argument, lower-court decisions (reported at 771 F.2d 323 and 598 F. Supp. 1316) holding that an Indianapolis antipornography ordinance violated the First Amendment (Hudnut v. American Booksellers Association, 106 S. Ct. 1172 [1986]). Justices Burger, Rehnquist, and O'Connor would have heard argument. The Indianapolis ordinance defined pornography as the "graphically explicit subordination of women, whether in pictures or in words" and treated violations of its provisions as civil rights violations enforceable through the city's Office of Equal Opportunity. Women (or men, children, or transsexuals who could "prove injury in the same way that a woman is injured") could file complaints against those trafficking in pornography. Violations also included coercing others to perform in pornographic works or forcing pornography on anyone; the ordinance also created a right of action against a maker or seller of pornography by anyone injured by someone who had read or seen pornography.

7. 450 U.S. 464 (1981).
8. 106 S. Ct. 2399 (1986).
9. The only disagreement among the justices concerned the circumstances under which the acts of an employee's supervisors or agents were attributable to the employer for liability purposes. Five justices, led by Justice Rehnquist, declined to issue a definitive rule on employer liability; four (Marshall, Brennan, Blackmun, and Stevens) believed that the EEOC's guidelines on sexual harassment correctly stated the applicable principles of employer liability.
10. 106 S. Ct. at 2406.
11. *Id.* at 2407.
12. 417 U.S. 484 (1974).
13. 429 U.S. 125 (1976). *Gilbert* was a Title VII case, but the Court relied directly on *Geduldig* in its holding that pregnancy discrimination is not sex discrimination.
14. In 1978 the Court decided that an employer's policy that denies previously acquired seniority to women who take maternity leave does violate Title VII, but held that the same employer's policy of making sick leave unavailable for pregnancy-related illness did not violate the act, citing *Gilbert.* (Nashville Gas Co. v. Satty, 434 U.S. 136 [1977]). Congress promptly amended Title VII to reject the approach to pregnancy taken by the Court in *Gilbert.* The amendment, known as the Pregnancy Discrimination Act (or PDA), provided that "the terms 'because of sex' or 'on the basis of sex' shall include . . . because of or on the basis of pregnancy, childbirth or related medical conditions" and directed that "women affected by pregnancy, childbirth or related medical conditions shall be treated the same for all employment related purposes . . . as other employees similar in their ability or inability to work . . ." (42 U.S.C. sec. 2000e[k]). The Court acknowledged and effectuated this congressional directive in Newport News Shipbuilding & Dry Dock Co. v. Equal Employment Opportunity Commission, 462 U.S. 669 (1983).

As Chief Justice Burger left the Court, two additional pregnancy cases were pending that tested whether the PDA and a federal unemployment-insurance law could be interpreted to permit or require, respectively, special favorable treatment of pregnant working women. *See* California Fed. Sav. & Loan v. Guerra, No. 85–494; Wimberly v. Lab. & Ind. Rel. Comm'n of Mo., No. 85–129.
15. 410 U.S. 113 (1973).
16. The Burger Court restricted the states' interference with access to contraceptives, as well. In Griswold v. Connecticut, 381 U.S. 479 (1965), a case predating the Burger era, the Court held that a Connecticut law preventing the sale of contraceptives violated married persons' right to marital privacy. The Burger Court carried *Griswold* one step further,

holding that single persons are likewise protected in their access, free of state interference, to contraceptives. (Eisenstadt v. Baird, 405 U.S. 438 [1972]). It completed its work in Carey v. Population Services International, 431 U.S. 678 (1977), which struck down a New York law making it illegal to sell or distribute contraceptives to minors, for anyone other than a pharmacist to sell contraceptives to adults, and for anyone to display or advertise contraceptives.

17. Planned Parenthood of Missouri v. Danforth, 428 U.S. 52 (1976).

18. Bellotti v. Baird, 443 U.S. 622 (1979).

19. H.L. v. Matheson, 450 U.S. 398 (1981); Planned Parenthood Ass'n of Kansas City, Mo., Inc. v. Ashcroft, 462 U.S. 476 (1983).

20. 462 U.S. 416 (1983). Akron was also the occasion of Justice O'Connor's debut on the abortion question. She wrote a dissenting opinion sharply criticizing the doctrinal underpinnings of Roe.

21. 106 S. Ct. 2169 (1986). The majority, however, had dropped from six to five. Chief Justice Burger broke ranks with the Akron majority, which he had joined, and, declaring that the Court had traveled too far from Roe, concluded: "If Danforth and today's holding really mean what they seem to say, I agree that we should reexamine Roe" (id. at 2192).

22. 448 U.S. 297 (1980) (upheld the Hyde Amendment's exclusion of even medically necessary abortions from federal funding of medical treatment for the poor). Williams v. Zbaraz, 448 U.S. 358 (1980), the companion case to McRae, held that a state is not required to pay for medically necessary abortions for which reimbursement is unavailable under the federal Hyde Amendment. See also Maher v. Roe, 432 U.S. 464 (1977); Poelker v. Doe, 432 U.S. 519 (1977).

23. Doe v. Bolton, 410 U.S. 179 (1973), the companion case to Roe, constituted the Court's first attempt to explain how the consideration of women's health was to be analyzed. In that case the Court held unconstitutional, among other provisions, requirements that first-trimester abortions be performed in an accredited hospital, be approved by a hospital committee, and have the concurrence of two physicians other than the patient's own doctor. The Court's invalidation of these requirements did not deter states from attempting other limitations on abortion procedures.

24. Ashcroft, supra note 19. In Thornburgh, supra note 21, however, the Court struck down a second-physician requirement where the statute failed to create an exception for emergency abortions.

25. Akron, supra note 20 at 423; Thornburgh v. American College of Obstetricians and Gynecologists, supra note 21.

26. 106 S. Ct. at 2178.

27. Most recently, Justice O'Connor made such an assertion in her dissenting opinion in Akron.

28. 106 S. Ct. at 2183.

29. See report on arguments in Thornburgh in 54 U.S. L. Week 3356 (Nov. 26, 1985).

30. 414 U.S. 632 (1974).

31. The only other Supreme Court case to apply the reasoning of *LaFleur* was Turner v. Department of Employment Security, 423 U.S. 44 (1975), in which the Court struck down a state law foreclosing pregnant women from collecting unemployment insurance without regard to whether or not they were able and available for work.
32. 106 S. Ct. at 2185.
33. 441 U.S. 380 (1979).
34. 463 U.S. 248 (1983).
35. 441 U.S. 347 (1979).
36. 453 U.S. 37 (1981).
37. Department of Defense Authorization Act of 1981, S. Rep. No. 826, 96th Cong., 2d Sess., reprinted in 1980 U.S. CODE CONG. & AD. NEWS 2646, 2647, 2649.
38. 416 U.S. 351 (1974).
39. *See also* Schlesinger v. Ballard, 419 U.S. 498 (1975) (Court upheld law giving male officers shorter time than female officers to achieve promotion or face discharge, on the ground that longer time given women was to compensate them for disadvantages they faced in the military; Court's ruling thus justified one legislative discrimination on the ground that it was made necessary by other legislative discriminations); Califano v. Webster, 430 U.S. 313 (1977) (per curiam) (Court upheld Social Security law giving women a more favorable benefit calculation than men upon retirement on ground that the extra benefits were designed to compensate women for employment discrimination; in fact, the favorable benefit calculation was the inadvertent side effect of a three-year reduction in the retirement age for women but not men, which opponents feared would result in early mandatory retirement for working women). *Cf.* Weinberger v. Wiesenfeld, 420 U.S. 636 (1975); Califano v. Goldfarb, 430 U.S. 199 (1977); and Mississippi Univ. for Women v. Hogan, 458 U.S. 718 (1982), in all of which the Court struck down sex-based laws after concluding that they were not passed in order to make up for past discrimination against women.
40. 442 U.S. 256. The Court relied on Washington v. Davis, 426 U.S. 229 (1976), and Arlington Heights v. Metro. Housing Dev. Corp., 429 U.S. 252 (1977), which made a similar point in the race discrimination context.
41. *See, e.g.*, Dothard v. Rawlinson, 433 U.S. 321 (1977), in which the Court struck down the state's height and weight requirements for prison guards because they disproportionately excluded women from the job and were not justified by business necessity. In another part of this case, the Court upheld the exclusion of women from guard positions in the male maximum-security prison. *See supra* note 6.
42. The Court is unlikely to facilitate current attacks on the wage gap. Its opinion in Corning Glass Works v. Brennan, 417 U.S. 188 (1974), signifies its generous approach to interpretation of the federal Equal Pay Act of 1963, but that act, however liberally construed, will never reach beyond guaranteeing equal pay for essentially the same jobs, a problem of rela-

tively minor proportions. The major source of the gap is the extensive sex segregation of the U.S. labor market and the generally lower wage structure of the female-intensive jobs. The Court has ruled that intentional wage discrimination violates Title VII—in County of Washington v. Gunther, 452 U.S. 161 (1981), it ruled that jail "matrons" whose employer calculated the value of both their jobs and the jobs of male guards and then deliberately set their wages, but not those of the guards, below the assessed value, stated a Title VII claim. But it is unlikely to entertain claims based on what it called "the controversial concept of comparable worth"—claims for increased wages on the basis of a comparison of the intrinsic worth of one's job with that of different jobs in the same organization or community (452 U.S. at 166), or even to uphold claims that practices, such as basing wages on market rates, violate Title VII because of their disproportionately negative effect on women. Such comparable-worth claims have been rejected by lower courts; the successes have come from state legislatures and city councils.

43. *See, e.g.,* U.S. Commission on Civil Rights, *A Growing Crisis: Disadvantaged Women and Their Children* (CLEARINGHOUSE PUB. NO. 78 [May 1983]).

8. Activism without Equality

1. *See, e.g.,* E. GOFFMAN, ASYLUMS, (1971); JOINT COMMISSION ON MENTAL HEALTH AND MENTAL ILLNESS: ACTION FOR MENTAL HEALTH (1961).
2. Lynch v. Baxley, 386 F. Supp. 378 (M.D. Ala. 1974); Lessard v. Schmidt, 349 F. Supp. 1078 (E.D. Wisc. 1972).
3. 352 F. Supp. 781, 784 (M.D. Ala. 1971), 344 F. Supp. 1341 (M.D. Ala. 1971), 344 F. Supp. 373 and 387 (M.D. Ala. 1972), *aff'd sub nom.* Wyatt v. Aderholt, 503 F.2d 1305 (5th Cir. 1974).
4. 357 F. Supp. 752, 764 (E.D.N.Y. 1973), *consent judgment approved sub nom.* NYSARC v. Carey, 393 F. Supp. 715 (E.D.N.Y. 1975).
5. A. DEUTSCH, THE MENTALLY ILL IN AMERICA (2d ed. 1949).
6. D. WEXLER, MENTAL HEALTH LAW, MAJOR ISSUES 12 (1981).
7. A. STONE, MENTAL HEALTH LAW: A SYSTEM IN TRANSITION 1 (1975).
8. REPORT TO THE PRESIDENT, THE PRESIDENT'S COMMISSION ON MENTAL HEALTH 4 (1978).
9. *See, e.g.,* Jackson v. Indiana, 406 U.S. 715 (1972).
10. 441 U.S. 418 (1979).
11. *Id.* at 429.
12. *Id.* at 430.
13. 422 U.S. 584 (1979).
14. 422 U.S. 588 (1979).
15. *See, e.g.,* D. Bazelon, *Institutionalization, Deinstitutionalization and the Adversary Process,* 75 COL. L. REV. 8997 (1975); A. Dershowitz, *Psychiatry in the Legal Process: A Knife That Cuts Both Ways,* 4 TRIAL 29

(Feb.-Mar. 1968); J. Ellis, *Volunteering Children: Parental Commitment of Minors to Mental Institutions*, 62 CALIF. L. REV. 840 (1974); B. Ennis and P. Litwack, *Psychiatry and the Presumption of Expertise: Flipping Coins in the Courtroom*, 62 CALIF. L. REV. 693 (1974).

16. O'Connor v. Donaldson, 422 U.S. 563, 576, 586 (1975).
17. *Id.* at 586.
18. 457 U.S. 309, 315, 316 (1982).
19. *Id.* at 315, 316.
20. *Id.* at 316, 317.
21. *Id.* at 318.
22. *Id.* at 326, 327.
23. *Id.* at 331 n. 1.
24. *See* Bell v. Wolfish, 441 U.S. 520 (1979).
25. 457 U.S. at 330.
26. *See* Association of Retarded Children of North Dakota v. Olson, 561 F. Supp. 473 (D.N.D. 1982), *aff'd*, 713 F.2d 1385 (8th Cir. 1983); Society for Good Will to Retarded Children v. Carey, 572 F. Supp. 1300 (E.D.N.Y. 1983), *rev'd in part*, 737 F.2d 1239 (2d Cir. 1984).
27. Scott v. Plante, 691 F.2d 634 (3d Cir. 1982).
28. 737 F.2d 1239 (2d Cir. 1984).
29. 457 U.S. at 322, 323 (1982).
30. *See, e.g.*, E. GOFFMAN, ASYLUMS (1961); W. Wolfensberger, *The Origin and Nature of Our Institutional Models*, in CHANGING PATTERNS IN RESIDENTIAL SERVICES FOR THE MENTALLY RETARDED (rev. ed. R. Kugel & A. Shearer 1976); S. Herr, *Civil Rights, Uncivil Asylums and the Retarded*, 43 CIN. L. REV. 679 (1974).
31. Community Mental Health Centers Act of 1963, 42 U.S.C. §§ 2681 *et seq.*
32. 451 U.S. 1 (1981).
33. 612 F.2d 84 (3d Cir. 1979).
34. 42 U.S.C. § 6010.
35. *Id.*
36. 451 U.S. at 18, 19, 20, 27.
37. *Id.* at 54.
38. Pennhurst State School & Hospital v. Halderman, 465 U.S. 89 (1984).
39. *See* Shapiro, *Wrong Turns: The Eleventh Amendment and the Pennhurst Case*, 98 HARV. L. REV. 61 (1984).
40. *See* Andrulis and Mayade, *American Mental Health Policy: Changing Directions in the 80's*, 34 HOSP. & COMM. PSYCH. 601–6 (July 1983).
41. 29 U.S.C. § 794; 20 U.S.C. §§ 1402 *et seq.*
42. 105 S. Ct. 3249 (1985).
43. *Id.* at 3257–58. For a detailed description of the development of the different equal protection standards, see Williams, *Sex Discrimination: Closing the Law's Gender Gap*, supra pp. 109–124.
44. This is ironic, in light of the Supreme Court's near-emasculation of the DD Act in Pennhurst v. Halderman, discussed earlier.

45. Frontiero v. Richardson, 411 U.S. 677, 687 (1973).
46. 105 S. Ct. at 3268–69.
47. This ruling will almost inevitably apply with equal force to the mentally ill, the aged, and others who are not currently treated as quasi-suspect classes.
48. 105 S. Ct. at 3259–60.
49. *Id.* at 3258.
50. *See, e.g.,* S. Rep. No. 93–319, 93d Cong. 1st Sess. at 2 (1973).
51. J. Parry, *A Review of the Burger Court's Disability Decisions, Part II,* 9 MENTAL & PHYSICAL DISABILITY LAW REPORTER 1 (Jan.–Feb. 1985).
52. 442 U.S. 379 (1979).
53. 105 S. Ct. 712 (1985).
54. *Id.* at 720.
55. 465 U.S. 624 (1984).
56. *See* Pennsylvania Ass'n for Retarded Citizens v. Pennsylvania, 343 F. Supp. 279 (E.D. Pa. 1972); Mills v. Board of Education, 348 F. Supp. 866 (D.D.C. 1972).
57. 20 U.S.C. § 1401 *et seq.,* especially § 1412. At the time P.L. 94–142 was enacted, Congress found that only 40 percent of handicapped children were receiving appropriate educational services. *See, e.g.,* H.R. Rep. No. 93–805, 93d Cong., 2d Sess. (1974).
58. *See, e.g.,* Battle v. Commonwealth of Pennsylvania, 629 F.2d 269 (3d Cir. 1980), *cert. den.,* 452 U.S. 968 (1981) (programs in excess of 180 days required in certain circumstances); Irving Independent School District v. Tatro, 468 U.S. 883 (1984) (clean intermittent catheterization is a related service); S-I v. Turlington, 635 F.2d 342 (5th Cir. 1981), *cert. den.,* 454 U.S. 1030 (1984) (expulsion of handicapped child not permitted; disciplinary action must be treated as a change in placement and due process afforded).
59. 458 U.S. 176 (1982).
60. *Id.* at 203.
61. *Id.* at 206, 207.
62. 468 U.S. 883 (1984).
63. 20 U.S.C. § 1401(17).

9. The "Police Practice" Phases of the Criminal Process and the Three Phases of the Burger Court

1. CHOPER, KAMISAR, AND TRIBE, THE SUPREME COURT: TRENDS AND DEVELOPMENTS 1978–79 339 (1979).
2. *See* Kamisar, *The Warren Court (Was It Really So Defense-Minded?), The Burger Court (Is It Really So Prosecution-Oriented?), and Police Investigatory Practices,* in THE BURGER COURT: THE COUNTER-REVOLUTION THAT WASN'T 62, 68 (V. Blasi ed. 1983).
3. *See infra.*

4. Kirby v. Illinois (1972) and United States v. Ash (1973), both discussed *infra*.
5. 384 U.S. 436 (1966).
6. *See* Kamisar, *supra* note 2, at 68, 78–81, 86–91.
7. *See, e.g.,* Franks v. Delaware, 438 U.S. 154 (1978) (rejecting the contention that one may never challenge the truthfulness of factual statements made in a police affidavit supporting a search warrant as "nothing more than a frontal assault upon the exclusionary rule itself"); Delaware v. Prouse, 440 U.S. 648 (1980) (rejecting the argument that "random stops" of an automobile for license and registration checks need not be subject to any Fourth Amendment restraints); Payton v. New York, 445 U.S. 573 (1980) (although a majority of the states passing on this question had upheld this practice, invalidating state statutes permitting the police to enter a suspect's home without a warrant to make a routine felony arrest); and Ybarra v. Illinois, 444 U.S. 85 (1980) (holding that a valid warrant to search a tavern and the person of the bartender did not authorize the police to invade "the constitutional protections possessed individually by the tavern's customers").

   Of course, not all the search-and-seizure cases decided in favor of the defense fit neatly into the "second phase" of the Burger Court era. *See* two such cases in what I call the "first phase": Gerstein v. Pugh, 420 U.S. 103 (1975) (holding that the Fourth Amendment requires prompt judicial review of the legality of warrantless arrests as a prerequisite to "extended restraint on liberty" following such arrests); and Brown v. Illinois, 422 U.S. 590 (1975) (rejecting the view that the giving of the *Miranda* warnings should purge the taint of any preceding illegal arrest). *Brown* was reaffirmed in Dunaway v. New York, 442 U.S. 200 (1979), and Taylor v. Alabama, 457 U.S. 687 (1982).

8. Massiah v. United States, 377 U.S. 201 (1964)—as clarified and expanded by two Burger Court decisions, Brewer v. Williams, 430 U.S. 387 (1977) (the "Christian burial speech" case), discussed at length in KAMISAR, POLICE INTERROGATION AND CONFESSIONS 139–224 (1980), and United States v. Henry, 447 U.S. 264 (1980), discussed extensively in W. White, *Interrogation Without Questions: Rhode Island v. Innis and United States v. Henry*, 78 MICH. L. REV. 1209 (1980)—holds that once adversary judicial proceedings have commenced against an individual (for example, once he has been indicted or arraigned), government efforts to "deliberately elicit" incriminating statements from him, whether done openly by uniformed police officers or surreptitiously by "secret agents," are impermissible. Even though these efforts do not constitute "custodial interrogation" within the meaning of *Miranda*, they violate the individual's right to counsel. *See also* Maine v. Moulton, 106 S. Ct. 477 (1985) (*Massiah* doctrine applies to crimes for which defendant had already been charged even though state had legitimate reasons for intercepting conversations in regard to its investigation of possible other uncharged offenses). *But see* Kuhlmann v. Wilson, 106 S. Ct. 2616 (1986) (*Massiah*

doctrine not applicable when defendant makes statements to a secret government agent posing as a cellmate when agent made no effort to stimulate conversations about the crime charged; "defendant must demonstrate that the police and their informant took some action, beyond merely listening, that was designed deliberately to elicit incriminating remarks").

9. *See* Kamisar, *supra* note 2, at 90–91. This essay was completed in the summer of 1982. See also Israel, *Criminal Procedure, The Burger Court, and the Legacy of the Warren Court,* 75 MICH. L. REV. 1320 (1977); Saltzburg, *Foreword: The Flow and Ebb of Constitutional Criminal Procedure in the Warren and Burger Courts,* 69 GEO. L. J. 151 (1980). But see Arenella, *Rethinking the Functions of Criminal Procedure: The Warren and Burger Courts' Competing Ideologies,* 72 GEO. L. J. 185 (1983); Pye, *Constitutional Adjudication in Criminal Procedure: Of Symbolism and Covert Overruling,* in 1986 PROCEEDINGS OF CANADIAN INSTITUTE OF ADVANCED LEGAL STUDIES; Rudovsky, *Criminal Justice: The Accused,* in OUR ENDANGERED RIGHTS 203 (Dorsen ed. 1984).

10. F. Allen, *American Criminal Procedure: Why the Dominance of Judge-Made Law?,* in POLICE PRACTICES AND THE LAW 1, 6 (1982).

11. *See* Rhode Island v. Innis (1980) and Edwards v. Arizona (1981), both discussed *infra.*

12. All nine cases had been decided below in favor of the defendant. In the Supreme Court the government won seven. Illinois v. Gates, discussed *infra,* was probably the most important. Moreover, the two cases the government "lost"—United States v. Place, 462 U.S. 696 (1983) (approving, under certain circumstances, warrantless seizure of personal luggage from custody of owner on less than "probable cause" and viewing "dog-sniffing" of luggage not a "search" within meaning of Fourth Amendment) and Florida v. Royer, 460 U.S. 491 (1983) (certain police-citizen "contacts" or "encounters," such as asking a person at an airport to identify himself and show his driver's license or airline ticket, not a "seizure" within meaning of Fourth Amendment)—advanced views that should prove quite useful to law-enforcement officials in the years ahead. Thus I concur in Judge Charles Moylan's conclusion that on the search-and-seizure front the government gained seven victories and suffered nothing more than "a couple of ties." *See* Criminal Law Rep. at 2408–09 (Aug. 17, 1983). All nine cases are carefully analyzed in LaFave, *Fourth Amendment Vagaries (of Improbable Cause, Imperceptible Plain View, Notorious Privacy, and Balancing Askew),* 74 J. CRIM. L. & CRIMINOLOGY 1171 (1983).

13. LaFave, *supra* note 12, at 1222.

14. 468 U.S. 897 (1984). *See also* the companion case, Massachusetts v. Sheppard, 468 U.S. 981 (1984).

15. At first blush, Tennessee v. Garner, 105 S. Ct. 1694 (1985)—holding that a police officer's slaying of an unarmed, "nondangerous" fleeing felon, to prevent his escape, is an "unreasonable 'seizure' " within the meaning

of the Fourth Amendment—seems to run counter to the recent search-and-seizure trend. But I share the view that *Garner*, which strikes me as more of a *substantive* criminal-law case—when is the police slaying of a fleeing felon justifiable homicide?—than a criminal *procedure* case, is an "aberration." *See* Note, *The Supreme Court, 1984 Term*, 99 HARV. L. REV. 4, 254 (1985). The invalidated statute did reflect the common-law rule, authorizing the use of deadly force, if necessary, to apprehend *any* fleeing felon. But the policies adopted by the police departments themselves were "overwhelmingly . . . more restrictive than the common-law rule . . . only 7.5 percent of departmental and municipal policies explicitly permit the use of deadly force against any felon; 86.8% explicitly do not" (105 S. Ct. at 1705).

It is also hard to avoid the conclusion that the Court was heavily influenced by an *amicus* brief filed by the Police Foundation, joined by nine national and international associations of police and criminal justice professionals and more than thirty law-enforcement chief executives, which concluded that "laws permitting police officers to use deadly force to apprehend unarmed, non-violent fleeing felony suspects actually do not protect citizens or law enforcement officers, do not deter crime or alleviate problems caused by crime, and do not improve the crime-fighting ability of law enforcement agencies" (Brief for Police Foundation, p. 11, quoted in *Garner*, 105 S. Ct. at 1705), and "are responsible," *inter alia*, "for unnecessary loss of life" and "for friction between police and the communities they serve, resulting in less effective law enforcement" (brief, *supra*).

16. 467 U.S. 649 (1984).
17. 105 S. Ct. 1285 (1985), discussed *infra*.
18. WILKINSON, SERVING JUSTICE: A SUPREME COURT CLERK'S VIEW 146 (1974).
19. *See* Grano, *Kirby, Biggers and Ash: Do Any Constitutional Safeguards Remain Against the Danger of Convicting the Innocent?*, 72 MICH. L. REV. 719, 723–24 (1974) and authorities discussed therein.
20. United States v. Wade, 388 U.S. 218 (1967); Gilbert v. California, 388 U.S. 263 (1967); Stovall v. Denno, 388 U.S. 293 (1967).
21. United States v. Wade, 388 U.S. at 235–36.
22. 406 U.S. 682 (1972).
23. 413 U.S. 300 (1973).
24. Neil v. Biggers, 409 U.S. 188, 198–201 (1972). *See also* Manson v. Brathwaite, 432 U.S. 98, 110–14, 117 (1977).
25. Manson v. Brathwaite, 432 U.S. 98, 110.
26. *See* F. Allen, *The Judicial Quest for Penal Justice: The Warren Court and the Criminal Cases*, 1975 U. ILL. L. F. 518, 541–42; Grano, *supra* note 19, at 722.
27. *See, e.g.*, WHITEBREAD, CRIMINAL PROCEDURE: AN ANALYSIS OF CONSTITUTIONAL CASES AND CONCEPTS 4 (1980).
28. GRAHAM, THE SELF-INFLICTED WOUND 157 (1970). *See also* LIEBERMAN, MILESTONES! 200 YEARS OF AMERICAN LAW 326 (1976).

29. *See* F. Allen, *supra* note 26, at 537–38, 540. Whether the Court should have required the police, wherever feasible, to make tape or verbatim stenographic recordings of the reading of rights, the waiver transaction, and any subsequent interrogation, thus adding fuel to the criticism that it was "legislating," is surely one of those "damned if it did" and "damned if it didn't" issues.

30. 106 S. Ct. 1135 (1986).

31. *Id.* at 1140.

32. O'Connor, J., joined by Chief Justice Burger and White, Blackmun, Powell, and Rehnquist, JJ.

33. 106 S. Ct. at 1143, 1144, 1147–48, n. 4.

34. Although the specific issues the Court addressed are difficult ones and dissenting Justice Stevens, joined by Brennan and Marshall, JJ., made out a powerful case for a contrary result, I think the majority opinion is based on a plausible reading of *Miranda*. When advised of his rights, Burbine chose neither to remain silent nor to ask for a lawyer, but, unbeknown to him, his sister asked a lawyer to represent him. Under the circumstances, I believe the Court's position, although arguable, is defensible: "Once it is determined that a suspect's decision not to rely on his rights was uncoerced, that he at all times knew he could stand mute and request a lawyer [but chose to do neither], and that he was aware of the state's intention to use his statements to secure a conviction, the analysis is complete and the waiver is valid as a matter of law" (106 S. Ct. at 1142).

35. 401 U.S. 222. For strong criticism of *Harris, see* LEVY, AGAINST THE LAW 149–63 (1974); Dershowitz and Ely, *Harris v. New York: Some Anxious Observations on the Candor and Logic of the Emerging Nixon Majority,* 80 YALE L. J. 1198 (1971); Stone, *The Miranda Doctrine in the Burger Court,* 1977 SUP. CT. REV. 99, 106–15.

36. 420 U.S. 714 (1975), criticized in Stone, *supra* note 35, at 125–29.

37. 420 U.S. at 723.

38. Even more disturbing than *Harris* and *Hass* is their recent extension to permit the use of a defendant's prior silence when he chooses to take the stand in his own defense. *See* Jenkins v. Anderson, 447 U.S. 231 (1980). In Fletcher v. Weir, 455 U.S. 603 (1982) (per curiam), the Court held that even a defendant's *post*arrest silence (so long as he was not given the *Miranda* warnings) could be used to impeach him if he chooses to testify at trial.

   Both *Jenkins* and *Weir* distinguished Doyle v. Ohio, 426 U.S. 610 (1976), which deemed it a violation of due process to use a defendant's silence for impeachment purposes when the defendant remained silent *after* being given the *Miranda* warnings. But the use of *post*arrest silence in a case like *Weir* also seems unfair. The implied promise contained in the *Miranda* warnings that a person's silence will not be used against him is derived not from the *Miranda* opinion, but from the self-incrimination clause itself. Many, if not most, people associate the right to remain silent with *an arrest*—a view widely disseminated by the media. *Miranda* has become part of the popular culture. Why should it matter whether knowledge of the right to remain silent is imparted by the police or absorbed from our "common culture"?

39. 417 U.S. 433 (1974).
40. *See* Friendly, *The Bill of Rights as a Code of Criminal Procedure*, 53 CALIF. L. REV. 929, 954–55 n. 135 (1965).
41. *See* 417 U.S. at 444–46.
42. *See* the discussion in KAMISAR, *supra* note 8, at 21–25, 69–76. *See also* Schulhofer, *Confessions and the Court*, 79 MICH. L. REV. 865, 867–78 (1981).
43. Miranda v. Arizona, 384 U.S. at 457–58 (emphasis added).
44. *See* 417 U.S. at 444–45.
45. *See* Stone, *supra* note 35, at 118–19.
46. 417 U.S. at 444.
47. *See* 384 U.S. at 444, 458, 467, 469.
48. *Id.* at 479 (emphasis added).
49. 446 U.S. 291 (1980).
50. 446 U.S. at 300–1.
51. *See* W. White, *supra* note 8, at 1223. For a discussion of how narrowly some courts interpreted "interrogation" prior to *Innis*, *see* KAMISAR, *supra* note 8, at 156 n. 21. In *Innis* itself, as the dissents pointed out, the Court gave its new definition of "interrogation" a questionable application to the facts before it.
52. 451 U.S. 477 (1981).
53. The *Edwards* case sharply, if somewhat obscurely, distinguished Michigan v. Mosley, 423 U.S. 96 (1975), which holds that if a suspect asserts his right to remain silent and the police cease questioning on the spot, they may "try again" at a later interrogation session if they satisfy certain conditions, such as resuming questioning only after the passage of a significant amount of time and giving the suspect a fresh set of warnings at the outset of the second session. Precisely what conditions must be met for the police to "try again" is left painfully unclear by *Mosley*. *See* the discussion in Stone, *supra* note 35, at 130–37.
54. 451 U.S. at 484–85 (emphasis added). *Edwards* was applied (or, arguably, extended) in Michigan v. Jackson, 106 S. Ct. 1404 (1986) (request for counsel in appearance before arraigning judicial officer triggers *Edwards* rule). But *cf.* Oregon v. Bradshaw, 462 U.S. 1039 (1983) (arrestee's question to officer, "Well, what is going to happen to me now?" constitutes "initiation" of further communication within meaning of *Edwards*).
55. *See* 105 S. Ct. at 1291–93.
56. *Id.* at 1296.
57. *See* 384 U.S. at 455–58, 461, 467–69, 473–74, 476–79.
58. *See* 105 S. Ct. at 1303.
59. The record is bereft of any affirmative factual support for the view that the first statement *caused* Elstad to confess later. For another thing, the initial *Miranda* violation was arguably inadvertent. The result might

have been different if, for example, Elstad had asserted his right to counsel at the first meeting and the police had refused to honor that assertion. Finally, the second confession was not the product of *intentional exploitation* of the prior illegality by the police. There is no evidence that the police took advantage of the prior illegality in any way, such as confronting the defendant with his earlier statement at the police station or reminding him of his earlier statement during the drive to the stationhouse.

60. *See* 105 S. Ct. at 1293.

61. *See* 467 U.S. at 660.

62. 105 S. Ct. at 1293.

63. Stewart, *The Road to Mapp v. Ohio and Beyond: The Origins Development and Future of the Exclusionary Rule in Search-and-Seizure Cases,* 83 COLUM. L. REV. 1365, 1397 (1983).

64. In addition to the *Miller-Smith-Knotts* line of cases, discussed immediately below, *see* Oliver v. United States, 466 U.S. 170 (1984) (expansively reading the "open fields" exception to Fourth Amendment restraints); California v. Ciraolo, 106 S. Ct. 1809 (1986) (naked-eye aerial observation of defendant's fenced-in backyard within curtilage of home not a Fourth Amendment "search"); Dow Chemical Co. v. United States, 106 S. Ct. 1819 (1986) (aerial photography of industrial manufacturing complex not a Fourth Amendment "search"); and United States v. Place and Florida v. Royer, both briefly summarized in *supra* note 12.

65. 425 U.S. 435, strongly criticized in LaFave, SEARCH AND SEIZURE: A TREATISE ON THE FOURTH AMENDMENT 409–417 (1978).

66. 442 U.S. 735, strongly criticized in CHOPER, KAMISAR, AND TRIBE, THE SUPREME COURT: TRENDS AND DEVELOPMENTS 1978–79 at 134–45 (1979) (remarks of Kamisar).

67. 460 U.S. 276, strongly criticized in LaFave, *supra* note 12, at 1174–78. But *cf.* United States v. Karo, 468 U.S. 705 (1984) (monitoring a beeper in a private residence not open to visual surveillance does constitute a "search").

68. 460 U.S. at 282.

69. *Id.* at 288 (Stevens, J., joined by Brennan and Marshall, JJ., concurring in the judgment).

70. 389 U.S. 347 (1967). *Katz* overruled the much-criticized 5–4 decision in Olmstead v. United States, 277 U.S. 438 (1928), which had held that wiretapping (or other forms of electronic surveillance) is neither a "search" nor a "seizure" and had viewed Fourth Amendment protection as turning on the presence of a physical penetration into enclosures. The *Katz* Court pointed out that "the Fourth Amendment protects people, not places" (389 U.S. at 351) and that, once this is recognized, "it becomes clear that the reach of that Amendment cannot turn upon the presence or absence of a physical intrusion into any given enclosure" (*id.* at 353).

71. The genesis of the *Carroll* doctrine was Carroll v. United States, 267 U.S. 132 (1925).

72. 453 U.S. 454 (1981).
73. *Id.* at 452 (concurring in the judgment in *Belton* and dissenting in Robbins v. California, 453 U.S. 420 (1981).
74. *See* generally Moylan, *The Automobile Exception: What It Is and What It Is Not—A Rationale in Search of a Clearer Label,* 27 MERCER L. REV. 987 (1976).
75. *See* Chambers v. Maroney, 399 U.S. 42 (1970); Cardwell v. Lewis, 417 U.S. 583 (1974); Texas v. White, 423 U.S. 67 (1975) (per curiam). For criticism of these developments, *see* Grano, *Rethinking the Fourth Amendment Warrant Requirement,* 19 AM. CRIM. L. REV. 603 (1982); Katz, *Automobile Searches and Diminished Expectations in the Warrant Clause,* 19 AM. CRIM. L. REV. 557 (1982); Moylan, *supra* note 74.
76. United States v. Ross, 456 U.S. 798 (1982).
77. 462 U.S. 213, extensively discussed and criticized in, *e.g.*, Kamisar, *Gates, "Probable Cause," "Good Faith" and Beyond,* 69 IOWA L. REV. 557 (1984); LaFave, *supra* note 12, at 1186–99; Wasserstrom, *The Incredible Shrinking Fourth Amendment,* 21 AM. CRIM. L. REV. 257, 274–75, 329–40 (1984). But see Grano, *Probable Cause and Common Sense: A Reply to the Critics of Illinois v. Gates* 17 MICH. J. L. REF. 465 (1984).
78. 462 U.S. at 232, 238.
79. *Id.* at 244 n. 13 (emphasis added).
80. *Id.* at 236–7, 244 n. 13.
81. 412 U.S. 218 (1973).
82. *Cf.* Escobedo v. Illinois, 378 U.S. 478, 490 (1964).
83. New Jersey v. T.L.O., 105 S. Ct. 733, 760 (1985) (schoolhouse search case) (dissenting opinion). Mapp v. Ohio, 367 U.S. 643 (1961), overruled Wolf v. Colorado, 338 U.S. 25 (1949) and imposed the Fourth Amendment exclusionary rule on the states as a matter of Fourteenth Amendment due process.
84. Weeks v. United States, 232 U.S. 383.
85. *See* the discussion of *Weeks* and other early search-and-seizure cases in Kamisar, *Does (Did) (Should) the Exclusionary Rule Rest on a "Principled Basis" Rather Than an "Empirical Proposition"?,* 16 CREIGHTON L. REV. 565, 598–604 (1983).
86. See *id.*; Schrock and Welsh, *Up from Calandra: The Exclusionary Rule As a Constitutional Requirement,* 59 MINN. L. REV. 251 (1974).
87. I share the view of the late Justice Stewart, who observed, Stewart, *supra* note 63 at 1395:

> [T]he evidence shows that exclusion does have a deterrent effect. We need only look to the dramatic increase in the number of search warrants issued in the years after the *Mapp* case [imposed the exclusionary rule on the state courts] for evidence that the Court's decision has had a tremendous impact on police practices. Police departments have sharply increased the amount of training they give their officers on how to comply

with the principles announced in the Supreme Court's fourth amendment decisions.

In discussions of whether the exclusionary rule significantly influences police behavior, the terms " 'deterrent' effects" or " 'deterrence' rationale" are frequently used. I think these terms are misleading. The exclusionary rule does not inflict a "punishment" on police who violate the Fourth Amendment and thus does not, and cannot be expected to, "deter" the police the way the criminal law is supposed to affect the general public. Because the police are members of a governmental entity, however, the rule influences them, or is supposed to influence them, by "systemic deterrence," *i.e.*, through a department's institutional compliance with Fourth Amendment standards.

Despite the popularity of the "deterrence" terminology, it seems more accurate and useful to call the exclusionary rule a *"counterweight"* within the criminal justice system or a *"disincentive"*—a means of eliminating significant incentives for making illegal searches, at least where the police contemplate prosecution and conviction. *See* Amsterdam, *Perspectives on the Fourth Amendment*, 58 MINN. L. REV. 349, 431 (1974).

88. 414 U.S. 338 (1974), extensively discussed and strongly criticized in Schrock and Welsh, *supra* note 86.

89. 414 U.S. at 348, 354, 349.

90. 428 U.S. 465 (1976).

91. 428 U.S. 433 (1976).

92. United States v. Leon, 468 U.S. 897; Massachusetts v. Sheppard, 468 U.S. 981. For commentary on these and related cases, most of it critical, *see* Alschuler, *"Close Enough for Government Work": The Exclusionary Rule after Leon*, 1984 SUP. CT. REV. 309; Bradley, *The "Good Faith Exception" Cases: Reasonable Exercises in Futility*, 60 IND. L.J. 287 (1985); Dripps, *Living with Leon*, 95 YALE L. J. 906 (1986); Duke, *Making Leon Worse*, 95 YALE L. J. 1405 (1986); LaFave, *The Seductive Call of Expediency: U.S. v. Leon, Its Rationale and Ramifications*, 1984 U. ILL. L. REV. 895 (1984); Wasserstrom and Mertens, *The Exclusionary Rule on the Scaffold: But Was It a Fair Trial?*, 22 AM. CRIM. L. REV. 85 (1984).

93. *See* Canon, *Ideology and Reality in the Debate over the Exclusionary Rule: A Conservative Argument for its Retention*, 23 S. TEX. L.J. 559, 563 (1982).

94. The available empirical evidence indicates that the "costs" of the exclusionary rule are relatively insubstantial. *See* COMPTROLLER GENERAL OF THE UNITED STATES, IMPACT OF THE EXCLUSIONARY RULE ON FEDERAL CRIMINAL PROSECUTIONS (1979); BROSI, A CROSS-CITY COMPARISON OF FELONY CASE PROCESSING (1979); Davies, *A Hard Look at What We Know (and Still Need to Learn) About the "Costs" of the Exclusionary Rule: The NIJ Study and Other Studies of Lost Arrests,*

1983 AM. B. FOUND. RESEARCH J. 611; Nardulli, *The Societal Costs of the Exclusionary Rule: An Empirical Assessment*, 1983 Am. B. Found. Research J. 585.

95. Tribe, *Constitutional Calculus: Equal Justice or Economic Efficiency?*, 98 HARV. L. REV. 592, 609 (1985).

96. *Cf.* Stevens, J., dissenting in *Leon*, 104 S. Ct. at 3456.

97. 104 S. Ct. at 3421.

98. *See* the discussion in LaFave, *supra* note 92 at 927–29.

99. *See* 104 S. Ct. at 3413, 2423.

100. *Id.* at 3414.

101. *Id.* at 3416.

102. INS v. Lopez-Mendoza, 468 U.S. 1032 (1984).

103. *Id.* at 1056 (White, J., dissenting).

104. *Id.* at 1060.

105. *Id.* at 1061.

106. *Id.* at 1043.

107. *Ibid.*

108. *Id.* at 1044.

109. "The INS's attention to Fourth Amendment interests cannot guarantee that constitutional violations will not occur, but it does reduce the likely deterrent value of the exclusionary rule" (*id.* at 1045).

110. The *Leon* Court, per White, J., quoted with approval, *see* 468 U.S. at 907 n. 6, Justice White's observation, *see* his concurring opinion in *Gates* (462 U.S. at 257–58), that the exclusionary rule "must bear a heavy burden of justification, and must be carefully limited to the circumstances in which it will pay its way by deterring official lawlessness." Because the *Leon* Court concluded that the exclusionary rule can have "no substantial deterrent effect" when the police have acted in "reasonable reliance" on a search warrant issued by a neutral magistrate that is subsequently determined to be invalid, it concluded that the rule "cannot pay its way in those situations" (468 U.S. at 907–8 n. 6).

111. *See* United States v. Janis, 428 U.S. 433, 449–53 and 450 n. 22 (1976); Stone v. Powell, 428 U.S. 465, 492 and n. 32 (1976).

112. *Cf.* CARDOZO, THE NATURE OF THE JUDICIAL PROCESS 51 (1925) (discussing "the tendency of a principle to expand itself to the limit of its logic").

113. According to one of the strongest defenders of the Burger Court's work in the criminal procedure field, Israel, *Criminal Procedure, the Burger Court and the Legacy of the Warren Court*, 75 MICH. L. REV. 1320, 1383–84 (1977):

> Difficulties [with *Miranda*] have arisen primarily in situations involving questioning "on the street." . . . [P]olice can easily identify what constitutes "custodial interrogation" where that concept is limited to questioning at the police station or

a similar setting. Also, in such a setting the message conveyed by the warnings is not one that concerns the police: the suspect ordinarily has been arrested and clearly recognizes that his situation is "serious." Indeed, the message of *Miranda* is one so frequently repeated in television dramas and actual post-arrest procedures that it is something the arrested person has come to expect.

In Berkemer v. McCarty, 468 U.S. 420 (1984) the Court held that "roadside questioning" of a motorist detained pursuant to a traffic stop does not constitute "custodial interrogation" for *Miranda* purposes and made it plain that a police officer who stops a person on the street to "investigate the circumstances that provoke suspicion" is not subject to the dictates of *Miranda*. Oregon v. Mathiason, 429 U.S. 492 (1977) (per curiam) and California v. Beheler, 463 U.S. 1121 (1983) (per curiam) demonstrate that even *police station* questioning designed to produce incriminating statements is not necessarily "custodial interrogation." In *Mathiason*, the suspect went to the station house after an officer requested that he meet him there and he agreed to do so. In *Beheler*, the suspect was said to have "voluntarily agreed to accompany police to the station house."

114. *See* text *supra* at notes 30–34.
115. United States v. Leon, 468 U.S. at 943 (Brennan, J., joined by Marshall, J., dissenting).

10. On Death Row, the Wait Continues

1. 408 U.S. 238 (1972).
2. 428 U.S. 153 (1976).
3. 428 U.S. 280 (1976).
4. 431 U.S. 633 (1977).
5. Coker v. Georgia, 433 U.S. 584 (1977).
6. Enmund v. Florida, 458 U.S. 782 (1982).
7. Lockett v. Ohio, 438 U.S. 586 (1978).
8. Gardner v. Florida, 430 U.S. 349 (1977).
9. Bullington v. Missouri, 451 U.S. 430 (1981).
10. Sullivan v. Wainwright, 464 U.S. 109 (1983).
11. Barefoot v. Estelle, 463 U.S. 880, 916 (1983).
12. 465 U.S. 37 (1984).
13. 347 U.S. 483 (1954).
14. 106 S. Ct. 1758 (1986).
15. Witherspoon v. Illinois, 391 U.S. 510 (1968).
16. McClesky v. Kemp, *cert. granted*, 106 S. Ct. 3331 (1986).

11. The Burger Court and the Prisoner

1. Holt v. Sarver, 300 F. Supp. 825 (E.D. Ark. 1969), 309 F. Supp. 362, *aff'd*, 442 F.2d 304 (8th Cir. 1971).
2. Gates v. Collier, 349 F. Supp. 881 (N.D. Miss. 1972).
3. OFFICIAL REPORT OF THE NEW YORK STATE SPECIAL COMMISSION ON ATTICA 3 (1972) ("ATTICA REPORT").
4. National Prison Project, JOURNAL 1 (Spring 1985).
5. ATTICA REPORT 60, 61–62.
6. Ruffin v. Commonwealth, 62 Va. (21 Gratt.) 790, 796 (1871); Coffin v. Reichard, 143 F.2d 443 (1946).
7. Washington v. Lee, 263 F. Supp. 327 (M.D. Ala. 1966), *aff'd*, Lee v. Washington, 390 U.S. 333 (1968); Johnson v. Avery, 393 U.S. 483 (1969); Houghton v. Shafer, 392 U.S. 639 (1968).
8. Haines v. Kerner, 404 U.S. 519 (1972); Wilwording v. Swenson, 404 U.S. 249 (1971); Preiser v. Rodriguez, 411 U.S. 475 (1973); Patsy v. Bd. of Regents of Fla., 457 U.S. 496 (1982).
9. Cruz v. Beto, 405 U.S. 319 (1972); Procunier v. Martinez, 416 U.S. 396 (1974); Younger v. Gilmore, 404 U.S. 15 (1971).
10. 365 U.S. 167 (1961).
11. For a summary of these and other cases, *see* KRANTZ, CORRECTIONS AND PRISONERS RIGHTS IN A NUT SHELL (2d ed. 1983).
12. Pell v. Procunier, 417 U.S. 817 (1974).
13. Richardson v. Ramirez, 418 U.S. 24 (1974).
14. Wolff v. McDonnell, 418 U.S. 539 (1974).
15. 384 U.S. 436 (1966).
16. Baxter v. Palmigiano, 425 U.S. 308 (1976).
17. Hewitt v. Helms, 103 S. Ct. 864 (1983); Superintendent v. Hill, 105 S. Ct. 2768 (1985).
18. Meachum v. Fano, 427 U.S. 215 (1976).
19. Houchins v. KQED, 438 U.S. 1 (1978).
20. Kleindienst v. Mandel, 408 U.S. 753, 762–63 (1972); Board of Education, Island Trees Union Free School Dist. No. 26 v. Pico, 457 U.S. 853 (1982) (Brennan, J., plurality).
21. Bell v. Wolfish, 441 U.S. 520, 560–61 (1979).
22. Hudson v. Palmer, 468 U.S. 517, 526 (1984) (emphasis added). *See also* Block v. Rutherford, 468 U.S. 576 (1984).
23. Davidson v. Cannon, 106 S. Ct. 686, 671 (1986).
24. Hutto v. Finney, 437 U.S. 678 (1978).
25. Rhodes v. Chapman, 452 U.S. 337 (1981); Bell v. Wolfish, *supra* note 21.
26. *See* Ramos v. Lamm, 450 U.S. 1041 (1981).
27. *See* Faulkner v. Wellman, 715 F.2d 269 (7th Cir. 1983), *cert. denied*, 468 U.S. 1217 (1984).

28. National Prison Project, *Status Report: The Courts and Prisons* (Feb. 20, 1986).

12. Close Reins on the Bureaucracy: Overseeing the Administrative Agencies

1. 397 U.S. 150 (1970).
2. 412 U.S. 699 (1973).
3. 426 U.S. 26 (1976); 468 U.S. 737 (1984).
4. 106 S. Ct. 2523 (1986).
5. 421 U.S. 560 (1975).
6. 105 S. Ct. 1649 (1985).
7. 467 U.S. 340 (1984).
8. 401 U.S. 402 (1971).
9. 448 U.S. 607 (1980).
10. 463 U.S. 29 (1983).
11. 454 U.S. 27 (1981).
12. 104 S. Ct. 2979 (1984).
13. 467 U.S. 837 (1984).
14. 106 S. Ct. 2360 (1986).
15. 106 S. Ct. 681 (1986).
16. 435 U.S. 519 (1978).
17. 410 U.S. 224 (1973).
18. 452 U.S. 490 (1981).
19. 462 U.S. 919 (1983).
20. EPA v. Mink, 410 U.S. 73 (1973); Renegotiation Board v. Bannercraft Clothing Co., 415 U.S. 1 (1974); Renegotiation Board v. Grumman Aircraft Engineering Corp., 421 U.S. 168 (1975); Administrator, FAA, v. Robertson, 422 U.S. 255 (1975); NLRB v. Robbins Tire & Rubber Co., 437 U.S. 214 (1978); Federal Open Market Committee v. Merrill, 433 U.S. 340 (1979); Kissinger v. Reporters Committee for Freedom of the Press, 445 U.S. 136 (1980); Forsham v. Harris, 445 U.S. 169 (1980); GTE Sylvania v. Consumer Products Safety Comm'n, 445 U.S. 375 (1980); Balderidge v. Shapiro, 455 U.S. 345 (1982); Department of State v. Washington Post, 456 U.S. 595 (1982); FBI v. Abramson, 456 U.S. 615 (1982); Federal Trade Commission v. Grolier, Inc., 462 U.S. 19 (1983); Department of the Air Force v. Weber Aircraft Corp., 465 U.S. 792 (1984); CIA v. Sims (1985).
21. NLRB v. Sears, Roebuck & Co., 421 U.S. 132 (1975).
22. Chrysler Corp. v. Brown, 441 U.S. 281 (1979); Consumer Product Safety Commission v. GTE Sylvania, Inc., 447 U.S. 102 (1980).
23. Department of the Air Force v. Rose, 425 U.S. 352 (1976).
24. 105 S. Ct. 1881 (1985).
25. 410 U.S. 73 (1973).

26. Freedom of Information Act Amendments of 1974, amending §§ (b) (1) and (b) (7).
27. Government in the Sunshine Act of 1976, amending 5 U.S.C. § 522 (b) (3).
28. Chrysler Corp. v. Brown, *supra;* Kissinger v. Reporters Committee, *supra;* GTE Sylvania, Inc. v. Consumers' Union, 445 U.S. 375 (1980). *GTE Sylvania* case was a procedural case, not going to the merits of a particular disclosure. But the effect of the ruling, which is not included in the fifteen government victories, is to make it more difficult for requesters to gain access.
29. GTE Sylvania, Inc. v. Consumers' Union, *supra;* Kissinger v. Reporters Committee, *supra.*
30. Sims v. CIA, *supra;* Forsham v. Harris, *supra;* Shapiro v. Drug Enforcement Administration, *cert. granted,* in tandem with Department of Justice v. Provenzano, 466 U.S. 926 (1984). Both of the latter cases became moot when Congress amended the Privacy Act, as part of the 1984 CIA Act cited in *Sims,* to make it clear that the government's position was contrary to Congress' original and present intent.

13. The Burger Court and Business

1. Craven, *Paean To Pragmatism,* 50 N.C.L. Rev. 977 (1972).
2. United States v. Columbia Steel Corp., 334 U.S. 495 (1948).
3. Fox, *The Modernization of Antitrust, A New Equilibrium,* 66 Cornell L. Rev. 1140, 1182 (1982).
4. Studies by the Staff of the Cabinet Committee on Price Stability (1969).
5. Mitchell, Speech before the Georgia Bar Association, Savannah, Ga. (June 6, 1969).
6. United States v. Arnold Schwinn & Co., 388 U.S. 365 (1967) (territorial customer restraints); Klor's v. Broadway-Hale Stores, Inc., 359 U.S. 207 (1959) (group boycotts); Northern Pac. Ry v. United States, 356 U.S. 1 (1958) (tie-ins).
7. Northwest Wholesale Stationers v. Pacific Stationery & Printing Co., 105 S. Ct. 2613 (1985).
8. Jefferson Parish Hosp. Dist. No. 2 v. Hyde, 466 U.S. 2 (1984).
9. Continental T.V. Inc. v. GTE Sylvania, Inc., 433 U.S. 36 (1977).
10. 465 U.S. 752 (1984).
11. Aspen Skiing Co. v. Aspen Highland Skiing Corp., 105 S. Ct. 2847 (1985).
12. 467 U.S. 752 (1984).
13. Perma Life Mufflers Inc. v. United States, 392 U.S. 134 (1968); United States v. Citizens & Southern National Bank, 422 U.S. 86 (1975).
14. 451 U.S. 557 (1981).
15. 334 U.S. 37 (1948).
16. 105 S. Ct. 3346 (1985).

17. Brown Shoe Co. v. United States, 370 U.S. 294 (1962).
18. State of Hawaii v. Standard Oil of California, 405 U.S. 251 (1972).
19. Continental T.V. Inc. v. GTE Sylvania, Inc., 433 U.S. 36 (1977).
20. *The Antitrust Decisions of the Burger Court*, 47 ANTI. L. J. 819, 821 (1978).
21. Sennott v. Rodman & Renshaw, 414 U.S. 926 (1973) quoting from Affiliated Ute Citizens v. U.S., 406 U.S. 128, 151 (1972) and SEC v. Capital Gains Research 375 U.S. 180, 186, 187 (1963).
22. Blue Chip Stamps v. Manor Drug Stores, 421 U.S. 723, 739, 740 (1975).
23. *Id.* at 762.
24. 425 U.S. 185, 215, 216 (1976).
25. 444 U.S. 11, 28, 29 (1979).
26. 445 U.S. 222, 247, 248 (1980).
27. 463 U.S. 646, 667, 668, 677 (1983).
28. 446 U.S. 680, 713, 714 (1980).
29. 375 U.S. 180, 195 (1963).
30. As quoted in MAYER, THE LAWYERS (1967) at 516.

14. The Burger Court and Labor-Management Relations

1. 105 S. Ct. 3064 (1985).
2. 407 U.S. 539 (1972).
3. Amalgamated Food Employees Union v. Logan Valley Plaza, 391 U.S. 308 (1968); NLRB v. Babcock & Wilcox Co., 351 U.S. 105, 113 (1956).
4. 407 U.S. at 547.
5. 424 U.S. 507 (1976).
6. 416 U.S. 267 (1974).
7. 444 U.S. 672 (1980).
8. 406 U.S. 272 (1972).
9. 417 U.S. 249 (1974).
10. *Id.* at 255.
11. 465 U.S. 513 (1984).
12. *Id.* at 529.
13. 452 U.S. 666 (1981).
14. *Id.* at 679.

15. Showing Workers Who's Boss

1. 386 U.S. 171 (1967).
2. 386 U.S. at 182.
3. 424 U.S. 554 (1976).
4. 460 U.S. 212 (1983).
5. 451 U.S. 679 (1981).

6. 451 U.S. 56 (1981).
7. 462 U.S. 151 (1983).
8. 105 S. Ct. 190 (1985).
9. 461 U.S. 731 (1983).
10. 452 U.S. 666 (1981).
11. National Labor Relations Board v. Yeshiva University, 444 U.S. 672 (1980).
12. 465 U.S. 513 (1984).
13. 445 U.S. 1 (1980).
14. 465 U.S. 822 (1984).
15. *Olin Corp.*, 268 NLRB 573 (1984); *United Technologies*, 268 NLRB 557 (1984).
16. 414 U.S. 368 (1974).
17. 412 U.S. 1 (1973).
18. 467 U.S. 526 (1984).
19. 457 U.S. 102 (1982).
20. 424 U.S. 1 (1976).
21. Summers, *Democracy in a One-Party State: Perspectives from Landrum-Griffin*, 43 MD. L. REV. 93, 116 (1984).
22. 456 U.S. 431 (1982).
23. *See, e.g.*, Sullivan v. Laborers, 707 F.2d 347 (8th Cir. 1983); Adams-Lundy v. Flight Attendants, 731 F.2d 1154 (5th Cir. 1986).

NOTES ON CONTRIBUTORS

HERMAN SCHWARTZ is a professor of law at The American University, Washington, D.C. He was Chief Counsel to the Senate Antitrust and Monopoly Subcommittee and Chief Counsel for Revenue Sharing, Department of the Treasury. The first person called in to mediate the Attica prison uprising in 1971, he founded the American Civil Liberties Union Prisoners Rights Project in 1969 and has served as Chairman of the New York State Commission of Corrections (1975–76). He is also an authority on the law and practice of electronic surveillance.

BURT NEUBORNE, professor of law at New York University, served as legal director of the American Civil Liberties Union from 1982 to 1986. He has argued Supreme Court cases ranging from the legality of the Vietnam War to the constitutionality of voting and speech restrictions. His scholarly works include *Political and Civil Rights in the United States* (Vols. I and II; with Norman Dorsen, Paul Bender, and Sylvia Law) and *The Myth of Parity*.

LYLE DENNISTON is the Supreme Court reporter for the *Baltimore Sun*. A newspaperman since 1948, he is a contributing writer and regular columnist for the *Washington Journalism Review*, a contributing editor and regular columnist for *American Lawyer* magazine, a legal commentator for the MacNeil/Lehrer NewsHour, and the author of *The Reporter and The Law: Techniques of Covering the Courts* (1980). He is an adjunct professor of law at the Georgetown University Law

Center and a member of the Advisory Committee of the Center for Communications Law Studies at Catholic University.

SIDNEY ZION writes frequently on the Supreme Court for *The New York Times Magazine* and other publications. He is the author of *Read All About It!* and was formerly editor of *Scanlan's Monthly*, legal correspondent for *The New York Times*, and an Assistant United States Attorney.

MORTON H. HALPERIN is director of the Washington Office of the American Civil Liberties Union and of the Center for National Security Studies. The author of a number of books and articles on the relation between national security and civil liberties including *Freedom v. National Security* (1977), he is a recipient of a MacArthur Foundation Fellowship. He is a former Deputy Assistant Secretary of Defense and served in 1969 on the staff of the National Security Council.

NORMAN REDLICH is Dean and Judge Edward Weinfeld Professor of Law at the New York University School of Law. He has taught constitutional law for twenty-eight years, is the author of a constitutional law casebook, and has served as corporation counsel of the City of New York (1972–74). He is co-chair of the Commission on Law and Social Action of the American Jewish Congress, which has been involved in many of the cases discussed in his chapter; the views expressed are his own.

HAYWOOD BURNS is Vice-Provost and Dean for Urban and Legal Programs, City College of New York, and President of the National Lawyers Guild. He is also counsel to the firm Rabinowitz, Boudin, Standard, Krinsky & Lieberman and Chair Emeritus of the National Conference of Black Lawyers.

WENDY W. WILLIAMS is an associate professor of law at Georgetown University. Before becoming a teacher, she practiced law in San Francisco with Equal Rights Advocates, a public-interest law firm specializing in sex discrimination issues.

NORMAN S. ROSENBERG, director of the Mental Health Law Project, Washington, D.C., was formerly an assistant professor of law, State University of New York at Buffalo. He has participated as counsel or *amicus curiae* in *Wyatt v. Stickney, Mills v. Board of Education, Parham v. J.R.*, and other cases dealing with the issues discussed in his chapter, lectures to and advises disability-case lawyers throughout the United States, has consulted with numerous state and federal agencies, and has served on a court-appointed review panel.

YALE KAMISAR, Henry K. Ransom Professor of Law at the University of Michigan, is author of *Police Interrogations and Confessions* (1980) and coauthor of six editions of two widely used casebooks, *Modern Criminal Procedure* (1965, 6th ed. 1986) and *Constitutional Law: Cases, Comments and Questions* (1964, 6th ed. 1986). He is also coauthor of a five-volume series, *The Supreme Court: Trends and Developments* (1979–84).

MICHAEL MELTSNER has participated in several hundred capital cases. He is the author of *Cruel and Unusual: The Supreme Court and Capital Punishment* (1973). A former first assistant counsel of the NAACP Legal Defense and Education Fund, Inc., and former dean of Northeastern University School of Law in Boston, he is now a professor at that school.

ALAN B. MORRISON is the director of the Public Citizen Litigation Group, an organization which he founded with Ralph Nader in 1972. Among his Supreme Court victories were the 1983 decision striking down the legislative veto and the 1986 case declaring the Gramm-Rudman Deficit Reduction Act unconstitutional. Mr. Morrison, who was a visiting professor of law at Harvard during 1978–79 and who also taught there in 1980–86, was rated by the *National Law Journal* as one of America's 100 most powerful lawyers in 1985; in 1986 the

National Journal listed him as one of the 150 most influential people on federal policies in the United States.

JERRY S. COHEN was the chief counsel and staff director for the Senate Antitrust and Monopoly Subcommittee for five years under the late Senator Philip Hart. He has written or coauthored two books, *America, Inc.* (1971) and *Power, Inc.* (1976). In his law practice he specializes in antitrust and other business litigation.

HERBERT E. MILSTEIN was chief enforcement attorney at the Securities and Exchange Commission and has conducted a private law practice for the last sixteen years. He specializes in securities litigation.

DAVID M. SILBERMAN, a former law clerk to Justice Thurgood Marshall and Judge David Bazelon, is Associate General Counsel of the AFL-CIO.

ARTHUR FOX, a labor law expert, began his career at the National Labor Relations Board. Since 1972, he has been affiliated with the Public Citizen Litigation Group in Washington, D.C., where he represents primarily individual workers, union reform caucuses, and unions.

INDEX